MW00851676

MORALITY
AND
GOD'S
LOVE

High School Framework Course 6

BRIAN SINGER-TOWNS

saint mary's press

Thanks and Dedication

A very special thank you to our student contributors: Mattias and Karla from Seton Catholic Preparatory School in Chandler, AZ; Victoria and Mike from Red Bank Catholic High School in Red Bank, NJ; and Demetrios from Our Lady of the Hills College Preparatory School in Kerrville, TX.

Dedicated to my parents, Mick and Trudy, whose moral compass has always been straight and true.

The Subcommittee on the Catechism, United States Conference of Catholic Bishops, has found that this catechetical high school text, copyright 2021, is in conformity with the *Catechism of the Catholic Church* and that it fulfills the requirements of Course 6 of the *Doctrinal Elements of a Curriculum Framework for the Development of Catechetical Materials for Young People of High School Age.*

Nihil Obstat: Dr. John Martens, PhD
Censor Librorum
November 20, 2020

Imprimatur: † Most Rev. Bernard A. Hebda
Archbishop of Saint Paul and Minneapolis
November 29, 2020

The nihil obstat and imprimatur are official declarations that a book or pamphlet is free of doctrinal or moral error. No implication is contained therein that those who have granted the nihil obstat or imprimatur agree with the contents, opinions, or statements expressed, nor do they assume any legal responsibility associated with publication.

Cover image: © Markus Pfaff / Shutterstock.com

The content in this resource was acquired, developed, and reviewed by the content engagement team at Saint Mary's Press. Content design and manufacturing were coordinated by the passionate team of creatives at Saint Mary's Press.

Printed in the United States of America

1170 (PO6881)

ISBN 978-1-64121-118-5

CONTENTS

UNIT 1

Foundational Principles for Christian Morality

HOW DO I KNOW WHAT IS "GOOD"?

LOOKING AHEAD

The way I act, being good, determines my reputation. Your reputation follows you everywhere you go, so you must put your best foot forward whenever interacting with someone. Spiritually, Knowing the right thing to do requires following the commandments and having strong morals, although this isn't always easy to do. Having a good reputation isn't the only reason why it matters how I act, but it does motivate me to always try to Know what is good and to act the best I can.

MIKE
Red Bank Catholic High School

CHAPTER 1
Moral Choices and God's Plan

WHY DOES IT MATTER HOW I ACT?

SNAPSHOT

Article 1

Created for Love and Happiness

Are you happy? Not just the momentary feeling you get when someone pays you a compliment or when you eat your favorite ice cream . . . but deep down are you at peace, a peace that would last even if you lost your cell phone? Are you filled with a love and gratitude that stays with you even when life doesn't go your way? Here's an important spiritual truth to base your life on: God made us to live in loving communion with him and with one another. Only by doing so will we experience true peace and happiness.

God's Revelation made known to us through Scripture and Tradition is based on one core truth: God created human beings to live in loving relationship with him. Stop and think about this for a moment. It is easy to take this amazing truth for granted. God, the Creator of the universe, the all-powerful, all-knowing Mystery who is beyond anything we can understand or imagine, wants to be in loving communion with us for all eternity. We should never take this lightly or for granted; it is the reason the Psalms are filled with praise and thanksgiving: "So that my glory may praise you / and not be silent. / O LORD, my God, / forever I will give you thanks" (30:13).

TAKE IT TO GOD

God, I've tried to change,
over and over again with the same results.
I end up in the same place I started
only more discouraged than before.
So I place myself in your loving hands
and acknowledge that I am powerless to change without your grace.
Give me the desire that I need to change my life
to turn away from sin and turn toward you.
For I trust that with your help all things are possible,
even the conversion of my stubborn heart.
All praise to you.
Amen.

Let's explore this fundamental truth further with a thought experiment. Let's think about how different things would be if God had a different purpose in creating human beings. For example, some ancient people believed that the gods (they often believed in more than one god) created human beings for the gods' amusement. Or they believed that human beings were created to feed the egos of the gods by worshipping them. If this were indeed the reason human beings were created, what would it mean for how we live? It could certainly mean some of the following things, and you could probably come up with many other implications:

- We would be at the mercy of the gods' changing whims and desires. An action that might please your god today could change tomorrow and leave you doing the wrong thing.
- Because the gods' value system is self-centered, focused on feeding their own egos and desires, then we human beings would imitate those values and would focus on only our own egos and desires.
- We would be in competition with other people for the gods' attention and rewards.
- Our understanding of love would be fundamentally changed. Rather than being freely given and freely received, love would have to be earned. This would make love relationships open to manipulation and difficult to trust.

Living in such a world doesn't sound like much fun, does it? But some people reading this might say, "Wait, that's the world I live in!" The sad reality is that as a result of Original Sin, many people do not know the truth about God. And even when we know the truth, the effects of Original Sin make it difficult to live as God calls us to live. We see this in many of the false values in the world: greed, dishonesty, revenge. This is why idolatry, the primary sin against the First Commandment, is probably the most prevalent sin in our world. Our lips confess belief in the one true God, but our actions indicate that we are living the values of false gods, gods that do not exist.

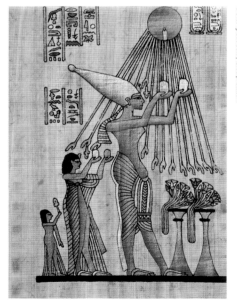

© Jose Ignacio Soto / iStockphoto.com

People in some cultures believed that they needed to keep their gods and goddesses happy through offerings and sacrifices.

But there's good news! Even though human beings lost the original state of perfect, loving communion that Adam and Eve enjoyed, God has been at work throughout history to restore us to full communion with him. The life, death, Resurrection, and Ascension of Jesus Christ are the fulfillment of God's saving plan. When we make choices to follow Christ, we participate in God's saving plan and will know true peace and happiness, a peace and happiness that the world cannot give.

© DisobeyArt /shutterstock.com

We are made in God's image with a soul, intellect, and free will. What does that mean for you?

Created in God's Image and Likeness

Another fundamental truth revealed in Genesis makes it clear what our relationship with him should be like: "Then God said: 'Let us make human beings in our image, after our likeness'" (1:26). In making us in his image, God spiritually connects us to himself and destines us for eternal happiness. We are endowed with a soul that allows us to be in true, loving communion with him, both now and for all eternity. Let's look briefly at the nature of the soul and two of its faculties: intellect and free will.

At our conception, we are given a spiritual **soul**, a divine gift that is unique to human beings. Our soul is the innermost aspect of ourselves. It is immortal, and it is what animates our bodies and makes us human. The soul and the

---

soul ➤ Our spiritual principle, it is immortal, and it is what makes us most like God. Our souls are created by God at the moment of our conception. It is the seat of human consciousness and freedom.

body are not two different natures, however. Because the body and soul are completely united, they form a single nature—a human nature. Our soul will live on after our death until it is united with our resurrected body at the Last Judgment. Having a soul means that God has given us the ability to be in communion with him in a way that is not limited by time or space.

God also gives every human person the gift of **intellect**. Intellect does not mean having a high IQ. Having intellect means that we have the ability to see and understand the order of things that God has established. Our intellect allows us to distinguish between what is truly good and what only appears to be good. Having an intellect means that God has given us the ability to understand how to be in communion with him.

The gift of **free will** makes it possible for us to choose the good that our reason enables us to understand. Because of human freedom, our actions are not predetermined by instinct or DNA (although these and other factors do impact our decision-making ability). Because we have free will, we are each individually responsible for our actions and accountable for our moral choices. Having free will means that we have the ability to choose to be in loving communion with God or the opposite—that is, we can misuse our freedom and reject him. Our free will is a clear sign that God is not manipulative; he does not force us to love him. True freedom is a manifestation of the image of God present in every person.

Our soul, with its intellect and free will, gives us a special dignity and a special place in God's plan. They orient us toward God and make it possible for us to be in a loving relationship with him that is unique among all his creatures. But to paraphrase the comic-book hero Spiderman, "With great gifts comes great responsibility." Our intellect and free will also make it possible for us to turn away from God. Thus, we now turn to the tragic side of salvation history, the reality of Original Sin and our separation from God. We must understand our history so that we can learn from it. ✳

HMMMMMM. . .   Why does having a soul, intellect, and free will also give us a unique responsibility for caring for creation?

intellect ➤ The divine gift that gives us the ability to see and understand the order of things that God places within creation and to know and understand God through the created order.

free will ➤ The gift from God that allows human beings to choose from among various actions, for which we are held accountable. It is the basis for moral responsibility.

Article 2

Genesis, Chapter 3: Freedom and Original Sin

Monique was struggling to understand the idea of Original Sin in her religion class. "So," she asked her teacher, "you're saying that because Adam and Eve disobeyed God thousands of years ago, we have to suffer for that too?" Her teacher smiled in understanding. "I get why this seems unfair," he replied, "but don't forget that this is a symbolic story told to teach us a spiritual truth, not a scientific reality. This spiritual truth is profound. It teaches that we are all connected to one another throughout time and space. The good and the evil that we do impacts others, even across great distances of time and space. It's a mystery, but that first sin has the greatest impact of any sin in history. Doesn't that kind of make sense?"

Although God wants each of us to live in perfect communion with him, he doesn't force us to do so. Every person who has ever lived is free to accept or to reject God and his will for us. Adam and Eve, our first parents, exercised this freedom in the biblical account of the Garden of Eden (see Genesis, chapter 3).

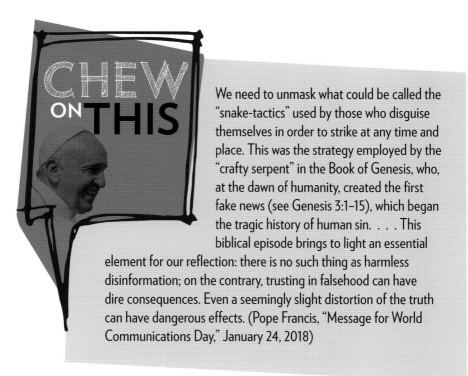

CHEW ON THIS

We need to unmask what could be called the "snake-tactics" used by those who disguise themselves in order to strike at any time and place. This was the strategy employed by the "crafty serpent" in the Book of Genesis, who, at the dawn of humanity, created the first fake news (see Genesis 3:1–15), which began the tragic history of human sin. . . . This biblical episode brings to light an essential element for our reflection: there is no such thing as harmless disinformation; on the contrary, trusting in falsehood can have dire consequences. Even a seemingly slight distortion of the truth can have dangerous effects. (Pope Francis, "Message for World Communications Day," January 24, 2018)

They chose to go against God's plan for them to live in perfect communion with God, with each other, and with all of creation. Their decision to eat the forbidden fruit affects each of us, everyone who came before us, and all those who will come after us.

Human Freedom and Moral Choice

Adam and Eve experienced the same choice that all humans have had to face: whether to choose what is good or to choose what is evil. And if Adam and Eve had a tough time resisting their forbidden fruit, how much more challenged are we by the world we live in? Every day, we are surrounded by thousands of messages that tell us that true happiness is found in the number of friends we have, the kind of phone we use, the clothes we wear, and what our body looks like. The pursuit of popularity, pleasure, and wealth are temptations that distract us from the authentic happiness that comes from true, loving relationships with God and with one another.

But that's where our free will comes in. Unlike animals, whose instinct drives their actions, we can think about the moral aspects of our behavior both before and after we act. Our free will allows us to choose to act in ways that are consistent with God's plan for us to live in loving relationship with him and with one another. We can choose to resist those temptations that lead us away from God, because we are free to do so. Of course, freedom also means that we are responsible for the choices we make, especially in religious and moral matters. Freedom and responsibility go hand in hand.

MAKE IT SO

Consider this scenario. Grace had never been popular with her classmates. She'd always been seen as just a little different. On the last day of the semester, the teacher needed to leave the room for a few minutes. There was a dish of candy on her desk that hadn't been there before. Several of Grace's classmates urged her to take some of the candy because it must be out for them—even though the teacher hadn't said that. They said they'd take some too, if Grace did. Grace liked the attention, and she also liked candy. But she doubted whether she should really take some without the teacher's okay. What might be limiting Grace's ability to choose freely? If you were there, what would you advise Grace to do? Why?

Certain factors may affect our freedom when making a moral decision. For example, we might be ignorant of a rare side effect that a prescription drug will have on our behavior. Psychological factors, such as fear, can drive us to do things we would otherwise never think of doing. Likewise, strong social pressures may lessen the moral responsibility for some of our actions. These are not excuses for acting badly, but they are a recognition that we are not always acting with perfect freedom when we make moral decisions. Although circumstances may weaken our ability to choose good over evil, our free will—and the responsibility that comes with it—cannot be taken away.

The Results of Sin

Read the consequences that God pronounced for the snake, Eve, and Adam after their sin, in Genesis 3:14–19. These verses are examples of the literary style **etiology**. Ancient peoples used etiologies to explain why things are the way they are. In this etiology, because of their sinful choices, the snake has to crawl on its belly, Eve will now suffer pain in childbirth, and Adam will have to work hard to grow food for survival.

© Dance60/Shutterstock.com

The biblical authors used etiologies to explain why snakes crawl and childbirth is painful. What stories does your family use to explain family customs or behaviors?

etiology ➤ A story that explains something's cause or origin.

Do not expect biblical etiologies to be scientific explanations about the causes of things. Rather, they creatively illustrate spiritual truths, rooted in the deep faith of the ancient Israelites. In this case, the spiritual truth is that there are negative consequences for our lives when we choose to disobey God.

This truth applies all the more to the condition we call **Original Sin**, another consequence of Adam and Eve's disobedience of God. We are all affected by Original Sin: "Adam and Eve transmitted to their descendants human nature wounded by their own first sin and hence deprived of original holiness and justice" (*Catechism of the Catholic Church*, number 417). Adam and Eve did not receive their state of **original holiness** for themselves alone but for all of human nature. Thus, when they sinned, their sin did not affect just them but also their human nature, which was passed on to all their descendants.

© Claudiad / iStockphoto.com

God did not create human beings for death. How would you explain God's plan for humanity to someone who had never heard of Christ's saving work?

Original Sin ➤ From the Latin *origo*, meaning "beginning" or "birth." The term has two meanings: (1) the sin of the first human beings, who disobeyed God's command by choosing to follow their own will and thus lost their original holiness and became subject to death, (2) the fallen state of human nature that affects every person born into the world, except Jesus and Mary.

original holiness ➤ The grace given to Adam and Eve in their original state by which they lived in close friendship with God.

Because of Original Sin, our human nature is wounded. Our relationship with God was broken with the loss of the grace of original holiness. We no longer walk in the garden with God as a close friend. Even though God greatly desires our friendship, we struggle to find him and trust him. With the loss of this friendship, we lost the grace of **original justice**, which was the harmony within ourselves, with one another, and with all creation. In our intellect, we experience difficulty knowing and understanding things we should easily know, like God's Law. Moral decisions are more difficult and confusing. This is the wound of ignorance. Our will is weakened and we have an inclination to sin, called **concupiscence**. We also experience suffering and death as a result of Original Sin. What God had warned Adam about has come true: "From that tree you shall not eat; when you eat from it you shall die" (Genesis 2:17).

Thanks be to God that these effects of Original Sin can be overcome by our faith in Christ and the grace that is given through the sacraments. ✳

HMMMMM. . . Where do you see the negative consequences of sin in the world today?

original justice ➤ The original state of Adam and Eve before the Fall. Due to their friendship with God, they were at harmony within themselves, with each other, and with all creation.

concupiscence ➤ The tendency of all human beings toward sin, as a result of Original Sin.

Article 3

The Beatitudes: New Life in Christ

If you have ever tried to make a positive change in your life, you probably discovered how hard it can be. Whether committing to spending more time in prayer, working harder in school, or getting more physical exercise, the majority of people give up on such commitments within a month! The effort required to change seems too much for us, and we give up.

Now think about God. After the Fall, he did not abandon humankind. The inspiring stories of the Old Testament reveal to us that after Adam and Eve's sin, God was at work to get human beings to turn away from sin and to turn toward him. He called Abraham to be the father of a Chosen People. Through Moses, he formed a sacred covenant with his Chosen People and gave them Divine Law to teach them how to live as a holy people. He gave them rituals and the priesthood so they could unite with him and with one another in prayerful worship. When the people failed to keep their covenant commitments, God called judges, kings, and prophets to lead them back to him. You might be justified in thinking that if anyone has reason to give up on us, surely it is God.

But God never gives up on humanity, both communally and individually. You have studied **salvation history** and the **Paschal Mystery** in other courses. You know how God the Father sent his only begotten Son as his ultimate saving act. You know how Jesus Christ saves us from sin and death through his suffering, death, Resurrection, and Ascension. You know that those who believe in Christ have new life in the Holy Spirit. The battle against sin and death has been won. In light of this reality, every person in the world faces a question only he or she can answer: Will you answer Christ's call to place your faith in him?

---

salvation history ➤ The pattern of specific events in human history in which God clearly reveals his presence and saving actions. Salvation was accomplished once and for all through Jesus Christ, a truth foreshadowed and revealed throughout the Old Testament.

Paschal Mystery ➤ The work of salvation accomplished by Jesus Christ mainly through his Passion, death, Resurrection, and Ascension.

This is a painting from the Church of the Transfiguration on the top of Mount Tabor in Israel. The tablet that Moses is holding and the light around his forehead symbolize the divine truth provided by God's Law.

Called to Beatitude

Perhaps you have never thought about what your goal in life is. Lots of people don't give it much thought. We just go with the flow, doing whatever our family and friends are doing. Advertising and social media often guide what we want and how we act. And then one day, something happens that makes us wake up and ask: "What am I doing with my life? What is going to bring me true happiness?" Hopefully, we ask these questions sooner than later! Unfortunately, for some people, this doesn't happen until they've experienced a great loss or have gone into a deep depression. God doesn't wish this for us, of course. He'd much rather we seriously listen to the truths he has revealed when we are young. An important revealed truth is that the Beatitudes can help us find our purpose in life and become the people God wants us to be.

In calling us to place our faith in him, Christ calls us to an entirely new vision of life. This vision is expressed in the Beatitudes. You will find these in Matthew 5:3–12 and Luke 6:20–26. If you haven't read them in a while, look them up and read them again. They present a vision of life that is radically different from the vision of life held by many people, both in Jesus' time and in our time. Just consider the meaning of the first beatitude in Matthew: "Blessed are the poor in spirit, / for theirs is the kingdom of heaven" (Matthew 5:3). Being poor in spirit is the opposite of being self-centered or egotistical. It means putting other people's needs before our own. It means trusting in God, not just in ourselves, for what we need. And living this way comes with a promise, that we shall be citizens of the Kingdom of Heaven, both in this life and for all eternity with God in Heaven.

The other seven beatitudes are just as radical in their implications. They illustrate the paradoxes of God's wisdom. It is only in looking to other people's needs that our deepest needs will be met. It is only in letting ourselves feel grief that we shall know God's comfort. It is only in being persecuted for doing what is right that we shall be worthy of Heaven. As we begin to understand the meaning of each beatitude, we start to see the incredible life that Christ calls us to as his disciples. That life we might call a life of **beatitude**.

© Adam Jan Figel / shutterstock.com

Which of the Beatitudes makes you feel most like you have found your purpose in life?

The Beatitudes teach us our vocation as Christians, the goal of our existence. We call this goal by different names: coming into the Kingdom of God, the beatific vision, entering into the joy of the Lord, being adoptive children of God (also called divine filiation), or entering into God's rest. By living the Beatitudes, we begin to experience on Earth the happiness that God has wanted human beings to know from the beginning of creation. A life of beatitude purifies our hearts and prepares us for the eternal happiness and joy that will come when we enter into perfect communion with the Holy Trinity in Heaven.

---

beatitude ➤ Our vocation as Christians, the goal of our existence. It is true blessedness or happiness that we experience partially here on Earth and perfectly in Heaven.

Living the Beatitudes	
Beatitudes (Matthew 5:3–12)	**Modern Meaning**
Blessed are the poor in spirit, for theirs is the kingdom of heaven.	Be humble; do not be attached to material possessions; trust in God to provide all that you need.
Blessed are they who mourn, for they will be comforted.	Be aware and supportive to other people's hardships and losses; do not ignore someone who is suffering.
Blessed are the meek, for they will inherit the land.	Respect other people's freedom, and be gentle in your relationships; do not be pushy or manipulative.
Blessed are they who hunger and thirst for righteousness, for they will be satisfied.	Treat other people with respect, and work for justice for all people and the Earth itself; do not participate in unjust systems and structures.
Blessed are the merciful, for they will be shown mercy.	Forgive yourself and others, even those who have hurt you the most; do not hold on to grudges.
Blessed are the clean of heart, for they will see God.	Practice charity (loving kindness), chastity (sexual purity), and love of truth (orthodoxy); do not expose yourself to the things—especially the addictive things—that will harm your heart, body, and faith.
Blessed are the peacemakers, for they will be called children of God.	Be a peacemaker and a bridge-builder by listening to those with different ideas and opinions and seeking truth wherever it might be found; never let anger alone guide your actions.
Blessed are they who are persecuted for the sake of righteousness, for theirs is the kingdom of heaven.	Do what is right and speak the truth, even if it means some people, including your family and friends, will disagree with you or get upset.
Blessed are you when they insult you and persecute you and utter every kind of evil against you (falsely) because of me. Rejoice and be glad, for your reward will be great in heaven.	If you do all these things, you will not be popular with everyone, but you will find true peace and true happiness, both in this life and in the next!

Living the Beatitudes brings meaning to our moral choices. For example, the Beatitudes promise that we will know happiness by embracing the hardships of life, not by avoiding them. They promise that we will know true joy by pursuing righteousness (or justice) and peace, not by pursuing wealth, fame, or power. Finally, even though we shall know the joy God intends for us only partially in this life, the Beatitudes promise that we shall know it completely in Heaven.

CATHOLICS MAKING A DIFFERENCE

Saint Martin de Porres (1579–1639) was born in Peru in the sixteenth century. His father was a Spanish nobleman, and his mother was a freed African slave. His family lived in poverty because Martin's father abandoned him and his mother. Perhaps worse, Martin was ridiculed and demeaned because of his mixed race. Because of Peruvian law at the time, he was not allowed to become a full member of the Dominicans, despite his deep desire to join this religious order. As a lay volunteer, Martin was assigned only the most menial tasks, which he did with love and grace. Eventually, he became a Dominican brother and was made head of the Dominican infirmary where he had an incredible healing ministry. Treating slave and nobleperson alike, Martin lived the Beatitudes of Christ by becoming one with those who endured poverty, grief, and persecution.

The Holy Trinity: Our Compass and Our Strength

Through our Baptism, we are already on our way to living a life of beatitude. Through the Sacrament of Baptism, Original Sin and all personal sin are washed away, removing our separation from God. We die to sin and the false promises of Satan, which lead only to unhappiness and eternal death. We are reborn to a new life in Christ, which leads to true happiness and eternal life. As baptized people, we trust God to do for us what we cannot do by ourselves.

God provides us with what we need to live the Beatitudes. Through Scripture and Tradition, he provides the compass, showing us the way to live as disciples. Through the graces given in Baptism, the Eucharist, and the other sacraments, we are provided with the strength we need. Called by God the Father, empowered by the Holy Spirit, and guided by the teaching and example of Jesus Christ, the Son of God, we constantly grow closer to the Holy Trinity through our moral choices. God alone reveals to us that he is Father, Son, and Holy Spirit. The mystery of the Holy Trinity is the central truth of the Christian faith. Through grace, we move toward the goal of Christian life, which is union with the Holy Trinity in Heaven.

Living the Beatitudes isn't the easiest way to live. Jesus himself acknowledges this: "Enter through the narrow gate; for the gate is wide and the road broad that leads to destruction, and those who enter through it are many. How narrow the gate and constricted the road that leads to life. And those who find it are few" (Matthew 7:13–14). At times, it will be tempting to give up trying to live a moral life. We can come up with a thousand reasons to justify a decision we know deep down is wrong. But even if we give in to temptation, God never gives up on us. Since Adam and Eve's sin, God has been at work, gently calling us to true happiness and joy. We must put our faith in Jesus Christ and never stop asking God to be our compass and our strength. ✳

© Sorin Popa / shutterstock.com

Scripture and Tradition provide the divine compass that shows us the way to live a life of beatitude.

HMMMMM. . .

Which of the Beatitudes do you find the most challenging to accept or to live out?

Article 4

Justification and Sanctification

Why should we be good? Do you do good things so that you can win the reward of Heaven? Or is being good a result of putting your faith in Jesus? Maybe you've had discussions on this question with someone who has asked whether you believe we are saved by our faith or by our (good) works.

In past centuries, these questions have been the cause of angry disagreement between some Christians. Thankfully, ecumenical discussions in the last few decades have resulted in greater clarity about these questions and in wider recognition of the truth that God has revealed: We are saved through God's work, not our own efforts. Our primary goal in Christian morality is to collaborate with God's grace, not to try to earn our way into Heaven.

Justified by the Grace of Christ

In his Letter to the Romans, Saint Paul spends a lot of time talking about how Christ saves us from sin and death. He argues that sin entered the world through the sin of Adam and Eve. Since then, every human being—except Mary—has been guilty of sin and is unworthy of sharing in God's holiness. The Old Law, rather than saving us, actually condemns us, because no one has been able to follow it perfectly; but it does help make us conscious of our sin. Our good works cannot save us because by themselves they cannot restore our holiness.

Read Romans 5:12–21. In this section, Saint Paul compares the sin of Adam to the gift of grace we receive through Jesus Christ. He uses an argument style common among Jewish teachers of the time: If some human action has a negative or positive result, God's response to that action is that much greater and more wonderful! Using this type of argument, Paul teaches that even though Adam and Eve's sin brought a great evil into the world, how much greater is the good that comes from God's response! In Paul's own words:

> But the gift is not like the transgression. For if by that one person's transgression the many died, how much more did the grace of God and the gracious gift of the one person Jesus Christ overflow for the many. . . .
> For if, by the transgression of one person, death came to reign through that one, how much more will those who receive the abundance of grace

and of the gift of justification come to reign in life through the one person Jesus Christ. In conclusion, just as through one transgression condemnation came upon all, so through one righteous act acquittal and life came to all. (Romans 5:15,17–18)

The process by which God's grace frees us from sin and sanctifies us (makes us holy) is called **justification**. Think of it this way: through our faith in Christ and the Sacrament of Baptism, we become a new person, an adopted son or daughter of God who shares in Christ's righteousness. Through Christ's Passion and the sanctifying grace received at Baptism, Original Sin is erased. Though the consequences of Original Sin remain, we receive an even greater blessing than the original holiness enjoyed by Adam and Eve. Without the separation caused by sin, harmony with ourselves, with God, and with one another is again possible. God grants us this wonderful gift through Baptism because it is through our Baptism that we unite ourselves to Christ's Passion and share in his death and Resurrection.

© Bill Wittman / www.wpwittman.com

How is Baptism related to the process of justification? Why is it such a joyful sacrament?

---

justification ➤ God's action of bringing a sinful human being into right relationship with him. It involves the removal of sin and the gift of God's sanctifying grace to renew holiness.

Our justification, being made right again with God, is entirely a work of his grace in us. The Holy Spirit is the one who prompts us and moves us toward conversion of heart. His grace justifies us in Baptism, freeing us from Original Sin and personal sins, and his grace continues to make us holy, or **sanctifies** us, as we cooperate with him to do good and avoid evil. We are nourished and healed from sin on our journey by prayer and by his grace in the sacraments. As we become more and more holy, we become more like Christ. We bring glory to God here on Earth, and after our death we shall continue to give him glory in Heaven.

Making these ideas a little more concrete might be helpful. Consider the life of Saint Ignatius of Loyola (1491–1556), the founder of the Jesuit order.

In his early life, Ignatius was determined to become a distinguished nobleman, and he was not considered to be particularly religious. He enjoyed the pursuits of young nobles: gambling, sword fighting, and chasing women. But at the age of thirty, all his noble pursuits came to a halt when he was struck by a cannonball, in-juring both of his legs. This turned out to be an occasion for a special grace in his life.

© The Crosiers / Gene Plaisted, OSC

God's grace was active in Saint Ignatius of Loyola's life long before he was aware of it. Saint Ignatius allowed God's gifts of forgiveness and righteousness to bear great fruit in his life.

---

sanctify ➤ To purify or make holy.

The *Catechism of the Catholic Church* contains this quote from Saint Athanasius of Alexandria (c. 297–373): "The Son of God became man, so that we might become god" (number 460). Of course, he did not mean that we literally become God, but that through grace we are able to be united with God. The Eastern Catholic Churches call this process *theosis,* or deification, and it is similar to justification. There are three stages in the process of deification:

1. The first stage is *katharsis*, or purification. In this stage, we remove sin from our lives so that we can focus on God.

2. The second stage is *theoria*, or illumination. In this stage, we come to know and experience what it means to be fully human through our communion with Jesus Christ.

3. The last stage of the *process*, theosis, comes from a Greek word meaning "divinization." As we put into perfect practice the teachings of Jesus Christ, we become saints who are in the fullest communion with God that is possible in this life. Divinization will be fully realized only with our own resurrection.

During his long recuperation, Ignatius began reading about the life of Christ and the lives of the saints. Thus began his conversion. Ignatius came to believe that modeling one's life on the example of Christ was a worthy goal and eventually became convinced that such a life would be more satisfying than life in a royal court. He repented of his previous sins and was determined to change. A series of fortunate events led him to spend ten months living in simple circumstances while praying and studying the spiritual life. God had begun the process of justification in Ignatius's life. The rest of his life would be marked by the desire to discover God's will and to do it, despite numerous challenges and setbacks. Sanctified through the grace of God, Ignatius achieved true holiness. He was declared a saint in 1622. You can find more about the life of Saint Ignatius in a saints book or by asking a Jesuit priest or brother about him.

God's Work and Our Collaboration

The theological concept of **merit** is sometimes used to describe our standing in the eyes of God. In general, merit refers to the compensation owed by a community or to a community for the actions of its members. Merit can be a reward, or it can be a punishment. In the theological sense, having merit means that God sees us as justified persons, free from sin and sanctified by his grace. Or it can mean that God sees us in need of merit, that we have not accepted his forgiveness and grace.

© gawrav / istock.com

What is your answer to the question: Why be good?

It should be clear from all you have learned so far that "no one can merit the initial grace of forgiveness and justification, at the beginning of conversion" (*Catechism of the Catholic Church [CCC]*, number 2010). God takes the initiative for our salvation by freely choosing to share his love, his grace, and his forgiveness with us. God first initiates, and then we respond. If our response is the response of faith in Jesus Christ and the reception of Baptism, we become collaborators in God's saving work. So, the merit we have in the sight of God is first and foremost God's free gift to us and then we grow in merit through our active participation in his saving plan.

---

merit ➤ God's reward to those who love him and by his grace perform good works. To have merit is to be justified in the sight of God, free from sin and sanctified by his grace. We do not "merit" justification or eternal life; the source of any merit we have is due to the grace of Christ in us.

This brings us back to the original question: Why should we be good? We should be good because that is how God made us. We should be good because God has given us a share in his life and his love. We should be good because God has given us his grace to justify us and to sanctify us so that we can live in perfect communion with him and all the saints for all eternity. Any other reasons, such as trying to impress others, trying to gain social status, or even trying to earn our way into Heaven, will eventually backfire because they put us at the center of our moral choices rather than putting God at the center. ✳

HMMMMMM. . .

Why do people shy away from the idea of becoming holy?

1. Why are human beings unique among all of God's creation?

2. Briefly describe the three God-given gifts that allow us to live in true, loving communion with God.

3. What are some factors that can diminish our freedom and lessen the moral responsibility of our resulting actions?

4. What is concupiscence?

5. Describe what it means to live the Beatitudes.

6. How does God provide us with the direction and the strength to live a life of beatitude?

7. Define *justification*.

8. How do we gain merit in the sight of God?

UNIT 1

Can you identify the symbolism in this painting of Adam and Eve in the Garden of Eden?

1. Why are Adam and Eve naked?

2. What do the animals in the painting symbolize?

3. What is the meaning of the body language between Adam and Eve?

CHAPTER 2
The Law of God

HOW DO I KNOW HOW GOD WANTS ME TO ACT?

SNAPSHOT

Article 5
God's Eternal Law

Let's say one day you wake up and decide that you are going to walk backward for the rest of your life. At first, it is rough going. You trip a lot, run into things, and maybe confuse and upset a lot of people. But with practice, you get pretty good at it. You can get places just about as fast as everyone else, and you rarely trip or fall. People even get used to it and stop commenting on how strange you are. So you think you've proven there is nothing natural about walking forward. Except . . . a few years later, your knees start to hurt and you have constant headaches. Your doctor tells you it is from the unnatural stress you have placed on your knee joints from walking backward, and on your neck from constantly looking over your shoulder. Sooner or later, he says, you are going to require knee replacements if you keep walking backward. Going against God's natural order has consequences.

Let's put this in a moral context. You wake up one day and decide to tell at least one lie every day—usually something that will benefit you. At first, it is rough going. You aren't very good at it; people often catch you doing it and get upset. But over time, you get more polished. People catch you less often, and when they do, they just shrug it off because they are used to it. You think you have proven that there is nothing natural about telling the truth and few consequences for not doing so. Except . . . a few years later, you are engaged

to the person of your dreams. As you grow nearer your wedding date, your fiancé catches you telling a lie, and then another, and another. Your fiancé breaks off the engagement, announcing the decision to you by saying simply, "I cannot spend my life with a person I cannot trust." People always pay a price for going against God's natural order.

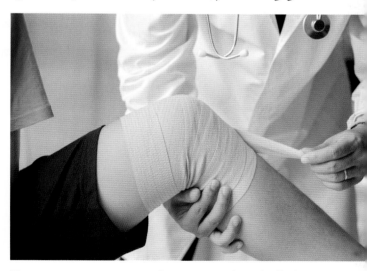

There are consequences to pay if we go against the order God establishes in Creation. These consequences can be physical, relational, and spiritual.

Eternal Law and Moral Law

These two stories are simple examples of the order in creation—an order that reflects God's will and purpose. Our loving Creator placed in his creation an order that reflects himself. We sometimes call this order Divine Law or **Eternal Law**. It is eternal because God is its source, and it is always true and never changes. God's Law governs the universe and directs it to its ultimate purpose. Every part of creation finds its purpose, its true end, in God's Eternal Law. And God has given human beings the gift of intellect by which we can understand and appreciate Eternal Law, even if only partially. We do this by using reason (the application of our intellect) and by listening to God's revealed truth.

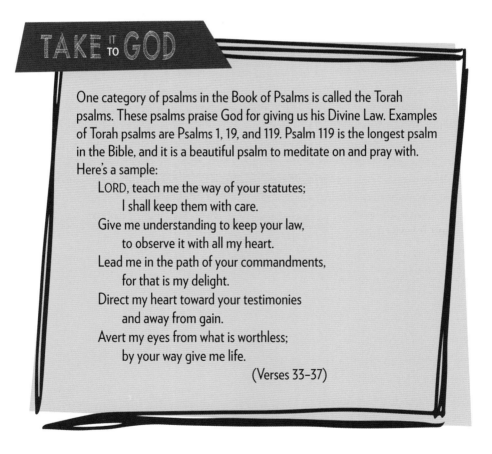

TAKE IT TO GOD

One category of psalms in the Book of Psalms is called the Torah psalms. These psalms praise God for giving us his Divine Law. Examples of Torah psalms are Psalms 1, 19, and 119. Psalm 119 is the longest psalm in the Bible, and it is a beautiful psalm to meditate on and pray with. Here's a sample:

LORD, teach me the way of your statutes;
 I shall keep them with care.
Give me understanding to keep your law,
 to observe it with all my heart.
Lead me in the path of your commandments,
 for that is my delight.
Direct my heart toward your testimonies
 and away from gain.
Avert my eyes from what is worthless;
 by your way give me life.

(Verses 33–37)

Eternal Law ➤ The order in creation that reflects God's will and purpose; it is eternal because it is always true and never changes. All other types of law have their basis in Eternal Law and are only true if they reflect the truth of Eternal Law.

Moral law comes from God and is a rational expression of Eternal Law. Moral law governs the relationships human beings have with God and with one another (for example, treat others as you would want them to treat you). We need moral law to guide us because we have the gift of free will. We can choose to act against Eternal Law and bring chaos, pain, and suffering into creation. We can also choose to act in ways that restore natural order and build up the Kingdom of God over all the Earth, bringing greater love and healing into creation.

Moral law reflects God's wisdom and love. It is the guidance and teaching he gives us that leads to the blessed life he wants for every person. Everyone can know moral law through the gift of our conscience. As a parent guides a child away from the dangers of the world, so God's moral law prevents us from falling prey to evil and urges us to do what is good. If we listen to our conscience and follow moral law, we will live in loving communion with God now and forever. This is why every person is obliged to follow moral law. ✳

This seedling can symbolize the order God has established in creation. How many natural laws can you name that govern the growth of this seedling and that are true for all seedlings?

HMMMMM... When have you seen people acting in ways that clearly don't make sense?

moral law ➤ The moral law is established by God and is a rational expression of Eternal Law. Moral law reflects God's wisdom; it is the teaching that leads us to the blessed life he wants for us.

Article 6

Natural Moral Law

Every person is born with an awareness of good and evil, right and wrong. Saint Thomas Aquinas describes this **natural law** as "nothing other than the light of understanding placed in us by God; through it we know what we must do and what we must avoid"[1] (*CCC*, number 1955). With the gift of reason, all people have the ability to recognize the moral law. Although as a result of the Fall, our minds no longer recognize its precepts clearly and easily, they remain written upon every human heart.

The founders of the United States acknowledged the existence of natural law in the Declaration of Independence, which proclaims that certain moral truths are self-evident. We just know them. It goes further to say that all human beings have fundamental rights and duties that cannot be taken away, including the pursuit of true happiness.

© US Capitol Collection, Washington DC, USA / Bridgeman Images

The Declaration of Independence appeals to natural law: "We hold these truths to be self-evident, that all men are created equal, that they are endowed by their Creator with certain unalienable Rights . . ."

---

natural law ➤ The moral law that can be understood through the use of human reason. It is our God-given ability to understand what it means to be in right relationship with God, other people, the world, and ourselves. However, our ability to know natural law has been clouded by Original Sin.

The Golden Rule is a good example of a natural moral law. Call it common sense or basic moral sense, but natural law dictates that we should treat people the way we want to be treated. Jesus reminds us of the wisdom of the Golden Rule (see Matthew 7:12), but Christians have no monopoly on it. Other great world religions, including Judaism, Islam, Buddhism, Hinduism, and Taoism, espouse it as well, although they may have a different way of saying it. Many people who profess no belief in God still adhere to the Golden Rule. The natural law is best summarized by the Ten Commandments, which God has given us that all might know the principles of natural law with ease, certainty, and without being mixed with error.

Because natural moral law is an expression of God's Eternal Law, it does not change with time. Regardless of the culture or religious belief, common principles bind us together and form the foundation for all other moral rules and civil laws. Any community that wishes to embody justice and goodness will develop civil laws that reflect—and do not contradict—natural law.

To summarize, natural law is part of our humanity—part of our nature. To be moral is to be fully human. The word *inhumane* expresses what happens when we do not live morally—that is, when we are no longer acting as human beings.

Natural Moral Law and the Church

The principles of the natural law were deeply rooted in Jewish consciousness. References to God's order in nature, his Law in our hearts, and the Ten Commandments are foundational to the Old Testament. Other ancient people were also aware of it. For example, Greek philosophy, particularly the teachings of the philosopher Aristotle, was one of the earliest expressions of natural law. Greek philosophy had a strong influence in the Roman Empire, so many early Christians were familiar with it. They drew upon their Jewish heritage and probably even made use of Greek philosophy in their teaching. We can see evidence of this in the New Testament. In the first chapter of the Letter to the Romans, Saint Paul explains why every person is responsible for the consequences of their sins.

> For what can be known about God is evident. . . . Ever since the creation of the world, his invisible attributes of eternal power and divinity have been able to be understood and perceived in what he has made. . . . And since they did not see fit to acknowledge God, God handed them over to their undiscerning mind to do what is improper. . . . Although they know the just decree of God that all who practice such things deserve death, they not only do them but give approval to those who practice them. (1:19-20,28,32)

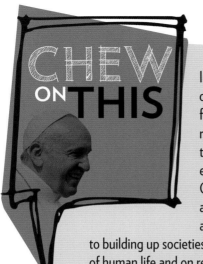

CHEW ON THIS

In the face of the spread of new forms of xenophobia (fear and hatred against foreigners) and racism, the leaders of all religions also have an important mission: that of spreading among the faithful the ethical principles and values inscribed by God on the heart of human beings, known as the natural moral law. It is about making and inspiring gestures which can contribute to building up societies founded on the principle of the sacredness of human life and on respect for the dignity of each person, on charity, on fraternity—which goes well beyond tolerance—and on solidarity.

In particular, may Christian Churches be humble and hard-working witnesses to Christ's love. Indeed, for Christians, the abovementioned moral responsibilities assume an even more profound meaning in the light of faith. ("Address of His Holiness Pope Francis to Participants at the World Conference on Xenophobia, Racism, and Populist Nationalism in the Context of Global Migration," September 20, 2018)

Essentially Paul is saying that knowledge of God and of the moral law is evident to every person through creation. So if we fail to acknowledge this and thus do not follow the natural moral law, we deserve God's just punishment.

Centuries later, Saint Augustine also appeals to the natural moral law to explain how all people, Christian or not, know in their hearts what is right. He uses the image of a king stamping his ring with the royal seal into wax as a metaphor for the way God stamps the seal of his Law into our hearts.

Where indeed are these rules written, wherein even the unrighteous recognizes what is righteous, wherein he discerns that he ought to have what he himself has not? Where, then, are they written, unless in the book of that Light which is called Truth? Whence every righteous law is copied and transferred (not by migrating to it, but by being as it were impressed upon it) to the heart of the man that works righteousness; as the impression from a ring passes into the wax, yet does not leave the ring. ("On the Trinity," Book XIV)

Unfortunately, as mentioned earlier, our ability to know the natural law is weakened because of Original Sin. Original Sin weakens our human nature, and we are subject to ignorance, suffering, and death. We have an inclination towards evil and towards choosing sin. Only through God's grace and revealed truth are we freed to fully know and carry out God's moral law. ✳

HMMMMM. . .

What are some universal moral truths that seem evident to you regardless of a person's religious identity?

Article 7

Law and the Old Testament

If you read the news headlines every day, it is painfully clear that not everyone obeys natural moral law. The presence of so much suffering caused by immoral human actions is a testimony that because of the effects of Original Sin, human beings reject the guidance of natural moral law. This does not mean that natural law is corrupt or missing from our hearts, only that we often reject it.

It is for this reason that God has revealed his moral law to us through Scripture and Tradition. This first takes place in the Old Testament of the Bible. The Law of Moses, also called the **Old Law**, is the first stage of God's Revelation to us about how we are to live as people made in his image. This Old Law is summarized in the Ten Commandments that God revealed to Moses on Mount Sinai (see Exodus 20:1–17). The Ten Commandments are also referred to as the **Decalogue**. They are a special expression of natural law, making clear through God's Revelation what he had already placed in the human heart.

© Sybille Yates / Shutterstock.com

Why is natural law not sufficient for human beings to live moral lives? Why is it necessary for God to reveal his Law through Scripture and Tradition?

Old Law ➤ Divine Law revealed in the Old Testament, summarized in the Ten Commandments. Also called the Law of Moses.

Decalogue ➤ The Ten Commandments.

The Torah and the Old Law

The Jewish name for the first five books of the Bible is the Torah. The Hebrew word *torah* is sometimes translated as "law," but it is better translated as "instruction." This helps us to remember that the primary purpose of the Old Law is to teach us how to live in right relationship with God and with one another. These are some of the kinds of laws you will find in the Torah:

- **The Covenant Code** (see Exodus 20:22–23:33) This set of laws immediately follows the Ten Commandments and is considered to be part of the Sinai Covenant in Exodus. The laws address slavery, personal injury, property damage, money, religious practices, and a few other topics. Many of them describe the punishment for breaking the law.
- **The Priestly Code** (see Leviticus, chapters 1–7 and 11–26) In general, these laws deal primarily with religious concerns, including instructions for proper worship.
- **The Holiness Code** (see Leviticus, chapters 17–26) This distinct section of the Priestly Code may have originally been for priests and later applied to all the people. The central theme of this set of laws is "Be holy, for I, the LORD your God, am holy" (19:2).

Keep in mind that all these laws must be interpreted in light of Jesus Christ's life and teachings.

The Ten Commandments

Imagine that the bishop of your diocese called people from all the parishes of the diocese together for a special, once-in-a-lifetime gathering. So many people were attending that the gathering had to be held outdoors at a huge stadium. People began gathering hours before the event was to start. Suddenly, before everything was scheduled to start, something dramatic happened. Clouds gathered in the sky, and brilliant flashes of lightning and loud peals of thunder filled the air. While this was happening, a small earthquake shook the ground, causing people to lean on one another to stay upright. Then just as suddenly as it began, all the noise and commotion stopped. As the bishop ascended the stage to begin the event, people turned to one another and said, "We better pay attention!"

This is close to what happened when God gave the Israelites the Ten Commandments. Take a look at Exodus 19:16–25. After the people arrived at Mount Sinai, they experienced a spectacular display of God's glory: thunder, lightning, trumpet blasts, earthquakes, and even an erupting volcano. It is the most dramatic appearance of God in the Bible, and it immediately precedes the proclamation of the Ten Commandments. Through these events, God was saying, "Pay attention, for these commandments are very, very important."

The Ten Commandments are found in the Book of Exodus (see 20:2–17) and the Book of Deuteronomy (see 5:6–21). They are part of the sacred covenant that God made with the Israelites, his Chosen People, at Mount Sinai. To understand the purpose of the Ten Commandments, we must first understand the purpose of the Sinai Covenant. We sometimes call this the Old Covenant to distinguish it from the New Covenant. But perhaps we should call it the Original Covenant because it is not "old" in the sense of being outdated. It is "old" in the sense that it was the Original Covenant God made with a special people. Jesus did not do away with this covenant, rather he fulfilled it.

First and foremost, the covenant was a relationship of love between God and his Chosen People. From the beginning, God has loved his people—including us—first. God tells Moses to tell the Israelites, "If you obey me completely and keep my covenant, you will be my treasured possession among all peoples, though all the earth is mine" (Exodus 19:5). Through the covenant, God sought to restore the loving communion that was lost through Original Sin, starting with the Israelites and then extending to all the people of the Earth. As part of the covenant, the Ten Commandments taught the Israelites how to live in loving relationship with God and with one another.

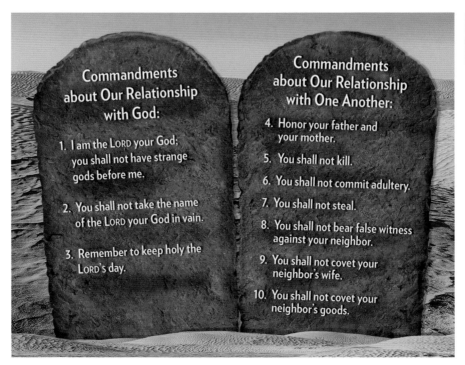

Commandments about Our Relationship with God:

1. I am the LORD your God; you shall not have strange gods before me.

2. You shall not take the name of the LORD your God in vain.

3. Remember to keep holy the LORD's day.

Commandments about Our Relationship with One Another:

4. Honor your father and your mother.

5. You shall not kill.

6. You shall not commit adultery.

7. You shall not steal.

8. You shall not bear false witness against your neighbor.

9. You shall not covet your neighbor's wife.

10. You shall not covet your neighbor's goods.

They summarized the many particular laws that follow in the books of Exodus and Deuteronomy, and they make up only a small percentage of the laws in the **Pentateuch**. Although many of these particular laws are no longer applicable to our culture, the moral principles expressed in the Ten Commandments are true in all places and all times.

Christians have always acknowledged the importance of the Ten Commandments. Strictly speaking, the Commandments address serious moral issues: idolatry, murder, theft, adultery. But they also embody moral principles that help us to address all the moral issues we face, including less serious issues that we still have an obligation to address morally. For this reason, many **catechisms** throughout the Church's history have used the Ten Commandments as the framework for teaching Christian morality. *The Catechism of the Catholic Church* uses this approach, as does this book.

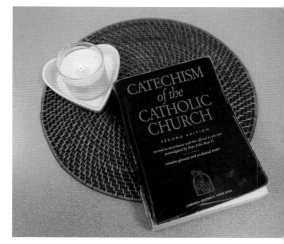

Why do the Ten Commandments continue to be a moral guide for many people?

Scripture teaches that our loving Father gives us his Law to lead us to a life of eternal happiness and to keep us from sin and evil. But as holy, spiritual, and good as the Old Law is, it is not enough to restore us to full communion with him. The Ten Commandments show what must be done, but they do not give us the strength, or the grace of the Holy Spirit, to do it. The Old Law is the first stage on the way to the Kingdom of God, preparing us for conversion and faith in Jesus. In this way, the Old Law is a preparation for the Gospel. ✳

 Which of the Ten Commandments is most violated in today's world?

Pentateuch ➤ A Greek word meaning "five books," referring to the first five books of the Old Testament.

catechism ➤ A popular summary, usually in book form, of Catholic doctrine about faith and morals and commonly intended for use within formal programs of catechesis.

Article 8

Law and the New Testament

God's Old Covenant with humanity is impossible to separate from the Old Law. So it should come as no surprise that when Jesus established the New Covenant he also taught a **New Law**, which fulfilled and completed the Old Law. This New Law, also called the Law of the Gospel, is the perfection of God's moral law, both natural and revealed. The New Law challenges us to be perfect in love by following the example of Jesus himself.

The Sermon on the Mount

Although Jesus' New Law is found in many different places throughout the Gospels, he taught the core of it in his Sermon on the Mount (see Matthew 5:1–7:29; see also Luke 6:20–49).

The location where this teaching took place is important because it makes connections between Moses and Jesus, between the Old Law and the New Law. Just as Moses delivered the Old Law to the people from a mountain as part of the Old Covenant, Jesus taught the New Law from a mountain (see Matthew 5:1) as part of the New Covenant.

The Sermon on the Mount starts with Jesus' proclaiming the Beatitudes. This is no accident. The values of the Beatitudes—poverty of spirit, meekness, mercifulness, righteousness, purity of heart, peacemaking, willingness to suffer for what is right—are the values we

Jesus' teaching attracted great crowds of people. Why is his teaching so inspiring when it is also so challenging to follow?

© Brooklyn Museum of Art, New York, USA / Bridgeman Images

New Law ➤ Divine Law revealed in the New Testament through the life and teaching of Jesus Christ and through the witness and teaching of the Apostles. The New Law perfects the Old Law and brings it to fulfillment. Also called the Law of Love.

I DIDN'T KNOW THAT!

The examples Jesus used about retaliation (Matthew 5:38–42) are unfamiliar to us but would have been very familiar to the people of his time. In Jesus' time, slave owners and landowners would show their displeasure with their slaves or workers with a backhanded slap (right hand on left cheek). Wealthy merchants would take poor people to court for their debts, taking from them even their clothing. Roman soldiers could require common people to carry their heavy (70-pound) packs for one mile. These are all examples of powerful people oppressing less powerful people. Jesus' directions are meant to shock the powerful into examining their oppressive actions.

need to live a moral life and to satisfy the desire for happiness that God has placed in our hearts. God's original promises in the Old Covenant find their fulfillment in the Beatitudes. By embracing the Beatitudes and living them out, we become citizens of the Kingdom of God. (The meaning of the Beatitudes is described in more detail in article 3.)

In the Sermon on the Mount, directly following the Beatitudes, Jesus teaches us an important purpose of living the New Law. He says that his followers should be the salt of the earth and the light of the world (see Matthew 5:13–14). These two metaphors emphasize that by living according to Christ's New Law, we can show others the way to true happiness and joy. We live by Christ's Law not only to bring ourselves into communion with God but also to show others the way to that communion.

Jesus then gives a series of teachings on topics such as avoiding anger, lust, revenge, and violence; loving our enemies; avoiding hypocrisy; giving generously; and trusting in God. Many of these teachings begin with Jesus saying, "You have heard that it was said . . ." after which he quotes a law from the Old Testament. Jesus then teaches the true meaning of that law. With this formula, Jesus is showing us that his New Law does not abolish or devalue the Old Law but instead releases its full potential. Let's consider one example:

> You have heard that it was said, "An eye for an eye and a tooth for a tooth."
> But I say to you, offer no resistance to one who is evil. When someone
> strikes you on [your] right cheek, turn the other one to him as well. If anyone
> wants to go to law with you over your tunic, hand him your cloak as well.
> Should anyone press you into service for one mile, go with him for two miles.
> (Matthew 5:38–41)

Does this strike you as a little crazy? What was Jesus saying here? Well, first he reminded his listeners that the Old Law limited the revenge you could take on someone who had hurt you. If someone put out your eye, the most you could do was put out their eye; you could not kill the person. But the New Law taught by Jesus calls us to greater love. The morality of the New Law witnesses to others the love of God through forgiveness, patience, and even outrageous generosity. Who can live this way? We can! Christ's New Law "is the grace of the Holy Spirit given to the faithful through faith in Christ" (*CCC*, number 1966). Through faith in Christ and the sacraments, and a life of prayers, the Holy Spirit provides the grace we need to live the New Law.

Other New Testament Moral Teachings

Besides Jesus' teachings in the Gospels, many of the letters, or epistles, of the New Testament contain moral teachings too. Often the letters address a particular moral situation, as the Apostles apply Jesus' New Law to their moral situations. Here are some examples:

Passage	Moral Teaching
Romans 12:9–21	general guidelines for moral living
Romans 13:1–7	respecting civil authority
Romans 14:13–23	whether to eat meat sacrificed to idols
1 Corinthians, chapter 13	defining what true love is
Ephesians 4:17–5:5	what it means to live according to the New Law
Ephesians 5:21–6:4 and Colossians 3:18–21	guidelines for family life
Colossians 3:5–17	vices to avoid and virtues to practice
Philemon	slavery

The Great Commandments: The Law of Love

An even shorter summary of the New Law is found in all three synoptic Gospels. In Mark, it is told like this:

> One of the scribes . . . asked him, "Which is the first of all the commandments?" Jesus replied, "The first is this: 'Hear, O Israel! The Lord our God is Lord alone! You shall love the Lord your God with all your heart, with all your soul, with all your mind, and with all your strength.' The second is this: 'You shall love your neighbor as yourself.' There is no other commandment greater than these." (12:28–31)

The two **Great Commandments** emphasize that the heart of the New Law is love. These two commandments were not new; they were part of the Old Law (see Deuteronomy 6:4–5 and Leviticus 19:18). You have probably noticed that the first Great Commandment, "Love God with all your heart, with all your soul, with all your mind, and with all your strength," is a pretty good summary of the first three commandments of the Decalogue. And the second Great Commandment, "Love your neighbor as yourself," summarizes the last seven commandments of the Decalogue.

MAKE IT SO

Janice serves on her county's board. The board faced a controversial issue about whether a local farm could exceed the county limits for the number of animals housed on the farm. Janice voted against increasing the limit, believing the danger to the water supply and air quality outweighed the benefit to the farm. After the vote, someone wrote a letter to the editor in the local newspaper. The letter severely and unfairly criticized Janice for her vote and even made fun of her—it was a symbolic slap in the face. Janice would see the letter writer at future meetings, possibly even at her church. How would you advise Janice in applying Jesus' Law of Love when she sees this person again? How could you apply the Law of Love when people make fun of you or tell lies about you?

Great Commandments ➤ Jesus' summary of the entire Divine Law as the love of God and the love of neighbor.

What is new about the Great Commandments is that Jesus pulls them out, highlights them, and says that these two are the first and the greatest of all the commandments. He is showing us that love is the foundation for properly understanding and interpreting all other moral laws. In a way, this doesn't make things easier. He is challenging us to live the commandments on a deeper level that calls for a total conversion of heart. But, ultimately, Jesus isn't raising the bar to make life harder for us. He calls us to a deeper love because he wants to give us the grace of the Holy Spirit, the very love of God in our hearts, to carry out his commandments. That is why the New Law is called the Law of Love. We aren't called to follow the commandments out of fear, but out of love, the love that is the gift of the Holy Spirit poured into our hearts.

To correctly understand the two Great Commandments, we must properly understand the spiritual meaning of this passage by focusing on what Jesus means by love. Jesus isn't talking about a do-whatever-feels-good-to-you kind of love. He is talking about a love that is based on God's Eternal Law. It is a love that is forgiving but also expects that we are working hard at being holy people. It is a sacrificial love that puts the good of others before our own comfort, just as we hope others would do for us. The Law of Love means that we hold ourselves to a high standard of moral living—God's standard.

(l) © monkeybusinessimages / iStock.com; (r) © DGLimages / iStock.com

How are the two Great Commandments interconnected? Why is it impossible to follow one without following the other?

The prophet Jeremiah describes in beautiful language the promise of the New Law, the Law of Love: "I will make a new covenant with the house of Israel. . . . I will place my law within them, and write it upon their hearts; I will be their God, and they shall be my people" (Jeremiah 31:31–33). It is truly amazing that God wrote the natural law into the hearts and minds of all people, made it even clearer in the Ten Commandments, and when we still didn't get it, the Father sent his Son, who became one of us to reveal the Law of Love, the perfection of the Divine Law. Now through our faith in Christ and Baptism, we receive the grace of the Holy Spirit, which enables us to live the two Great Commandments. And each time we receive the sacraments, we receive further grace, nurturing us to love God and to share his love with others. ✳

HMMMMMM. . .   Which of Jesus' "new laws" in the Sermon on the Mount do you find hardest to live out?

Article 9

Moral Law and the Church

"He's a Christian, but I know he goes out drinking most weekends." "She belongs to that big church in town, but she's the worst gossip in school." "They read the Bible every day, but they've never reached out to anyone with a helping hand."

Unfortunately, some people love to point out the flaws of others but seem more than willing to overlook their own shortcomings. Rather than sitting in judgment of others, we should reflect on how we can live more fully as Christ taught. None of us is perfect and without sin (see Romans 3:9–10), yet being Christian means we must strive to live in holiness and to be models of holiness for others, leading them to God. Saint Paul uses the concept of imitation to describe this: "So be imitators of God, as beloved children, and live in love" (Ephesians 5:1–2). "Join with others in being imitators of me" (Philippians 3:17). "You became imitators of us and of the Lord . . . so that you became a model for all the believers" (1 Thessalonians 1:6–7). To help us to be imitators of Christ, the Church's teaching authority guides us, and the sacraments strengthen us.

Two Types of Church Law

Why should you care what the Church teaches about the moral decisions you make? Think about it for a minute. The Church is the source of moral truth because of her union with Christ, the head of the Church, and because she is endowed with the Holy Spirit. Further, the Church's moral guidance is not driven

by profit or self-interest. The Church and its leaders are motivated by love; they want people to know the love and joy God intends for us. What other organization or group can make these same claims?

Christ has given the Church the responsibility of being a light to the world and a model of his New Law. The Church does this through the witness of her members and by teaching the world Christ's Law of Love. Also, the Church has her own laws to guide

"Jesus said . . . you are Peter, and upon this rock I will build my church. . . . I will give you the keys to the kingdom of heaven" (Matthew 16:17–19).

her members. The **Precepts of the Church** provide us with general guidance in living a Christian life, and the Church's **Canon Law** provides specific rules to maintain good order within the visible society of the Church.

The most basic of Church laws are called the Precepts of the Church. As you read them, you will notice that they primarily ask us to participate in the sacramental life of the Church and to participate in the Church's mission in the world. They are meant to be the minimum disciplines we must practice to ensure that we grow in love of God and neighbor. For example, they require us to receive the Sacrament of Penance and Reconciliation only once a year (but hopefully we would receive it more often than that).

Catholics are obligated to follow these precepts. Rather than seeing them as a burden, we should approach them as helpful reminders about how to live our faith in a deep and enriching way. They are really minimum requirements for being Catholic, asking us to participate in the rich faith life of the Church to receive the nourishment we need to live morally and to fulfill what it means to be a Christian.

The Precepts of the Church
1. Attend Mass on Sundays and holy days of obligation and rest from unnecessary labor on these days.
2. Confess your sins in the Sacrament of Penance and Reconciliation at least once a year.
3. Receive the Eucharist at least during the Easter season.
4. Observe the days of fasting and abstinence established by the Church.
5. Help to provide for the material needs of the Church according to your ability.

Canon Law is the law of the Church. *Canon* comes from the Greek word for "rule." Each individual law of the Church is called a canon. The canons are collected in a large book called *The Code of Canon Law*. Trained experts in Canon Law are called canonists or canon lawyers. These people often teach in seminaries and universities and work for bishops in diocesan offices.

Canon Law is concerned with the relationships among different members of the Church and with matters that affect the Church's mission. It governs

Precepts of the Church ➤ Sometimes called the Commandments of the Church, these are basic obligations for all Catholics, dictated by the laws of the Church and intended to guarantee for the faithful the indispensable minimum in prayer and moral effort.

Canon Law ➤ The name given to the official body of laws that provide good order in the visible body of the Church.

such things as norms for the celebration of the sacraments and public worship; norms for Catholic education; regulations for the administration of Church property; the rights and responsibilities of bishops, priests, deacons, consecrated religious, and the laity; and how to resolve conflicts among members of the Church. Canon Law even gives penalties that apply when certain canons are broken. Canon Law is of course based in Eternal Law and applies the truths of Eternal Law to life within the Church community.

The Magisterium and Moral Teaching

The moral guidance of the Church goes beyond the Precepts of the Church and Canon Law. God has given the **Magisterium**—the bishops of the world united with the Pope—the responsibility for passing on and teaching his revealed truth. Revelation includes moral truth, and so the Magisterium has the responsibility for teaching the fullness of the New Law of Christ first to the Church and to the entire world.

CATHOLICS **MAKING** A DIFFERENCE

© Alina Reybakh / Shutterstock.com

Living the Law of Love doesn't mean having to take on huge moral issues. Saint André Bessette (1845–1937) shows us how to do it as part of ordinary life. Brother André is a Canadian saint. He joined the Holy Cross Brothers in 1870, but due to ongoing illness, his duties consisted mainly of washing floors and windows, carrying firewood, and greeting visitors and tending to their needs. Many of these visitors experienced healings after he prayed for them, and his reputation spread. Brother André attributed these cures to Saint Joseph, to whom he had a great devotion. André eventually built a shrine to Saint Joseph in Montreal, using the nickels he received from giving students haircuts. Eventually, this humble shrine became a basilica with side altars filled with the crutches of people healed through his prayers. Over a million people paid their respects after his death in 1937. André was canonized by Pope Benedict XVI on October 17, 2010.

Magisterium ➤ The Church's living teaching office, which consists of all bishops, in communion with the Pope, the Bishop of Rome. Their task is to interpret and preserve the truths revealed in both Sacred Scripture and Sacred Tradition.

The Magisterium always applies Christ's moral teaching to modern situations. In recent times, they have given moral direction on such issues as genetic testing, the use of embryos in medical research, abortion, the death penalty, and immigration laws. When speaking on these issues, they apply natural law and reason to appeal to people of diverse faiths and beliefs. The people who make civil laws do not always accept the moral truth spoken by the Pope and the bishops, but the Church's voice must be an important part of the dialogue.

Catholics always have a special obligation to listen carefully to what the Pope and bishops say about moral matters. The Magisterium ensures that we stay faithful to the teaching of the Apostles in matters of faith and morals. When the Pope and the bishops agree on a matter of faith and morals, they speak with **infallibility**. This means that the Holy Spirit guides them to teach the truths, or doctrines, of our faith without error. Infallibility has three levels:

Level 1: Infallibility of the Deposit of Faith. The divinely revealed truths that are part of the Deposit of Faith and handed down through Scripture and Tradition are always true. These can be defined and explained by the Pope *ex cathedra* ("from the chair") or by the college of bishops when gathered at an Ecumenical Council. This level of infallibility also applies to individual bishops when they are teaching about the Deposit of Faith and their teaching is in union with the college of bishops and the Pope. We, the faithful, are required to give our assent and obedience to these teachings.

Level 2: Infallibility of Teaching on the Deposit of Faith. The Church's infallibility also extends to the doctrines that are necessary to explain and safeguard the truths contained in the Deposit of Faith. The doctrine of infallibility is one of these necessary teachings. Similar to the first level, infallible doctrines in this level can be declared by the Pope, or by the bishops in an Ecumenical Council, or they can be taught by individual bishops. We are required to give our assent and obedience to these teachings too.

Level 3: Other Authentic Teaching by the Magisterium. The Pope and bishops regularly release other teachings to deepen our understanding of Revelation in regard to faith and morals. These can be papal encyclicals, apostolic exhortations, teaching documents from Ecumenical Councils, and teaching documents released by bishops' conferences and individual bishops. These documents not only deepen our understanding of the revealed truths of faith but also safeguard us from false teachings. Though these teachings are not infallible and may further develop over time, we should give them our most serious consideration and presume their truth out of respect for the teaching office of the Church.✳

---

infallibility ➤ The gift given by the Holy Spirit to the Church whereby the Magisterium of the Church, the Pope and the bishops in union with him, can definitively proclaim a doctrine of faith and morals without error.

1. Why is every person obliged to follow moral law?

2. Name five different types or expressions of moral law.

3. Describe natural law.

4. Why is natural moral law important?

5. What law do the Ten Commandments summarize? What is another name for the Ten Commandments?

6. Why is the New Law called "New"?

7. Give an overview of the content of the Sermon on the Mount.

8. Describe the two types of Church law.

9. What is infallibility?

Hinduism
This is the sum of duty:
do not do to others what would
cause pain if done to you
Mahabharata 5:1517

Buddhism
Treat not others in ways
that you yourself would
find hurtful
The Buddha, Udana-Varga 5.18

Baha'i Faith
Lay not on any soul a load
that you would not wish to
be laid upon you, and
desire not for
anyone the
things you
would
not
desire for
yourself
Baha'u'llah, Gleanings

Confucianism
One word which sums up the
basis of all good conduct...
loving-kindness.
Do not do to
others what
you do not
want done
to yourself
Confucius, Analects 15.23

Islam
Not one of you truly believes
until you wish for others what
you wish for yourself
The Prophet Muhammad, Hadith

Taoism
Regard your neighbour's gain
as your own gain, and your
neighbour's loss as your own loss
Lao Tzu, T'ai Shang Kan Ying P'ien, 213-218

Judaism
What is hateful to you,
do not do to your neighbour.
This is the whole Torah;
all the rest is commentary
Hillel, Talmud, Shabbat 31a

Sikhism
I am a stranger to no one;
and no one is a stranger
to me. Indeed, I am
a friend to all
Guru Granth Sahib, p. 1299

THE GOLDEN RULE

Jainism
One should treat all
creatures in the world
as one would like
to be treated
Mahavira, Sutrakritanga

Christianity
In everything, do to others
as you would have them
do to you; for this is the
law and the prophets
Jesus, Matthew 7:12

Zoroastrianism
Do not do unto others
whatever is injurious
to yourself
Shayast-na-Shayast 13.29

Native Spirituality
We are as much alive
as we keep the earth alive
Chief Dan George

Unitarianism
We affirm and promote respect
for the interdependent
web of all existence
of which we are a part
Unitarian principle

Published by Paul McKenna
Copyright © Paul McKenna 2000
interfaithgold@gmail.com

WORLD RELIGIONS AND THE GOLDEN RULE

1. Which of these statements reminds you most of the Golden Rule from Christianity?

2. Why do so many of the world's religions have this concept as part of their teaching?

CHAPTER 3
Sin and Its Consequences

IS THERE REALLY SUCH A THING AS SIN?

SNAPSHOT

Article 10

Sin in the Old Testament

Is the word *sin* a part of your vocabulary? Sin is real. It is deliberately choosing to act in a way that is contrary to God's will. There are small sins and big sins, sins that mostly harm the person committing them (but never only that person) and sins that harm thousands or maybe even millions of people.

Some people claim that awareness of sin is disappearing from our society. Annual Gallup polls taken since 2002 indicate that the majority of the United States' population (varies between 64 percent and 82 percent) believe the country's moral values are getting worse. We could view this statistic as encouraging news because it means the majority of people in this country care

TAKE IT TO GOD

Have mercy on me, God, in accord with your merciful love;
    in your abundant compassion blot out my transgressions.
Thoroughly wash away my guilt;
    and from my sin cleanse me.
For I know my transgressions;
    my sin is always before me.
Against you, you alone have I sinned;
    I have done what is evil in your eyes. . . .
Cleanse me with hyssop, that I may be pure;
    wash me, and I will be whiter than snow.
You will let me hear gladness and joy;
    the bones you have crushed will rejoice.
Turn away your face from my sins;
    blot out all my iniquities.
A clean heart create for me, God;
    renew within me a steadfast spirit. . . .
My sacrifice, O God, is a contrite spirit;
    a contrite, humbled heart, O God, you will not scorn.
(Psalm 51: 3–6,9–12,19)

enough about morality to notice that it needs improving. Or we could view it as discouraging news because it means that even though a majority of people believe the country's moral values are declining, it doesn't seem to be making any difference!

Regardless of how aware our society is about sin, in the Bible sin is a prominent topic. The word *sin* and its variations occur 915 times in the New American Bible translation. The central focus of salvation history is how God saves us from sin and death. Sin entered the world through the sin of Adam and Eve. And with sin came death. Sin and death were not part of God's plan for human beings. Throughout history, God has worked to save us from our slavery to sin and death. Starting with his covenants with Noah, Abraham, and the Israelites, continuing through the preaching of the prophets, and culminating in the Paschal Mystery, the Bible tells how the miraculous power of God's saving love defeats sin and death once and for all.

Rebelling against God

One key idea about sin, especially in the Old Testament, is that sin is rebelling against God. This happens at the beginning of salvation history when Adam and Eve disobey God's direct command not to eat the fruit from the tree of the knowledge of good and evil (see Genesis 2:1–6). It is also a common theme in Exodus. The Israelites openly rebel against God by grumbling against him in the desert (see Exodus 16:2) and by creating and worshipping a golden calf (see Exodus, chapter 32). At the end of his life, Moses even says:

> Take this book of the law and put it beside the ark of the covenant of the LORD, your God, that there it may be a witness against you. For I already know how rebellious and stiff-necked you will be. Why, even now, while I am alive among you, you have been rebels against the LORD! (Deuteronomy 31:26–27)

The prophets spoke frequently about sin as a rebellious attitude toward God:

> Ah! Rebellious children,
>   oracle of the LORD,
> Who carry out a plan that is not mine,
>   who make an alliance I did not inspire,
>   thus adding sin upon sin.
>
>   (Isaiah 30:1)

But this people's heart is stubborn and rebellious;
> they turn and go away,
And do not say in their hearts,
> "Let us fear the LORD, our God."

> > > (Jeremiah 5:23–24)

"Son of man, you live in the midst of a rebellious house; they have eyes to see, but do not see, and ears to hear but do not hear. They are such a rebellious house!" (Ezekiel 12:2)

The Hebrew word most often used to express this idea is *pesha'*, which is translated as *transgression* or *rebellion* or *sin*. Why do we rebel against God? We rebel because we want life to be different than it is, and ultimately we want God to be different than he is; we want to be "in control." But rebelling against God is kind of like rebelling against the air or the sun. God is love and truth and life; we have no existence outside of him. Why rebel against that

The Israelites rebelled against God because they grew tired of waiting for Moses to return from the holy mountain. What are some reasons people rebel against God's Law today?

which makes life possible? Living a moral life means accepting God's Eternal Law as it is and not as we want it to be, and accepting God as he is and not as we want him to be. This is what Jesus meant when he said that we must have a childlike faith in the Kingdom of God (see Mark 10:14); we must trust that God loves us even more than we love ourselves.

Missing the Mark

The Hebrew word in the Old Testament most commonly translated as sin is *chatâ'*, a word that means "to miss," as in an archer missing his target. This concept points to another key understanding of sin, that sin is missing the goal of living a life in harmony with God's Eternal Law. This understanding of sin is slightly different than seeing sin only as an active rebellion against God because *chatâ'* indicates a desire to live according to God's will but failing in some of our attempts to do so. Some reasons for this failure are a lack of commitment, not setting our moral standards high enough, letting outside forces influence us—this list could go on and on.

Sin as an occasion of missing the mark happens throughout salvation history. In fact, many of Israel's greatest heroes were guilty of this. Here are just a few of the instances recorded:

- After God gives Gideon victories in battle, Gideon makes a golden idol, breaking the First Commandment (see Judges 8:27).
- The mighty judge Samson breaks the Law repeatedly: he marries a foreign woman, touches a dead lion's carcass, takes outrageous revenge, visits prostitutes, and reveals the secret of his divine power to another foreign woman (see Judges 14:1–16,19).
- The sons of the wise judge, priest, and prophet Samuel "looked to their own gain, accepting bribes and perverting justice" (see 1 Samuel 8:3).
- King David, known for his great faith in God, committed adultery and then arranged for the husband of the woman he got pregnant to be killed in battle (see 2 Samuel, chapter 11).
- King Solomon, known as one of the wisest men in the Bible, had many foreign wives and joined them in worshipping their foreign gods and goddesses (see 1 Kings 11:1–10).

The understanding that sin is missing the mark points out a reality that Saint Paul names in one of his letters: "What I do, I do not understand. For I do not do what I want, but I do what I hate" (Romans 7:15). Sometimes sin seems to have its own life within us; even when we want to do what is right, something in us makes us act wrongly. But realizing our inclination to act in this way can be an occasion of grace because missing the mark should make it

© avid_creative / iStockphoto.com

Rebellion can be good when protesting injustices, but it is never good when protesting against God's Law.

clear to us that we cannot overcome sin on our own power. We must ask for and trust in the grace of Christ given to us through the power of the Holy Spirit. We can find encouragement in these further words of Paul: "The Spirit too comes to the aid of our weakness. . . . We know that all things work for good for those who love God" (Romans 8:26,28).

Consequences of Sin

Under the Old Covenant, there was a tendency for the Israelites to think you would be punished for sin or rewarded for virtue in this life, rather than the next. Many thought that if you were prosperous, you must be free from sin. If you were suffering hardship, then God must be punishing you for your sins. Many also believed that God punished children for the sins of their parents, with seemingly contradictory teachings in the Old Testament itself (see for example Numbers 14:18 and Ezekiel 18:20). There was also the temptation, as there could be for us today, to think that God's punishment for sin is a type of vengeance he takes on us, or to think that once we have sinned, God totally forsakes us.

We see these misunderstandings reflected in some Old Testament passages. This does not mean that the Old Covenant was wrong, only that the Israelites did not fully understand it or live their Covenant with God. We must interpret these Old Testament passages in light of the whole Bible to properly understand them. When Jesus comes, he clarifies these misinterpretations and helps the people of his time, and us, to know and understand God's Covenant more clearly. Further, he and his heavenly Father send the Holy Spirit to provide the grace we need to live out God's Law. There are many linguistic styles and types of writing in Scripture, and we need the bigger picture to interpret them.

The Church Jesus founded also helps us to faithfully interpret Scripture and have greater clarity on what sin is and how its consequences play out in our lives. Contrary to these misunderstandings about the consequences for sin, the Church teaches us that we should not think of punishment for sin as some kind of vengeance inflicted on us by God; rather, punishment for sin flows directly from the nature of sin. Sin causes death—most importantly, spiritual death—which causes deep suffering in our souls. Further, our sins don't just harm us though; they injure others (including family members) but not as a punishment from God. By its very nature, our sin affects the entire community, just as our acts of virtue build up the entire community.

When we look at the whole of Scripture, we also see how God sometimes allows us to experience hardships so we might repent from sin and find God's mercy and healing. God often did this in the Old Testament to help the Israelites turn back to him after they sinned. And lest we think God forsakes us when we sin, on the contrary, God wants nothing more than to rescue us from sin, as evidenced by the saving mission of Jesus, who took on our sins and died for us that we might be restored to God's friendship. ✳

HMMMMM. . .

Which definition of sin speaks to you the most, rebelling against God or missing the mark? Why?

Article 11
Sin in the New Testament

"I'm just not sure I believe in sin," Jonas told Derek. The two friends were hiking while on a camping trip with their families. "I mean, people just make mistakes and don't always make the best choices when they're feeling strong emotions. Who am I to judge what's right or wrong for someone else?"

"Hmm," Derek mused. "So, you're saying that there are no absolute rights and wrongs? That you've never chosen to do something you know will hurt someone else out of spite or selfishness or just not caring? I guess you're a better person than I am! I know there are times I've fallen short of being the best I can be, and it's often because of a choice I've made."

"Well, when you put it that way," said Jonas, "it's kind of hard to argue with you."

New Testament Words for Sin

Hamartia is the most common Greek word used for *sin* in the New Testament. It means "falling short" and is essentially equivalent to the Hebrew word *chatâ'*. So the understanding of sin as "missing the moral mark" continues to be important in the New Testament.

© jentakespictures / iStockphoto.com

One result of sin is that it can lead to lawless situations or lawless communities that endanger human life and dignity.

Other Greek words associated with sin in the New Testament are *parap-toma* and *parabasis*, which can be translated as "transgression" (see Matthew 6:14–15 and Galatians 6:1), and *anomia*, which is usually translated as "lawlessness" (see 1 John 3:4). When we consider the meaning of these Greek words, an expanded understanding of sin emerges. Sin is not only missing the goal of living in accordance with God's will but also crossing a boundary established by God and breaking the natural law that is written on every human heart (see Romans 2:14–16). The result is that human beings live in lawless communities that do not reflect God's plan for humanity. Although these concepts can be found in the Old Testament, the New Testament provides some new teaching that deepens our understanding of the reality of sin.

New Testament Lists of Sins	
Several New Testament passages list sins that were common at the time the New Testament was written. How are these sins part of our culture? What other sins would you add to these lists?	
Matthew 15:19	"For from the heart come evil thoughts, murder, adultery, unchastity, theft, false witness, blasphemy."
Romans 1:29–31	"They are filled with every form of wickedness, evil, greed, and malice; full of envy, murder, rivalry, treachery, and spite. They are gossips and scandalmongers and they hate God. They are insolent, haughty, boastful, ingenious in their wickedness, and rebellious toward their parents. They are senseless, faithless, heartless, ruthless."
Galatians 5:19–21	"Now the works of the flesh are obvious: immorality, impurity, licentiousness, idolatry, sorcery, hatreds, rivalry, jealousy, outbursts of fury, acts of selfishness, dissensions, factions, occasions of envy, drinking bouts, orgies, and the like."

Light and Truth versus Darkness and Lies

In the Gospel of John, Jesus says this in response to some questions from the Pharisee Nicodemus:

And this is the verdict, that the light came into the world, but people preferred darkness to light, because their works were evil. For everyone who does wicked things hates the light and does not come toward the light, so that his works might not be exposed. But whoever lives with the truth comes to the light, so that his works may be clearly seen as done in God. (3:19–24)

Jesus is revealing an important insight about sin: every sin is a lie against the truth, a lie about what truly brings God's saving love and joy into the world. People sin because they have fooled themselves into believing that a sinful action will make them happy or fulfilled. They tell themselves that this little bit of cheating, this act of revenge, this physical pleasure, or this act of stealing will make them happy. And maybe it will for a while, but the feeling of happiness that comes from sin is not lasting, because sin does not lead to beatitude, the true and lasting happiness that comes from union with God.

This brings us to the second insight about sin in Jesus' statement, which is that sinful acts are done in darkness—not literal darkness, of course, but metaphorical darkness. You will meet some people who brag about their sinful actions, but these people are the exception. Most people keep their sins secret because they are ashamed of them, because deep in their hearts they know that their actions are lies against God's truth and are wrong.

Jesus says, "I am the light of the world" (John 8:12) and "I am the way and the truth and the life" (14:6). To escape the lies and darkness of sin, we must accept and follow Jesus Christ, the light and the truth.

In the Gospel of John, Jesus presents us with a clear choice: we can live in the darkness of sin, or we can live in the light of God's love.

Everyone Has Sinned

Another truth about sin made clear in the New Testament is that everyone, except Jesus and his mother, Mary, is affected by Original Sin and is subject to death and a weakened nature prone to evil because of this. This truth is implied in the Gospels, but it is made explicit in the writings of Saint Paul. For example, John the Baptist proclaims "a baptism of repentance for the forgiveness of sins" (Mark 1:4). Jesus implies that people in all nations have sinned when he charges the Apostles to continue his mission, saying, "Thus it is written that the Messiah would suffer and rise from the dead on the third day and that repentance, for the forgiveness of sins, would be preached in his name to all the nations" (Luke 24:46–47).

Saint Paul directly addresses this in his Letter to the Romans. Paul speaks at length about sin, its effects, and how we are freed from it. He teaches that Jews and Greeks (meaning all non-Jews) are "all under the domination of sin" (3:9). A few verses later, he says, "All have sinned and are deprived of the glory of God" (verse 23). A few chapters later, he makes the point again: "Therefore, just as through one person sin entered the world, and through sin, death, and thus death came to all, inasmuch as all sinned" (5:12). Paul is teaching the Romans and all believers that we all need the salvation that comes through faith in Jesus Christ.

Forgiveness

Both the Old and New Testaments speak about punishment for sin and also God's mercy; however, the teaching on forgiveness for sins takes on a more central focus in the New Testament. With the arrival of Jesus—the promised and long-awaited Messiah—in the New Testament, we read the Good News of the forgiveness of sins offered to us through the life, death, and Resurrection of Jesus, who took upon himself the sins of the whole world. We see Jesus teaching in parables about his mission to bring us forgiveness and inviting us to repent and believe in him and his power to save us.

Jesus is concerned about sin. He uses hyperbole—a literary style that uses exaggeration to make a point—to teach how serious sin is: "If your right eye causes you to sin, tear it out and throw it away. It is better for you to lose one of your members than to have your whole body thrown into Gehenna" (Matthew 5:29). But what Jesus emphasizes even more is that he has come to reach out to sinners and to forgive sin. Jesus proclaims, "I did not come to call the righteous but sinners" (9:13). He goes to the homes of people stigmatized as public sinners and dines with them (verse 10). He forgives the sins of the paralytic (see Luke 5:20), the sinful woman who washes his feet (see 7:48), and the woman caught in adultery (see John 8:11). He tells many stories—the Parable of the Lost Sheep (see Matthew 18:10–14),

The New Testament places great emphasis on God's forgiveness. The Church continues Christ's ministry of forgiveness through the Sacrament of Penance and Reconciliation.

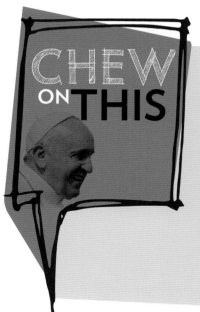

CHEW ON THIS

We are all sinners. Is this true? If any of you does not feel you are a sinner, raise your hand. . . . No one. We all are sinners. We sinners, with forgiveness, become new creatures, filled by the spirit and full of joy. Now a new reality begins for us: a new heart, a new spirit, a new life. We, forgiven sinners, who have received divine grace, can even teach others to sin no more. (Pope Francis, "General Audience," March 30, 2016)

the Parable of the Unforgiving Servant (see verses 21–35), the Parable of the Prodigal Son (see Luke 15:11–32)—that show his power to forgive sins and God's desire to save us from our sins.

Jesus also emphasizes how critical it is that his followers practice loving forgiveness. In the Sermon on the Mount, he teaches, "As you judge, so will you be judged" (Matthew 7:2). In giving us the Lord's Prayer, he emphasizes this: "forgive us our debts, as we forgive our debtors" (6:12). When Peter asks how many times we should be willing to forgive someone who sins against us, Jesus tells Peter we must forgive not seven times, as Peter suggests, but seventy-seven times (see Matthew 18:22)—meaning an unlimited number. Jesus shared the power to forgive sins in God's name with his Apostles (see John 20:22–23). This wonderful gift in which sins are forgiven in God's name is still with the Church today in the Sacrament of Penance and Reconciliation.

This emphasis on forgiving sin is the heart of the New Law, the Law of Love. Christ teaches us that God is primarily waiting to forgive us, not to condemn us. God loves us so much that he wants us to be free from the burden of sin, from the shame, the isolation, the hungers that are never satisfied. This freedom can happen only if we accept God's forgiveness and die to sin through Baptism and live a life of faith in Christ. Then we will be given the grace to forgive ourselves. After that, we will be given the grace to forgive others, as hard as that may be to do at times.

The Consequences of Sin

The New Testament is clear about the ultimate consequences of sin. In his Letter to the Romans, Paul says, "For the wages of sin is death, but the gift of God is eternal life in Christ Jesus our Lord" (6:23). Paul is confirming the teaching of the Old Testament—sin leads to death. We have all sinned and we all will die. But Paul adds something new: Death is not the end! Because of his obedient, loving sacrifice, Jesus Christ opened the doors to life after death, eternal life in Heaven for all who believe in him.

Jesus' work of salvation does not mean that Heaven is guaranteed for all people. In the Parable of the Last Judgment, Jesus teaches that the penalty for those who fail to live the Law of Love is the "eternal fire prepared for the devil and his angels" (Matthew 25:41). For those who live a life of unrepented sin, Hell is the ultimate consequence.

In his earthly teaching, Jesus corrects some misunderstandings about the consequences of sin, such as that every bad thing that happens to us is a punishment from God. When his disciples ask him, "Who sinned, this man or his parents, that he was born blind?" Jesus replies, "Neither he nor his parents sinned" (John 9:2–3). In another place, Jesus says about some Galileans who were killed by Pilate: "Do you think that because these Galileans suffered in this way they were greater sinners than all other Galileans? By no means!" (Luke 13:2–3). From passages like this, we learn that the bad things that happen to us are not always a punishment from God, and he does not directly punish people's children for their parents' sins

Similarly, Jesus teaches that just because some people are blessed with material wealth does not mean that they are living a life pleasing to God. In the Parable of the Rich Man and Lazarus (see Luke 16:19–31) and the Parable of the Rich Fool (see 12:16–21), Jesus makes it clear that being materially blessed in this life does not necessarily mean you will be rewarded in the next. ✳

HMMMMMM. . .   What are your thoughts on forgiveness and its importance?

Article 12
Requirements for Sin

To truly understand a concept, it often helps to start with a definition of the words associated with that concept. Definitions force us to be clear and consistent about what we believe. They provide a common language and a common understanding so that we can intelligently discuss abstract concepts and complex realities. Sin is one of those complex realities. Sin can be about serious matters and less serious matters. Some actions almost everyone agrees are sinful in all circumstances, and other actions may or may not be sinful depending on the circumstances and the intention behind the action. All this makes it challenging to define sin in a single, clear statement.

Fortunately, God guides the Church to truth and clarity, and the Church guides us in our understanding of sin and what is sinful.

A Definition of Sin

The glossary of the *Catechism of the Catholic Church* gives this definition for *sin*:

> [Sin is] an offense against God as well as a fault against reason, truth, and right conscience. Sin is a deliberate thought, word, deed, or omission contrary to the Eternal Law of God. In judging the gravity of sin, it is customary to distinguish between mortal and venial sins. (Page 899)

The first part of this definition sums up almost everything we have discussed about Scripture's teaching on sin. Sin is primarily an offense against God; it is rebellion against God's will and his desire that we live in loving communion with him and with one another. It is a rejection of God's love for us. When we sin, we put our will before God's will, our desires before God's desires. We make ourselves the center of the universe. This is the exact opposite of the obedience of Jesus Christ, who "humbled himself, becoming obedient to death" (Philippians 2:8).

Sin is also an offense against the truth of God's Eternal Law and against the gift of reason that we use to understand natural law. It is a betrayal of right conscience, which is the sure knowledge of what is right and wrong that we are working to develop within our hearts. Sin is a rejection of the gifts that God has provided us to live a life pleasing to him, a life devoted to his Law of Love. Sin leaves us wounded in body, mind, and soul, and wounded in our relationships with God and others.

Sin is the result of a deliberate thought, word, or deed. The hurt caused by sinful words can be just as damaging as a physical attack.

The *Catechism's* definition also makes clear what kind of things can be sins. Sin can be a deed or act, of course. But sin can also be a word. Words can be used to reject God, to tell lies, or to hurt other people through gossip, libel, or cruel remarks. Thoughts can also be sins—not the thoughts that enter our heads unbidden and we quickly dismiss, but the thoughts of revenge, lust, envy, or domination that we dwell on and keep alive. These thoughts are real, they are in our control, and they negatively affect our relationships with God and with one another. The *Catechism's* definition is clear that thoughts and actions must be deliberate to be sinful; they cannot be accidental or unintended.

What Makes Something a Sin?

Three elements determine the morality of any human act: (1) the **object**, that is, the specific thing the person is choosing to do, (2) the **intention** of the person doing the action, and (3) the **circumstances** surrounding the act.

---

object ➤ In moral decision-making, the object is the specific thing—an act, word, or thought—that is being chosen.

intention ➤ The intended outcome or goal of the person choosing the object when making a moral decision.

circumstances ➤ The specific conditions or facts affecting a moral decision. Circumstances can increase or decrease the goodness or evil of an action.

In determining whether a human act is morally good or morally bad, we must consider all three elements together. For an act to be morally good, the object, intention, and circumstances must all be good. The circumstances play a secondary role, as they can affect the person's moral freedom.

Consider a situation in which Marj is organizing a fundraiser to help earthquake victims. Marj wants to keep everyone's focus on the suffering people, so she stays in the background, not making a big deal about the work she is doing. In this case, Marj's act is morally good because both the object (raising money for charity) and the intention (helping people who are in need) are good.

On the other hand, let's say Orlando is also organizing a fundraiser to help earthquake victims. Unlike Marj, Orlando's only reason for doing this is to draw attention to himself. He uses every opportunity to get his picture in the news and to talk about himself. The object of Orlando's act (raising money for charity) is good, but the intention (Orlando's pride) is bad. This makes Orlando's act sinful. Doing the right thing for the wrong reasons will not make your actions morally good.

© m-imagephotography / iStockphoto.com

Rudy is interviewing for a job and he's asked you to be one of his character references. Rudy used to have occasional seizures caused by a medical procedure. However, for the last year, he's been on a new medication and he's been seizure-free. The new job requires Rudy to use some heavy machinery, which would be a real disaster if Rudy had a seizure while operating them. "I really want this job," Rudy tells you, "and since I've been seizure-free for a year, you don't need to mention them." The problem is that the reference form asks if you know of any reason why Rudy might not be able to perform his job. Considering the three elements of a moral act—the object, the intention, and the circumstances—what do you do?

Why does a person's intention matter when they are performing an objectively good act?

The circumstances surrounding a situation can affect how good or bad an act is. For example, let's say Marj's friends are pressuring her to take more credit for her fundraising work. Under these circumstances, the goodness of Marj's actions is even greater because she is resisting that pressure.

A final consideration is that some actions are evil in themselves, and they are always wrong to choose. Good intentions or special circumstances can never make these actions morally good or even less evil. Put simply, you cannot do an action that is evil in itself, even if some good might come from it. Rape would be one example of an action that is always wrong. Circumstances such as being drunk or being pressured by peers to commit this act will never make such a choice less evil. Other examples of actions that are always morally wrong are adultery, murder, and blasphemy. These things are never morally right—ever. ✳

HMMMMM. . .

How could an action objectively be a sin, but the person doing it might be innocent of committing a sin?

Article 13

Types of Sin

You may have seen it happen. Two students get into a fight in a school hallway, and everyone just stops and watches, not wanting to get involved. A classmate is unfairly talking down another classmate, and others just listen without coming to the person's defense. A neighbor kicks and beats his dog, and other neighbors ignore its cries without reporting the abuse. Are those who are ignoring these sinful behaviors guilty of sin? Are some of these sins so serious that they separate us completely from God?

Sins of Commission and Omission

Some people fall into the trap of believing that we are only responsible for the sins we directly commit, sins that are the direct result of our deliberate thoughts, words, or deeds. We call these kinds of sins **sins of commission**. But the *Catechism* also talks about **sins of omission**. A sin of omission occurs when we fail to do something that is required by God's moral law.

I DIDN'T KNOW THAT!

Many Catholic saints had sinful pasts before they became committed to Christ. You know that Saint Peter denied Christ and that Saint Paul persecuted Christians. But did you know that Saint Olga (879–969), the first canonized Russian saint, had hundreds of people killed when she became the first woman ruler of Russia? Saint Vladimir (956–1015) murdered his half brother and built a temple to a false god. Saint Mary of Egypt (344–421) was sexually promiscuous before her conversion. Blessed Bartolo Longo (1841–1926) was a satanic priest. These saints are a testimony to the power of God's grace and forgiveness. Remember, there is nothing you can do that can separate you from God's love if you seek his forgiveness and reconciliation.

sin of commission ➤ A sin that is the direct result of a freely chosen thought, word, or deed.

sin of omission ➤ A sin that is the result of a failure to do something required by God's moral law.

For example, let's say you witness a classmate egging a neighbor's house. Later your neighbor comes over and asks your family if they saw anything. You say nothing because you do not want to get your classmate into trouble. You did not directly tell a lie, so are you guilty of a sin? Yes, you are guilty of a sin of omission because you are required by the Eighth Commandment to tell the truth and instead you withheld it.

Mortal Sin and Venial Sin

Sins can have different degrees of severity (or what the *Catechism* calls "gravity"). The most basic distinction in this regard is between mortal sins and venial sins. A **mortal sin** is a serious offense against God, one that destroys within us the virtue of charity, which helps us to love God and our neighbor. A mortal sin involves serious immoral acts, or what the Church calls "grave matter." The Ten Commandments specify the issues that constitute grave matter. Jesus referred to the Ten Commandments when he spoke to the rich young man who asked him how to inherit eternal life (see Mark 10:19). Jesus implied to the young man that sins against the Ten Commandments, if unrepented, would keep us from eternal life. This is the reason they are called mortal sins; mortal means "death," and these sins have the power to cause eternal death—that is, eternal separation from God.

For a sin to be a mortal sin, the person committing it must have full knowledge of the immorality of the act and give their complete consent to doing it. They must know how wrong an action is and then deliberately and freely choose to do it. A person cannot unintentionally commit a mortal sin. Accidentally seeing a few answers on your classmate's test is not a mortal sin.

Venial sins are less serious than mortal sins because they do not destroy our relationship with God and our ability to love. But they do damage these things. Venial sins involve a lesser degree of evil, or they may be seriously wrong acts committed without full knowledge of just how wrong they are. Or a venial sin may involve a seriously wrong act, such as failing to attend Mass on Sunday (a sin against the Third Commandment), which is lessened by some circumstance, such as sleeping through your alarm after staying out too

---

mortal sin ➤ An action so contrary to the will of God that it results in a complete separation from God and his grace. As a consequence of that separation, the person is condemned to eternal death. For a sin to be a mortal sin, three conditions must be met: the act must involve a grave matter, the person must have full knowledge of the evil of the act, and the person must give full consent in committing the act.

venial sin ➤ A less serious offense against the will of God that diminishes one's personal character and weakens but does not rupture one's relationship with God.

When might cheating on a test be a venial sin? When might it be a more serious sin?

late the night before. With God's grace, charity can repair the damage to our relationship with God caused by venial sins.

Venial sins are closely associated with **vices**. Vices are the opposite of **virtues**, which are habits of good actions. When we keep repeating sins, even venial ones, we are in danger of forming bad habits, called vices. The danger of developing a vice is that it makes it easier to sin without seriously thinking about it. Ultimately, this makes it easier to commit mortal sin. Let's return to the example of cheating on a test. Let's say that one day you just don't have time to study properly, and you "accidentally" see an answer on someone else's test for a question you aren't sure of, and you use it. This approach turns out to be so simple and effective that you repeat this sin by copying an answer or two on other tests. You are developing a vice for cheating. Then one day someone offers you a complete test with all the answers, stolen from a teacher's file. This is a serious sin, but the vice you have developed for cheating makes it hard to resist the temptation.

---

vice ➤ A practice or habit that leads a person to sin.

virtue ➤ A habitual and firm disposition to do good.

The Seven Deadly Sins

Church doctrine identifies and cautions against seven particularly harmful sins. They are sometimes referred to as **capital sins**—meaning "most serious or influential"—because they lead to and reinforce all sorts of other sinful actions, thoughts, and omissions. The capital sins, all of which are sins against God, are deadly in that they increase our tendency to sin and cause us to turn away more and more from God. For example, the capital sin of envy can lead to spreading rumors about people who have more than you do or to lying or stealing to get the things you want. Here is a list of the seven deadly sins with present-day definitions:

The Seven Deadly (Capital) Sins	
Pride	Believing you are better than others, often resulting in despising or disrespecting other people. Pride is the root of all sins, including those of disobedience committed by Satan and Adam and Eve.
Greed (Covetousness)	Greediness; hoarding money and things
Envy	Resentment that we direct at others who have some success, thing, or privilege that we want for ourselves
Anger (Wrath)	Strong anger that makes us want to seek revenge and prevents reconciliation.
Lust	Undisciplined, unchecked desire for self-enjoyment, especially of a sexual nature
Gluttony	Excessive eating or drinking
Sloth	Habitual laziness; failing to put forth effort and take action

Do you struggle with any of these sins? Have you noticed in your own experience that these seven sins make it hard to resist other sins? One way to overcome the struggle against sin is through the practice of the human virtues. Virtues are firm attitudes, stable dispositions, and the habitual perfection of our intellect and our will that guide our actions according to reason and faith.

---

capital sins ➤ Seven sins that lead to and reinforce other sins and vices. The seven are traditionally called pride, covetousness (greed), envy, anger (wrath), gluttony, lust, and sloth.

Human virtues develop in us through practice. Practice helps us harness the power of grace within us, and the more we practice, the easier it is to make good moral decisions and achieve our God-given potential. By choosing to do what is good, we grow in virtue and become increasingly disposed to choose what pleases God and to seek communion with him.

© Lightspring / Shutterstock.com

The seven capital sins, such as gluttony, can be deadly. Which capital sin is the most prevalent in our culture?

Christian morality, then, is being the person God created you to be—a person who chooses to be good. You grow into a moral person by choosing good acts, carefully examining your motives to be sure your intentions are good, and avoiding circumstances that lessen your ability to choose freely. Choosing to act morally and avoiding sin have many benefits, including greater self-esteem, healthier relationships with others, and a deeper sense of the love of God coming through loud and clear in your life. ✳

HMMMMM. . .

Which capital sin(s) do you struggle with the most? Which virtues can you cultivate to help with your struggle?

Article 14
Social Sin

"After our religion class, I've been thinking about how hard our culture makes it to keep from sins like cheating, gossiping, being greedy, and having premarital sex," said Camille. "Then I started to realize how my sins and the sins of so many people altogether have big effects on society! Think about the terrible wars and political conflicts that are happening because of the sins of greed. Think about the struggle of refugees because of prejudice. And think about the huge number of abortions and broken families because of the lack of respect for life and dignity!"

"Yeah and then there's how we spend so much money on ourselves when there are so many people in need!" added Josh. "And what about the ways we contribute to problems with our environment, like pollution poisoning our air and water and even the threat of global climate change? Who knows how our sins can shape the world around us!"

Social Sins and Unjust Social Structures

Many sins, like the sins Camille and Josh are talking about, seem to infect societies. Things like war and the resulting refugees, pollution, unlivable wages, abortions, euthanasia, lack of health care, and so on become accepted as normal attitudes or actions by a significant number of people in that society. We could also point to how, even though slavery has ended in the United States, people of color are still much more likely to live in poverty, experience prejudice and violence from authorities, and end up in prison. These are just some of the better-known examples; many others could be listed.

Connected to this are injustices that seem to be the result of social structures that allow and support the causes of the injustice. Examples include people without jobs when others are overworked, people without homes when there could easily be enough homes for everyone, people who go hungry when supermarkets are full of food. You could probably add many more examples.

These sins fall under a category called **social sin**. Social sin is connected to the Gospel teaching on **social justice**. This article introduces the main concepts, and later articles speak to some specific issues of social justice.

---

social sin ➤ The impact that every personal sin has on other people; sin that directly attacks others' life, freedom, dignity, or rights; and the collective effect of many people's sins over time, which corrupts society and its institutions by creating "structures of sin."

social justice ➤ The defense of human dignity by ensuring that essential human needs are met and that essential human rights are protected for all people.

Human Dignity and the Common Good

Every person is created in the image of God. Therefore, every human being has infinite worth and dignity because we all share God's worth and dignity. No other thing, no amount of money, no building project, no scientific discovery, no new technology is more important than preserving the life and dignity of a single person. Every group, every culture, every nation—if it wants to be just—must make preserving the dignity of each person the highest priority in its planning, its laws, and its organizational structure.

Every community or group must respect and protect the rights and dignity of every person.

It is an essential part of human nature that we live in societies. God did not create man and woman to live alone and isolated. The community of the family and community of the **state** are an important part of God's plan. The doctrine of the Trinity can help us to understand this. Recall that God is a communion of three Divine Persons, living in perfect love and harmony. Because we have been created in God's image, our human communities should reflect the love and harmony of the Holy Trinity. Human communities must

---

state ➤ Any organized political authority in a specific area, such as a kingdom, a nation, a country, or a state within a country.

support our spiritual life and orient us toward, or at a minimum not get in the way of, our ultimate goal: eternal communion with God in Heaven. Communities do this by being attentive to what the Church calls the **common good**.

The Pastoral Constitution on the Church in the Modern World (*Gaudium et Spes*, 1965) gives excellent guidance on this topic. It defines the common good as "the sum of those conditions of social life which allow social groups and their individual members relatively thorough and ready access to their own fulfillment" (number 26). In other words, we ensure the common good by making sure that all persons' basic needs are met and their human rights are respected.

Papal Encyclicals on Social Sin		
Many popes have addressed the reality of social sin through teaching letters called encyclicals. Here are three important ones.		
Encyclical	Pope	Major Themes
"On the Condition of Labor" ("*Rerum Novarum*")	Pope Leo XIII, 1891	Addresses the Church's right to speak on social issues, and the rights and duties of workers and employers. Supports unions and the just wage.
"On Christianity and Social Progress" ("*Mater et Magistra*")	Pope Saint John XXIII, 1961	Says modern society is becoming more complex and interdependent. The gap between rich and poor nations threatens society, as does spending on nuclear weapons. When necessary, governments must act on these problems to protect the common good.
"On Care for Our Common Home" ("*Laudato Sí*")	Pope Francis, 2015	The first encyclical to focus on the environment and its destruction comprehensively. Brings attention to the way we have harmed the Earth through consumerism, pollution, environmental destruction, and global warming. Calls on all people to take swift and unified action to care for creation.

common good ➤ Social conditions that allow for all citizens of the Earth, individuals and families, to meet basic needs and achieve fulfillment.

Every person is equal in God-given dignity and has the same God-given rights. *The Church in the Modern World* goes on to say what some of the needs and rights are that must be made available to all people: "everything necessary for leading a life truly human, such as food, clothing, and shelter; the right to choose a state of life freely and to found a family, the right to education, to employment, to a good reputation, to respect, to appropriate information, to activity in accord with the upright norm of one's own conscience, to protection of privacy and rightful freedom even in matters religious" (number 26).

Although each individual and every community group has a responsibility to create and support institutions that improve the quality of human life, the political community has a specific responsibility to do so. States have the authority and responsibility to defend and promote the common good; it is the primary reason they exist. This authority comes from God.

A concept related to the common good is social justice. Social justice is the defense of human dignity by ensuring that essential human needs are met and that essential human rights are protected. A society that preserves the common good is practicing social justice.

CATHOLICS **MAKING** A **DIFFERENCE**

One of the most significant ways creation is being damaged by human beings today is the destruction of the Amazon rainforests. The Amazon rainforests produce 20 percent of the world's oxygen, so its loss affects the whole planet. Over 20 percent of the rainforest has been destroyed by logging and burning since the 1970s, and the rate of loss keeps increasing. The bishops of Latin America, both individually and as a group, are working for an end to the destruction. "We urge the governments of the Amazonian countries, especially Brazil and Bolivia, the United Nations and the international community to take serious measures to save the lungs of the world," the bishop's council (CELAM) said in an official statement. "If the Amazon suffers, the world suffers." (*Catholic News Service,* August 23, 2019)

Defining Social Sin

We are now ready to define *social sin*. Social sin is not one person's individual sin, but it is rooted in personal sin. Social sin is the collective effect of many people's personal sins. So if one employer pays a woman less than he pays a man for doing the same job, this is his personal sin. But if many employers in a city, state, or country pay women less than they pay men for doing the same jobs, they have created a situation of social sin. They are each guilty of personal sin, but they have produced a social condition in which injustice is accepted and tolerated. This is why many of the "isms"—racism, sexism, ageism—are often also instances of social sin.

©Romolo Tavani / Shutterstock.com

What responsibility do we have to fight social sin? How can we fight social sins such as environmental destruction, racism, poverty, and abortion?

Social sin happens when a sinful attitude or action becomes so commonly accepted that it goes unchallenged by most people. An example of this could be when a country's resources are concentrated in the hands of a few wealthy people while large numbers of people have barely enough to survive. Social sin can actually become a part of society's law. For example, there were states in the United States that had laws mandating that black Americans and white Americans live in separate neighborhoods and use separate public restrooms and separate seating on public transportation. That these laws ever existed points to the long-standing racial prejudice that had become (and sometimes still is) part of our laws and practices. Such established norms or laws are sometimes called structural sin or institutional sin, indicating that a social sin has become part of the fundamental attitudes, laws, and practices that make up the structure of society.

What are some of the worst social sins that are occurring in the world right now?

UNIT 1

1. Briefly describe two key understandings of sin found in the Old Testament.

2. What are some of the misunderstandings of sin reflected in the Old Testament?

3. Why does Jesus say that sin is about lies and darkness?

4. Name three things that Jesus teaches about forgiveness.

5. Define *sin*.

6. What three things determine whether a human act is a sin?

7. What is the difference between a mortal sin and a venial sin?

8. What is the relationship between personal sin and social sin?

9. Give three examples of social sin.

ART STUDY

THE SEVEN DEADLY SINS

1. Can you identify each of the seven deadly sins in this modern depiction?

2. Which sin is portrayed more as a social sin?

3. Do you think it is common for all seven deadly sins to be present in a single home?

UNIT 1 HIGHLIGHTS

CHAPTER 1   Moral Choices and God's Plan

God Gives These Gifts to Every Human Being

Soul: Our spiritual principle. It is immortal, it is the seat of human consciousness and freedom, and it is what makes us most like God.

Made in God's Image

Free will: The gift from God that allows human beings to choose from among various actions, for which we are held accountable.

Intellect: The divine gift that gives us the ability to see and understand the order in creation and to know God through the created order.

Justification: The Scales Are in Our Favor!

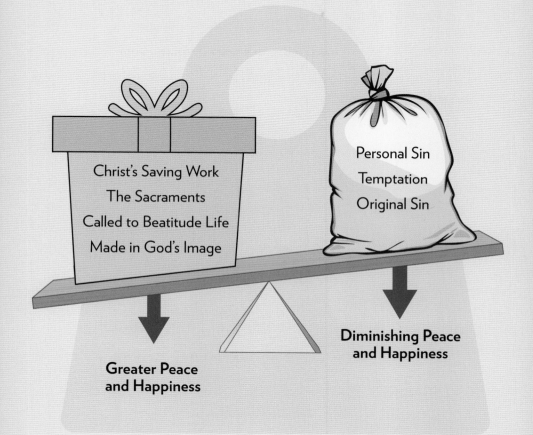

Christ's Saving Work
The Sacraments
Called to Beatitude Life
Made in God's Image

Personal Sin
Temptation
Original Sin

**Greater Peace
and Happiness**

**Diminishing Peace
and Happiness**

CHAPTER 2   The Law of God

The Expressions of Eternal Law

Natural Law

- Moral law that can be understood through our intellect and reason
- Available to every person

Old Law

- God's Law revealed in the Old Testament
- Summarized in the Ten Comandments delivered by Moses

New Law (Law of Love)

- Fufillment of the Old Law as revealed by Christ
- Taught by Jesus in the Sermon on the Mount
- Characterized by the Beatitudes

Great Commandments

Taught by Jesus as:
- Love God with your whole self.
- Love your neigbor as yourself.

The Old Law and the New Law

The New Law deepened and extended the meaning of the Old Law. The Great Commandments summarized both the Old and the New Laws.

The Old Law

The New Law

The Great Commandments

1. I am the LORD your God; you shall not have strange gods before me.
2. You shall not take the name of the LORD your God in vain.
3. Remember to keep holy the LORD's day.

"The sabbath was made for man, not man for the sabbath." (Mark 2:27)

"Love the Lord, your God with all your heart and with all your soul and and with all your mind." (Matthew 22:37)

4. Honor your father and your mother.
5. You shall not kill.
6. You shall not commit adultery.
7. You shall not steal.
8. You shall not bear false witness against your neighbor.
9. You shall not covet your neighbor's wife.
10. You shall not covet your neighbor's goods.

"You have heard that it was said to your ancestors, 'You shall not kill; and whoever kills will be liable to judgment.' But I say to you, whoever is angry with his brother will be liable to judgment." (Matthew 5:21–22)

"You shall love your neighbor as yourself." (Matthew 22:39)

CHAPTER 3   Sin and Its Consequences

Understandings of Sin from the Bible

Old Testament:
Rebelling against God
and against his Law

**Old
Testament:**
Missing
the mark

**New
Testament:**
Falling short

New Testament:
Darkness

Is It a Sin?

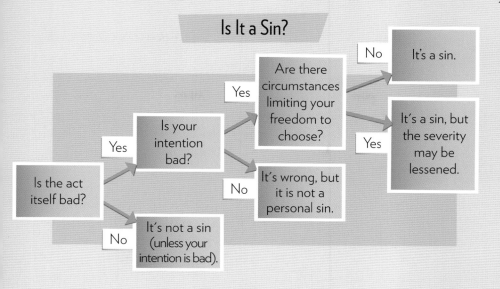

Is the act itself bad?

Yes → Is your intention bad?

No → It's not a sin (unless your intention is bad).

Yes → Are there circumstances limiting your freedom to choose?

No → It's wrong, but it is not a personal sin.

No → It's a sin.

Yes → It's a sin, but the severity may be lessened.

Types of Sin

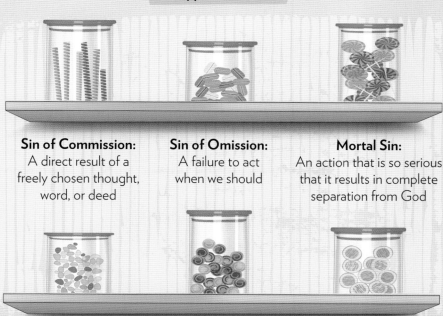

Sin of Commission:
A direct result of a freely chosen thought, word, or deed

Sin of Omission:
A failure to act when we should

Mortal Sin:
An action that is so serious that it results in complete separation from God

Venial Sin:
A less serious offense that weakens our relationship with God

Capital Sins:
Seven sins that lead to and reinforce other sins and vices

Social Sin:
The collective effect of many people's personal sins leading to social injustices that become widely accepted

UNIT 1

BRING IT HOME

HOW DO I KNOW WHAT IS "GOOD"?

FOCUS QUESTIONS

CHAPTER 1   Why does it matter how I act?

CHAPTER 2   How do I know how God wants me to act?

CHAPTER 3   Is there really such a thing as sin?

MIKE
Red Bank Catholic High School

Reading this unit reminds me that I should always live as God wants us to and remain in a loving relationship with him. Because human beings have been gifted with free will and intellect, it is up to our decision-making ability to know what is good and do it. Our primary goal in Christian morality is to collaborate with God and his graces. God will always help us and guide us in making the right decision. He provides many guides to help us, including the Ten Commandments, the Beatitudes, and the Golden Rule. Even so, I will still make mistakes, but God will always forgive me.

REFLECT

Take some time to read and reflect on the unit and chapter focus questions listed on the facing page:

- What question or section did you identify most closely with?

- What did you find within the unit that was comforting or challenging?

UNIT 2

Honoring God

DOES IT REALLY MATTER HOW I THINK ABOUT GOD?

LOOKING AHEAD

UNIT 2

How I think about God is very important. We need to understand that God loves us and sees us as his children, not as slaves or evil beings. He wants the best for us and does what is best for us even when it seems like the opposite is happening. I wish I knew more about how my understanding of God affects my actions and my life. I also would like to know if the Church has a specific stance about how we should see God, or is that left to our personal relationship with God?

DEMETRIOS
Our Lady of the Hills College
Preparatory School

CHAPTER 4
The First Commandment: Faith, Not Idolatry

IS THERE STILL SUCH A THING AS FALSE GODS?

SNAPSHOT

Article 15

Living the First Commandment

The first three commandments all have a common theme: loving and honoring God. They call us to love God above all else, to honor him by keeping holy names and holy things sacred, and to show our devotion by honoring the Lord's Day. Jesus, who is himself God, summarized the first three commandments with the first of his Great Commandments: "Hear, O Israel! The Lord our God is Lord alone! You shall love the Lord your God with all your heart, with all your soul, with all your mind, and with all your strength" (Mark 12:29–30).

Let's begin with the First Commandment: "I am the Lord, your God. You shall not have strange Gods before me." This is the starting point of our moral life. It calls us to put our faith in God alone. There is no other god, no other creature, no other thing that is worthy of our complete faith and adoration. There is no one and nothing else that can save us from sin and death. The opposite of placing our faith in God is idolatry, which is placing our faith, hope, and love in something that is not God.

UNIT 2

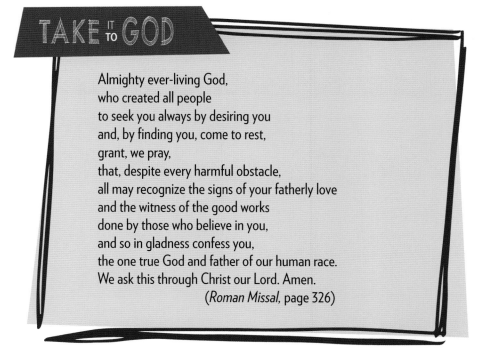

TAKE IT TO GOD

Almighty ever-living God,
who created all people
to seek you always by desiring you
and, by finding you, come to rest,
grant, we pray,
that, despite every harmful obstacle,
all may recognize the signs of your fatherly love
and the witness of the good works
done by those who believe in you,
and so in gladness confess you,
the one true God and father of our human race.
We ask this through Christ our Lord. Amen.

(*Roman Missal*, page 326)

We face a great many temptations to sin against the First Commandment, more than you might think. Our culture is filled with messages that promise certain things will bring us true happiness and fulfillment. Experiences and substances provide temporary highs. It is tempting to chase after these things, to make them the center of our lives. We may not worship idols made in the image of Baal and Asherah, but idolatry is alive and well in our time.

Putting God First

A Christian politician gave an interview on the challenges he faced in integrating his faith and his political positions. He supported legislation that provided help for immigrants and people in poverty, legislation that protected the environment, and legislation providing health care for all people. He also opposed capital punishment, legalized abortion, and legalized euthanasia. He maintained these positions despite the criticism he received from people within his own political party. When asked why he did this, he answered simply, "My first and primary commitment is to God and his Law."

This politician was being faithful to the First Commandment: "I am the Lord, your God. You shall not have strange Gods before me." The First Commandment is first because it is the primary foundation for our lives and happiness. All the other commandments depend on the First Commandment. For example, why would you keep holy the Sabbath if you really didn't believe in God? Why would you always speak the truth if you didn't believe it was part of God's Eternal Law? Why would you not have as much sex as you want with whomever you want if you didn't believe that God established sacramental marriage as the only proper place for sexual intimacy?

© m-imagephotography / iStock.com

What does putting God first mean to you?

The First Commandment is a summons—a call for us to have faith in God, to put our hope in him, and to love him completely, without holding back anything. Obeying the First Commandment is not for the indecisive and weakhearted; it is an exciting journey that requires a complete commitment of heart, soul, and mind. You cannot say you believe in God and then trust a horoscope to guide your future. You cannot say you put your complete hope and trust in God and then live as though the only thing that matters in life is being the best athlete or having the highest grade point average no matter the cost. You cannot say you love God absolutely and not follow the guidance of the Church he established as his Body on Earth.

Sins against Faith, Hope, and Love

Living the First Commandment is a natural expression of the **Theological Virtues** of faith, hope, and love. If God is the unchanging source of all life and goodness, faithful in all his promises, how can we not put our faith in him? After Jesus Christ has shown us the depth of his Father's forgiveness and humility, how can we not place our hope in him? Knowing God's unconditional, saving love for us revealed in the Paschal Mystery, how can we not love him in return? These Theological Virtues are indeed gifts from God, gifts that we are called to embrace and live out. Sins against the First Commandment often follow when we fail to place our faith in God, to put our hope in his promises, and to love him with all our heart.

When we live lives marked by faith, hope, and love, we are guided by the truths taught by Divine Revelation. These truths are revealed by God through Scripture and Tradition and taught by the Church's Magisterium. Failing to accept the truths of our faith can lead to the sin of doubt, which is to either disregard the truths of faith or to question them without seeking to further understand them. This can lead even further to **heresy**, which is to deny an essential truth of our faith, or even **apostasy**, which is to reject the Christian faith completely. Avoiding doubt does not mean we won't have questions about the truths of faith. Seeking answers to those questions from your parish leaders, your parents, your religion teachers, and resources that clearly present

---

Theological Virtues ➤ The name given for the God-given virtues of faith, hope, and love. These virtues enable us to know God as God and lead us to union with him in mind and heart.

heresy ➤ The conscious and deliberate rejection by a baptized person of a truth of faith that must be believed.

apostasy ➤ The act of renouncing one's faith.

Church teaching is the way we grow deeper in faith! The fault is in ignoring those questions or seeking answers from those who disbelieve or lack true knowledge about our faith.

Placing our hope in God means to confidently expect his blessing in this life and the reward of Heaven in the next. We must avoid the sin of despair, which is to stop believing that God cares for us and that he will fulfill his promises to us. Religious despair is related to but different from psychological despair. Psychological despair can mean you believe that your life is pointless or meaningless. Religious despair is believing that a belief in God is meaningless or pointless. Neither kind of despair is good for us. When we are experiencing either kind, we should seek help from those who are prepared to assist us with these questions.

Placing our hope in God also means we must avoid the sin of presumption, which means believing we can be saved by our own efforts. Presumption can also mean believing God will save us even if we are not fully committed to reforming our lives and following his will. God's Revelation in Scripture and Tradition make it quite clear that we cannot save ourselves from sin and death. It also teaches us that even though God freely gives us his saving grace, we must be willing to cooperate with that grace!

© Bill Wittman / www.wpwittman.com

The First Commandment requires that we nurture our relationship with God. What are some of your practices for growing in your relationship with God?

CATHOLICS MAKING A DIFFERENCE

The Carmelites are a religious order devoted to giving witness to the presence of God in the world. They give witness to the First Commandment through their devotion to putting God first in their personal ministry and their shared life together. The English translation of their motto is "With zeal have I been zealous for the Lord God of Hosts." They are inspired by the prophet Elijah and by Mary of Nazareth, who both said yes to God, allowing God to bring hope and healing to the world through their lives. There are many famous Carmelite saints you have heard about in other books: Saint Teresa of Ávila, Saint John of the Cross, Saint Thérèse of Lisieux, and Saint Edith Stein. Today, the Carmelites work in many different ministries, serving as chaplains, counselors, missionaries, retreat directors, and peace and justice coordinators. Wherever they work, they give witness to the goodness and joy that come from putting God first in life.

UNIT 2

Loving God above everything else might seem quite obvious, but we should never think that love is easy or happens without struggle. We can fail in many ways to return God's love, such as through indifference, ingratitude, and refusing to fully commit to loving him (sometimes called lukewarmness, see Revelation 3:15–16).

The sin most contrary to the love of God is hatred of God, a sin of pride that involves the denial of God's goodness. This sin presumes that we are somehow knowledgeable enough to judge God and find him deserving of our hatred. It may seem difficult to conceive of someone hating God, but throughout history there have been people who have angrily claimed that God is responsible for the evil and suffering in the world. Perhaps motivated by their own pain, these people have not considered that human choices have caused most of the world's evil and suffering. In fact, our faith teaches that God suffers with those who suffer.

Undoubtedly, you desire to put your faith, hope, and love in God and to make him the most important thing in your life. The Church identifies the previously mentioned sins as warnings to not let down your guard and thus take the First Commandment for granted. We must regularly and intentionally nurture our relationship with God. This is an important key to living a moral life and why the gift of the Church is essential to our moral life.

Nurturing Your Relationship with God	
Participating in the sacraments and in the life of the Church is the best way to nurture and enrich our relationship with God. Here are some great ways to do this.	
Adoration	To adore God is to acknowledge him as our Creator, as our Savior, as never-ending Love, as the gift giver who provides everything we need for salvation. We offer adoration to God in all the Church's liturgies, especially in the Sacrament of the Eucharist.
Prayer	Prayer is the primary means through which we strengthen our relationship with God. Adoration is only the beginning of prayer; it focuses our attention on God. Prayer must also include praise and thanksgiving, intercession and petition, meditation and contemplation. We experience all these forms of prayer in the liturgy of the Church.
Sacrifice	Following Christ's example, we are called to lives of sacrificial love. We make sacrifices in many ways—by following the Church's guidelines for abstinence and fasting, by spending time with family and friends even when it is inconvenient, by accepting sickness and suffering with dignity and courage. In the Eucharist, we unite our sacrifice with Christ's perfect sacrifice and grow closer to him.
Promises and Vows	Just as God keeps his promises to us, we must keep our promises to him. For example, in the sacraments we make promises to God, such as promising to believe in him and to reject Satan, and promising to love, cherish, and be faithful to our spouse until death. We can also make personal promises to God, such as a promise to pray daily or to tithe. Our faith community supports us in keeping the promises and commitments we make to God.

Religious Freedom

Religious freedom is an issue connected to the First Commandment. Our belief in God and the religion we practice go hand in hand. Some people might ask, "If the revealed truths taught by the Catholic faith are so important to understanding the one, true God, wouldn't the Church want to require the Catholic faith as the religion for all people?" The answer is absolutely not. The Catholic Church is strongly against any state-mandated religion. We follow the example of God, who honors each person's free decision to accept God's gift of faith. If God does not force people into accepting faith, then certainly it would be wrong for us to do so.

tithe ➤ A commitment to donate a tenth or some other percentage of our income to the Church and other charitable causes.

Why must we work for religious freedom for all people in every nation?

UNIT 2

This means several things for believers. First, we must continually work to guard and promote religious freedom in all nations and states. All people, no matter where they live, must be free to choose how to live out their relationship with God. Second, we have a responsibility to share and promote the truths of the Catholic faith with the world. Although we respect other religions and the truth they may share with us, only the Catholic Church has the fullness of truth, which has been revealed by God. How can people of other faiths know this and choose it if we do not share it with them as clearly and confidently and humbly as possible? ✳

HMMMMM. . .

Why is it challenging for people to keep trust in God as the focus of their life?

Article 16

Idolatry in the Bible

Isa's grandfather loved to have her kayak with him whenever she could, and she liked it too. Once when they were unloading their kayaks, he saw Isa tuck her phone into her back pocket. "Why are you bringing that with you? You don't need your phone while we are out on the water."

Isa replied, "Just for emergencies, Grandpa."

He smiled at her and shook his head. "I worry about you and your friends. It seems like people always have their phones with them . . . at the dinner table, in the car, and even in the bathroom! I think people treat their phones like they are the center of their lives, like a god."

"I don't think that's true," Isa said. "It's just habit. Most people don't think much about God at all."

"Just because something is a habit, doesn't make it good for us," replied her grandfather. "And I'm not talking about worshipping Zeus or Athena. Seems like some of my friends make exercise a god. It's all they can think about, and they forget who gave them their bodies to begin with."

"Yeah, I get that," replied Isa. "Some of my friends are completely obsessed with having the most online friends or having the most likes on their posts. They can be so into it that they're completely in another world even when we're in the same room."

"One thing I've learned is that all those things I used to think were so important when I was younger ultimately just left me empty," said her grandpa. "For me now, it is all about connection—connection with you, my family, friends, nature, and ultimately God. The Bible is right about putting God first."

"I see what you're doing," Isa said. "And you don't have to convince me."

Original Meaning of the First Commandment

The full text of the First Commandment from the Book of Exodus reads like this: "I am the LORD your God, who brought you out of the land of Egypt, out of the house of slavery. You shall not have other gods beside me. You shall not make for yourself an idol or a likeness of anything in the heavens above or on the earth below or in the waters beneath the earth; you shall not bow down before them or serve them" (20:2–5). In its original context, the First Com-

---

idolatry ▶ The worship of other beings, creatures, or material goods in a way that is fitting for God alone. It is a violation of the First Commandment.

mandment focused on the sin of **idolatry**, which is the literal worship of gods and goddesses other than Yahweh. For the ancient Israelites, idolatry was a real and concrete thing. They had just come from slavery in Egypt, a kingdom that worshipped many different gods and goddesses. They were settling in a land where the native people, the Canaanites, worshipped many different gods and goddesses too. It would only be natural for them to also believe in a **pantheon** of divine beings.

The story of the Israelites worshipping the golden calf in Exodus, chapter 32, is intended to remind us just how tempting idolatry can be. When Moses took longer than expected to return to their camp, the Israelites made an image of the god **Baal** and worshipped it. Keep in mind that this happened soon after Moses had first given them the Ten Commandments! After reading

this chapter in Exodus, you might think: "How stupid could those Israelites have been? They just heard the warning against idolatry, and here they are making an image of a foreign god and worshipping it!" Recall, however, that they still did not completely understand believing in only one god. They still believed in other gods besides Yahweh. So, when Moses didn't appear as expected, they naturally turned to a god they were familiar with for comfort. Are we so different? When things don't go the way we want or expect, many people try to escape their disappointment or pain through food or shopping or sex or drugs and alcohol. As the Church often reminds us, our modern idols are just as prevalent as the old false gods and goddesses.

The rest of the Old Testament reveals how difficult it was for the Israelites to consistently worship Yahweh

In the Old Testament, idolatry was literally the worship of other gods and goddesses, such as the goddess Asherah. The Old Testament's books record that the Israelites frequently fell into this sin.

© Louvre, Paris, France / Bridgeman Images

UNIT 2

---

pantheon ➤ All of the gods of a people or religion collectively.

Baal ➤ The Canaanite god of rain and vegetation, often represented by a bull and worshipped in the "high places." He was considered a false god by the Israelites but worshipped by them when they fell away from the one true God.

alone. Yes, they offered sacrifice to Yahweh in the Temple, but they often fell into old practices of worshipping gods like Baal and **Asherah** (also called Ashtaroth). Here's one example from Judges:

> The Israelites again did what was evil in the sight of the LORD, serving the Baals and Ashtarts, the gods of Aram, the gods of Sidon, the gods of Moab, the gods of the Ammonites, and the gods of the Philistines. Since they had abandoned the LORD and would not serve him, the LORD became angry with Israel and he sold them into the power of the Philistines and the Ammonites. (10:6-7)

If you read the full passage (10:6–16), you will see that the Israelites repented of their idolatry and threw out their foreign gods. Unfortunately, they kept repeating this pattern, falling back into idolatry again and again.

The Israelites who eventually became the Jewish People have a rich witness of faith. Their belief in Yahweh was inspiring and at times heroic. Their faith prepared us for the coming of Christ, and it was their faith that Christ himself practiced. Still, throughout their early history, the Israelites struggled with **monotheism.** Yahweh might have been their God, but the gods and goddesses of the people around must have seemed just as real. So at times they also worshipped Baal, Asherah, and other gods and goddesses. They worshipped some of these gods and goddesses in sacred places where people prayed and offered sacrifice. Carved statues of these gods and goddesses were sometimes placed on home altars for prayer and protection—thus the prohibition against carven images in the commandment.

Some worship practices were particularly offensive, but they must have occurred, because they are mentioned in Scripture. The worship of Asherah included having sex with temple prostitutes to ensure good harvests (see Deuteronomy 23:18–19). The worship of Molech seemed to involve child sacrifice (see Leviticus 18:21).

God had to remind the Israelites again and again, with painful consequences, that he is all-powerful and the only God. Eventually, they learned their lesson. After the Exile, and certainly by the time of Jesus, Jews had come to the conclusion that there was only one God and that the gods and goddesses of other peoples were only myths.

Asherah (also called Astarte or Ashtoreth) ➤ The Canaanite goddess of love and fertility, often represented by a serpent and worshipped in sacred groves. She was considered a false god by the Israelites but also worshipped by them when they fell away from the one true God.

monotheism ➤ The belief in and worship of only one God.

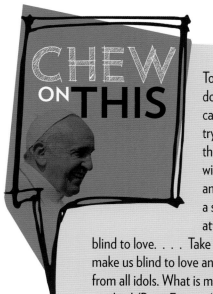

Today, I invite you to think: how many idols do I have and which one is my favorite? Because recognizing one's own forms of idolatry is the beginning of grace and puts one on the path of love. Indeed love is incompatible with idolatry. If something becomes absolute and supreme, then it is more important than a spouse, than a child or a friendship. Being attached to an object or an idea makes one blind to love. . . . Take this to heart: idols rob us of love, idols make us blind to love and, in order to truly love, we must be free from all idols. What is my idol? Remove it and throw it out of the window! (Pope Francis, "General Audience," August 1, 2018)

Do Catholics Worship Graven Images?

Although the First Commandment forbids us to worship images, like the golden calf, it is permissible, and indeed good, to use images like crucifixes, statues, pictures, or icons to symbolically represent the sacred and holy. If you have been in other Christian churches, you may have noticed that some are different from Catholic churches. Many have no statues, no vigil lights, and no stations of the cross, partly out of respect for the First Commandment.

Catholics have sometimes been criticized for the images in our churches because of the mistaken understanding that we worship these things. But we do not worship or adore these objects. We **venerate**, or give respect and honor to, saints, sacred objects, and images. Veneration is different from worship and adoration, which are meant for God alone. Veneration does not violate the First Commandment.

Idolatry in Today's World

Judaism, Islam, and Christianity are all monotheistic faiths. Today, no devout Christian, Jew, or Muslim would have a statue of Baal in their bedroom or secretly worship Asherah. Is the sin of idolatry a thing of the past? Not

---

venerate ➤ To show respect and devotion to someone or something.

according to Jesus. Recall the Sermon on the Mount. In it, Jesus teaches: "No one can serve two masters. He will either hate one and love the other, or be devoted to one and despise the other. You cannot serve God and mammon" (Matthew 6:24). In this teaching, Jesus is broadening our understanding of idolatry. *Mammon* means "wealth and riches." Idolatry is not just worshipping pagan gods and goddesses; it is letting something like money take the place that God should have in our lives. Read the next part of the Sermon on the Mount (Matthew 6:25–34) to see what Jesus says about relying on God alone.

Jesus focuses on money because people of his time thought money would bring them security and happiness. This is certainly true in our time too. But money isn't the only thing we idolize. The pursuit of success and fame can be a form of idolatry whether through sports, academics, or the arts. A good example would be a person who takes illegal performance-enhancing drugs or

sabotages a competitor in order to win. That person has crossed the line from participating in healthy competition to making winning and fame a god in their life.

Entertainment can also be a form of idolatry. Think of people who spend so much time in playing video games, watching television, or using social networking sites

Jesus said we cannot serve both God and mammon. How is money idolized in today's world?

that they neglect their family and friends, their grades, and even their health. Have those people made entertainment a god in their lives? Another form of idolatry is the pursuit of "things." Have you ever known someone who was obsessed with getting the latest phone, a particular car, certain clothes, or any other material thing?

Idolatry has a strong connection to the complex issue of addictions and obsessive behaviors. Our society has all kinds of recognized addictions—to alcohol, narcotics, sex, gambling, food, and even shopping. People with addictions have learned to turn to their addictive behavior when bored or stressed or hurting rather than to turn to God. This is the common thread in all these examples of modern idolatries: we turn to something that is not God to try

mammon ➤ An Aramaic word meaning wealth or property.

© DisobeyArt / Shutterstock.com

UNIT 2

What are the things that take our focus away from God and even from relationships with family and friends?

and find the happiness and fulfillment that can only come from God. As Saint Augustine of Hippo (354–430) once said, "Idolatry is worshipping anything that ought to be used, or using anything that is meant to be worshipped."

What are the signs that you have crossed the line from having a normal and healthy interest in something to making it an idol in your life? Here are some questions to consider:

- Has your focus on the thing in question (for example, sports, academics, video games, popularity, alcohol) affected your relationship with God? Has it caused you to spend less time in prayer, to miss Mass, to feel uncomfortable around members of your faith community?
- Has the thing in question affected your relationships with family and friends in unhealthy ways? Are you spending less quality time with them? Is it causing you to keep secrets?
- Is the thing in question taking over God's role in your life? Are you relying on it for your happiness more than you are relying on God for your happiness? Are you making your life choices based on its influence rather than making your life choices based on God's calling?

If your answers to some of these questions make you uncomfortable, it may be a sign that you need to assess your spiritual priorities and make some changes in your life. You can start by talking to a spiritual adviser, such as a priest or other minister in your church or school, and by making a renewed commitment to put God first in your life. ✳

HMMMMMM...

What are you tempted to make an idol in your life, to even take over the central place God should have?

Article 17

Other Sins against the First Commandment

The previous two articles discussed some of the most common sins against the First Commandment. Other sins against the First Commandment are less likely to be committed by the Christian faithful but have been widely practiced throughout human history. They fall generally into two categories: (1) superstition, which "is manifested in idolatry, as well as in various forms of divination and magic" (*Catechism of the Catholic Church [CCC]*, number 2138), and (2) irreligion, which can be thought of as the absence or rejection of the virtue of religion.

Superstition

Superstition is a deviation of true religion and can take many forms. One example is the practice of assigning magical power to certain practices or objects, such as charms or omens. When we see items like crystals or good luck charms as more than just decorations, as having the power to bring about a particular outcome, we are practicing superstition. Superstition can even make us depart from true prayer and worship of God. For example, while we can pray to God for our team to perform well during a game or for protection of the players, we should not so idolize winning that we treat sacred actions like the Sign of the Cross or saying prayers as a way to manipulate God to do our will. True prayer and worship of God come from a humble interior disposition, seeking our true good and the good of others.

Hobbies and games that lead individuals to believe in **magic** or the occult can be sinful. They too are not compatible with true Christian belief and worship of God. Believing in creatures, devices, or objects as if they have divine power is a serious sin. Satanism, astrology, palm reading, and attempts to call up the dead or see the future are all forms of the sin of **divination**. They are wrong because "they contradict the honor, respect, and loving fear that we owe to God alone" *(CCC*, number 2116).

---

superstition ➤ Attributing to someone or something else a power that belongs to God alone and relying on such powers rather than trusting in God; a sin against the First Commandment.

magic ➤ The belief in supernatural power that comes from a source other than God; a sin against the First Commandment.

divination ➤ The practice of seeking power or knowledge through supernatural means apart from the one true God; a sin against the First Commandment.

Why are palm reading and other forms of divination sins against the First Commandment?

Sins of Irreligion

One of the sins that falls under the category of irreligion is **sacrilege**, or the abuse of the sacraments, persons, things, or places that are consecrated to God. For example, some movies, TV shows, and celebrities poke fun at objects or actions that are specifically religious, whether Christian, Jewish, Muslim, or some other faith tradition. There is nothing funny about belittling the symbols and rituals of the faith.

Simony is another sin of irreligion. Simony describes the practice of buying and selling spiritual things and favors and is another sin against the First Commandment. A modern example of simony would be a television preacher's promising people miraculous cures if they send in a certain amount of money. Although it is permissible to expect a contribution for goods and services so that the ministers of God can earn a living, someone who tries to buy or sell spiritual power, or con unsuspecting people with promises of God's favor, is guilty of sin.

---

sacrilege ➤ An offense against God. It is the abuse of a person, place, or thing dedicated to God and the worship of him.

simony ➤ Buying or selling something spiritual, such as a grace, a sacrament, or a relic.

MAKE IT SO

Hilary has been into some strange things before, but now she's really gone fully weird. She found a link to an astrology site online, and she's completely into it. The other day, she wouldn't go to the movies because her horoscope said she should be careful of "exposing yourself to strong emotions." You even found out that Hilary's paying someone from the site for personal advice. "God made the sun and the stars and the planets," Hilary tells you. "Doesn't it make sense that he might use those to give you guidance?" How could you respond to Hilary or someone like her? What insights from the First Commandment and the Church's teaching could inform you? What superstitions or magical thinking might affect your thinking?

Atheism has become much more common in our time. Atheism is the denial of the existence of God and is an offense against the First Commandment. Atheism can have many faces, including the belief that humans aren't dependent on God. Atheism that attacks or mocks religious beliefs or is used by political leaders to persecute religious people must be condemned. On the other hand, there are many atheists who respect other people's religious beliefs, even though they do not believe in God themselves. Although these atheists do not practice any religion, they are still committed to protecting the dignity of the human person and strive to live moral lives based on care and concern for others.

Agnosticism is a cousin to atheism. Instead of declaring that there is no God, agnostics believe that it is impossible to prove God's existence. Thus, agnostics believe that one cannot know anything about God or his nature. Again, like atheists, many agnostics strive to live a moral life based on recognizing the dignity of others. They just believe they can do this without claiming definitive belief in God.

---

atheist; atheism ➤ One who denies the existence of God; the denial of the existence of God.

agnostic; agnosticism ➤ One who believes we cannot know anything about God's existence or his nature; the belief that we cannot know anything about God's existence or his nature.

Why have atheism and agnosticism been on the rise in the United States and other developed countries?

It is important to remind ourselves that we must avoid making simplistic judgments about the religious choices of other people. Jesus himself cautioned us against judging others: "Stop judging, that you may not be judged. . . . Why do you notice the splinter in your brother's eye, but do not perceive the wooden beam in your own eye?" (Matthew 7:1–3). The *Catechism* even suggests that Christians have some responsibility for people's choices to reject religion:

> Believers can have more than a little to do with the rise of atheism. To the extent that they are careless about their instruction in the faith, or present its teaching falsely, or even fail in their religious, moral, or social life, they must be said to conceal rather than to reveal the true nature of God and of religion.[1] (Number 2125)

This suggests that in our relationships with atheists and agnostics, we want to be in respectful dialogue, seeking to understand the reasons for their lack of belief, while also sharing the hope, joy, and strength we find through faith in God. ✳

 HMMMMM. . .   Which of these other sins against the First Commandment most concerns you? Why?

1. What is the heart of the First Commandment? How do we keep it?

2. What are two ways that we sin against the call to place our hope in God?

3. What is the original meaning of the First Commandment?

4. List some modern examples of the sin of idolatry.

5. Describe three ways people practice sinful excesses of religion.

6. What is atheism?

UNIT 2

© National Gallery, London, UK / Bridgeman Images

Worship of the Golden Calf (Exodus, chapter 32)

1. What questions or insights do you have after studying this painting?

2. How would you describe the feelings of the people depicted in the painting?

3. What clues in the painting show that this idolatry is not acceptable to God?

CHAPTER 5

The Second Commandment: Reverence, Not Profanity

WHY DOES IT MATTER HOW I USE GOD'S NAME?

SNAPSHOT

Article 18

Reverence: Responding to the Sacredness of God

Brian went to Mass regularly with his grandmother. His grandmother was advanced in years, and it was getting harder and harder for her to get around. Every week, Brian watched his grandmother enter the church and painfully genuflect toward the tabernacle before entering the pew. When Mass was over, she would genuflect again and then go to the tabernacle, where she would painfully kneel for a few minutes of prayer. One day, Brian asked his grandmother: "Grandma, why do you always genuflect and kneel in church? I'm sure God sees how hard it is for you and doesn't need you to do that."

His grandmother answered: "Of course God doesn't need me to do it. But I need to do it for God. Every time I genuflect or kneel in reverence to him, I remind myself of his love and care for me, and I remind myself of all he has done for me."

Is there someone in your life you cannot ever imagine disrespecting? Maybe it is a grandparent or an aunt or an uncle who has always loved and accepted you, or maybe it is a teacher, coach, priest, or youth minister who has always been wise, kind, and honest with you. You would never think to use these people's names as a curse or to involve them in some lie or wrongdoing.

So, if you hold this level of respect for people in your life, is it not just as important to treat God and his name with the same or even greater honor? God deserves our complete respect, and we should honor him in our every thought, word, and deed. This is what the Second Commandment, "You shall not take the name of the Lord your God in vain," is all about. Some people think it is just a command against swearing, but it is so much more than that.

© Voronin76 / Shutterstock.com

UNIT 2

Reverence versus Profanity

Showing reverence for God and his sacred name is the proper response of true faith. How else would we respond to the One who is the creator of all that is, to the One who is faithful in all his promises, to the One who is perfect love, to the One who suffered death on the cross to save us from sin and death? When we reverence God, we recognize that he is **sacred**, that he is not ordinary, that he is holy and just, and that he is worthy of our praise and adoration. We practice this reverence especially in sacred places, such as churches and shrines, and at sacred times, such as during the Eucharist or our private prayer.

But showing God reverence should not happen only at Mass once a week or when we take time to pray. We must also show reverence for God in all the words and actions of our daily life. We can do this by having reverence for creation, because creation reveals to us the wonder of God. We can also do this by treating all people reverently, because every person is made in God's image and likeness.

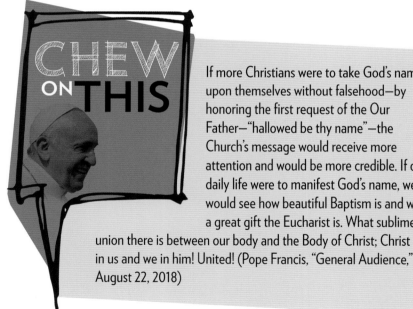

CHEW ON THIS

If more Christians were to take God's name upon themselves without falsehood—by honoring the first request of the Our Father—"hallowed be thy name"—the Church's message would receive more attention and would be more credible. If our daily life were to manifest God's name, we would see how beautiful Baptism is and what a great gift the Eucharist is. What sublime union there is between our body and the Body of Christ; Christ in us and we in him! United! (Pope Francis, "General Audience," August 22, 2018)

---

sacred ➤ The quality of being holy, worthy of respect and reverence; set apart for God.

The opposite of reverence is **profanity**. Profanity is more than just swearing or using vulgar language. It means to treat something that is sacred as if it were ordinary or meaningless. To treat God profanely or to live your life profanely is to miss the mark. (Remember the Bible's definition of sin?) It is a failure to live up to the high calling that we have as children of God: to love and honor all people and all things, and most especially God. Speaking profanely or living profanely is to settle for less than the best, to accept a second-rate way of life. It brings dishonor to God and to us.

The Name of God

The people of the Bible placed great value on names. A person's name usually indicated something special about a person, maybe something about their character or family. A person and their name were closely connected—to misuse a person's name was seen as causing a literal injury to them. Because of this ancient belief, people would not give their names casually to a stranger so God's Revelation of his personal name, Yahweh, to Moses (see Exodus 3:11–15)

In the Book of Exodus, God reveals his sacred name to Moses. Why is this such an important event in salvation history?

---

profanity ➤ Speaking disrespectfully about something that is sacred or treating it with disrespect.

was a big deal. It indicated God's trust in Moses and his Chosen People that they would not abuse his name. Jesus emphasized the importance of keeping his Father's name holy in teaching his disciples to pray: "Our Father in heaven, / hallowed (holy) be your name" (Matthew 6:9). Still today, many Jewish people will not say the personal name for God aloud out of respect for the sacredness of his name.

It is in this context that we should understand the Second Commandment, "You shall not take the name of the Lord your God in vain." To use God's name in vain means to use it for dishonorable or profane purposes. It is treating or using his name, which is holy and worthy of the greatest respect, as something ordinary, or even worse, for evil purposes. The people of the Bible would have seen this as not only dishonoring God's name but also dishonoring God himself. We should see it the same way.

TAKE IT TO GOD

Make a regular **examination of conscience** part of your prayer life. Here are some questions connected to the Second Commandment that you can use for an examination of conscience:

- Have I used vulgar, suggestive, or obscene speech?
- Have I used the name of God in cursing or swearing?
- Have I spoken about God, the Church, the saints, or sacred things with irreverence, hatred, or defiance?
- Have I talked disrespectfully about other people or myself?
- Have I behaved disrespectfully in church?
- Have I failed to keep vows or promises that I have made to God?
- Have I sworn by God's name either falsely (perjury) or rashly?

---

examination of conscience ➤ Prayerful reflection on, and assessment of, one's words, attitudes, and actions in light of the Gospel of Jesus; more specifically, the conscious moral evaluation of one's life in preparation for reception of the Sacrament of Penance and Reconciliation.

UNIT 2

The Names of God in the Old Testament		
The Hebrew names of God in the Old Testament have several different forms. Here are some of the variations.		
Hebrew	Literal Translation	Name Used in English Bible Translations
El	"God"	God
Elohim	"God" (plural form)	God
El Shaddai	"God, the One of the Mountains"	God Almighty
El Elyon	"God Most High"	God Most High
Yahweh	"I am who am"	LORD (with small caps)
Yahweh Sabaoth	"Lord of Hosts"	Lord Almighty

If you were to listen carefully to your own speech, the conversations of others, and the spoken media for an entire day, how many times do you think you would hear God's name? How many of those times do you think it would be used respectfully? All too often we hear people use the expressions "Oh, God!" "Jesus Christ!" or even "Holy Mother of God!" as a way to express humor, surprise, or anger. Rarely is it used in a situation where people really intend to call on our God and Savior. Using the name of God profanely is a sin and a sign that we are losing the awe and respect due to him.

The sinfulness of abusing God's name also extends to other names. Using the name of the Virgin Mary or the name of any of the saints in vain is also wrong. God calls us each by name, and so our names have great value. Every person's name is sacred in the sight of God. ✳

HMMMMMM... When and where do you experience people ridiculing good or holy things?

Article 19
Keeping Sacred Commitments

One of the most interesting paradoxes of the spiritual life is that we are most free after we have made a major commitment. Some people think of freedom as the ability to do whatever you want, whenever you want, with whomever you want. But the reality of trying to live that way is that people become trapped by having too many choices. They are always moving on to new experiences or relationships, always leaving their options open. People who live this way almost always end up not accomplishing anything that has lasting significance, and they rarely have relationships of real depth and meaning. Living life like this actually makes a person less free when it comes to loving and being loved and when it comes to making a meaningful difference in the world.

Saint John of the Cross (c. 1541–1591) once said, "Consider what it is God wants, and then do it." Only someone who fully commits—to a cause, to a particular work or ministry, or to a particular person or group—is truly free to live the full life God intends for us. When you think of people who are admired for their contributions to family life, sports, society, or the Church, what do they all have in common? Almost always, these people have been faithful to the commitments they have made. By making a complete commitment to a specific person, group, or cause, they are not distracted by other things. This leaves them freer to focus on being true to the person, the ministry, or the cause that God has called them to as their primary commitment.

Only someone who fully commits is truly free to live the full life God intends for us.

How is this related to the Second Commandment? The Second Commandment's original focus was the importance of being true to vows or commitments made in God's name. What did that mean for the ancient Israelites, and what does it mean for us today?

UNIT 2

Vows Made in God's Name

In the world of the ancient Israelites, individuals swore oaths to one another, and tribes or nations made **covenants** with one another. Today, we would probably call these agreements contracts and treaties. It is characteristic of these oaths and covenants that they were made in the name of the gods the people believed in. They called upon these gods to witness their agreement, and they believed that their gods would enforce these sacred promises and would bring punishment upon anyone who broke their oath or covenant agreement.

UNIT 2

We see examples of this type of oath frequently in the Bible. When Jacob and his Uncle Laban made a peace agreement, they concluded by saying, "May the God of Abraham and the God of Nahor [their ancestral deities], the God of their father, judge between us!" (Genesis 31:53). When King Saul finally understood that David would succeed him as king, he asked David to make an oath to spare his family: "Swear to me by the LORD that you will not cut off my descendants and that you will not blot out my name from my father's house" (1 Samuel 24:22).

The original meaning of the Second Commandment was to hold the name of God in great reverence and also to protect these sacred oaths and covenants the Israelites made in the sacred name of God. The Second Commandment warned them not to make these promises "in vain," meaning not to make a sacred oath or covenant about something trivial. And if they made a sacred oath

I DIDN'T KNOW THAT!

Is the word *god* a name or a description? Well, it is kind of both. The English word *god* has its origin in an early Germanic word *guthan*, which may be related to an earlier word meaning "to pour (an offering)." Or it may be related to a completely different earlier word meaning "to call, to invoke (a sacrifice)." No one knows for sure! What we do know is that when the word is lowercased *(god)*, we are using it as a designation for a divine being. But when a people of faith capitalize the word, they are referring to the one true God—like a name.

---

covenant ➤ A solemn agreement between human beings or between God and a human being in which mutual commitments are made.

or covenant, they better fully intend to keep that promise. The second part of the commandment warns: "For the LORD will not leave unpunished anyone who invokes his name in vain" (Exodus 20:7). As was discussed in the previous article, invoking God's name was serious business, and people had better be serious when they did it.

Making an oath on the Bible emphasizes the importance of keeping sacred commitments.

In the Sermon on the Mount, Jesus reinforces the importance of keeping commitments:

> Again you have heard that it was said to your ancestors, "Do not take a false oath, but make good to the Lord all that you vow." But I say to you, do not swear at all; not by heaven, for it is God's throne; nor by the earth, for it is his footstool; nor by Jerusalem, for it is the city of the great King. Do not swear by your head, for you cannot make a single hair white or black. Let your "Yes" mean "Yes," and your "No" mean "No." Anything more is from the evil one. (Matthew 5:33–37)

Jesus is saying that we should be so honest in everything we do and say that there is no need to use God's name in making an oath. It should be assumed that as his disciples we will tell the truth and keep our important commitments.

Sacred Commitments Today

The practice of making sacred oaths in the name of God isn't just an ancient practice. It is part of public life in the United States and many other countries. Politicians swear to fulfill their public duties with their hand on the Bible while calling upon God's help. Judges swear to uphold the law of the land in the same way. Witnesses in a courtroom usually swear to tell the truth, saying, "So help me God." These are all sacred oaths, and to break these oaths is a serious sin. Because we make them publicly in God's name, breaking them implicates God in our failure or lie.

We make sacred oaths in the context of liturgy and prayer also, but we usually call them promises or vows. Often these are associated with one of the sacraments. In the Sacraments of Baptism and Confirmation, we promise to reject Satan and all his works and empty promises. In the Sacrament of Matri-

MAKE IT SO

Your friend Javier was recruited into a Los Angeles gang when he was only thirteen but left the gang when he was in his early twenties. He had witnessed and even done some terrible things and was glad to build a better life filled with hope and joy.

One day, a police officer and an assistant to the district attorney knocked on Javier's door. "We know you've left the life and are on a good path," they told him. "We need you to testify against your former gang leaders to stop the misery they are causing. We're not after you, you would have complete immunity and we would protect you from any reprisal."

"You don't understand," answered Javier. "I swore an oath not to betray the gang when I joined them. And even though they are guilty of many bad things, they were my family for many years. I can't break that oath."

How do you advise Javier to help him make the right decision? How does the Second Commandment inform you? Are there any promises and vows in your own life that you need to rethink?

mony, the bride and bridegroom promise to be true to each other until death, no matter what happens to them. In the Sacrament of Holy Orders, a man being ordained to the priesthood makes promises of celibacy and obedience to his bishop. Men and women who enter the consecrated life commit to the evangelical counsels by taking vows of chastity, poverty, and obedience. These are all sacred promises made in God's name, and breaking them is a serious sin. People should make these vows only after a time of prayerful discernment, being as sure as humanly possible that God is calling them to this particular vocation and commitment.

Besides these major vows we make during our lives, many people also make less serious promises to God. Often these promises are commitments to some kind of spiritual practice. For example, you might promise to watch less television during Lent. You might pledge to give a certain amount of money to charity every month or every year. You might commit to a regular time of prayer every day. These types of promises are important commitments to growing in our relationship with God, and we should do our best to keep them.

UNIT 2

Keeping Your Commitments to God

Personal prayer, regularly receiving the Sacraments of the Eucharist and Penance and Reconciliation, spiritual reading, and attending retreats are examples of spiritual practices that nurture and deepen our relationship with God and help us grow in understanding and living out Jesus Christ's moral teachings. Maintaining these practices is an important sacred commitment we make to God. Here are some suggestions from experienced leaders on keeping spiritual commitments.

What sacred promises do we make in the Sacraments of Baptism and Confirmation?

1. **Start with some "must dos."** Make a list of the practices you know you must do no matter what. The Precepts of the Church are a good place to start. These are the minimal requirements for living a Christian life. Do not let anything get in the way of these nonnegotiable commitments.

2. **Be realistic.** Some people become overenthusiastic in making new spiritual commitments. Instead of trying one new thing, they want to try six. Unless you join a monastery, it is unlikely that you can fit a lot of new spiritual commitments into your life all at the same time. If you are feeling the need to grow in your relationship with God by adding new spiritual practices to your nonnegotiables, make a commitment to try one new spiritual practice at a time.

3. **Make a commitment for forty days.** Forty is an important symbolic number in the Bible. One reason is that forty is the number of days and nights Jesus spent in the desert fasting and praying (see Matthew 4:1–2). If you decide to try a new spiritual practice, such as reading a chapter of the Bible a day, make a commitment to do it for forty days. Decide on the time and place, and stick to it. It takes forty days for a new spiritual practice to start to become a habit. ✳

HMMMMMM. . .   In your opinion, what is the most serious and important vow a person can make in their life?

Article 20
Other Sins against the Second Commandment

Perhaps you have seen these stories in your in your news feed. A Christian group conducts anti-gay protests at public funerals, supposedly in the name of God. People firebomb or shoot at mosques, again in the name of God. Well-known preachers claim to speak for God in saying that some act of nature is God's punishment for some type of sin. Or people take an oath in the name of God to tell the truth and then proceed to lie or tell half-truths on the witness stand or in performing their public duties. These are examples of either blasphemy or perjury, which are sins against the Second Commandment.

UNIT 2

To attack, destroy, or deface a sacred object or holy place is a sin against the holiness of God, protected by the Second Commandment.

Blasphemy and Perjury

Far worse than a casual curse is using the name of God, of Jesus Christ, of the Virgin Mary, or of the saints in an intentionally offensive way. This is called **blasphemy**. Blasphemy could be expressing hatred of God or defiance against him either publicly or privately. It is like saying, "I know better than God." Some common ways blasphemy is committed today include using God's name as an excuse to cover up a crime, to excuse a sin, or to claim that a spoken word or action is in the name of God when it is clearly against God's will. For example, some so-called Christian groups or individuals say that God wants them to commit acts of terrorism against elected officials or public institutions.

Blasphemy is a grave sin. In Jesus' time, blasphemy was considered so serious that a person could be put to death as punishment. Jesus' claim to be the Messiah and the Son of God was considered blasphemous by those who wanted to kill him. Although in our society today we would not put someone to death for blasphemy, perhaps we have become too used to the offensive use of God's name.

CATHOLICS **MAKING** A DIFFERENCE

© REUTERS/News.com

Catholics in over twenty-five cities across the United States celebrate a Red Mass every year. The Red Mass is a special liturgy attended by Catholic and non-Catholic judges, lawyers, law clerks, law professors, and other legal professionals at the start of the legal year. These judicial leaders are publicly asking God to help them honor their vows to seek justice with honesty and integrity. One of the better-known Red Masses is the one celebrated each fall in Washington, DC. It is attended by justices of the Supreme Court, members of Congress, the diplomatic corps, the Cabinet, and sometimes, the president of the United States. During a Red Mass, special prayers ask the Holy Spirit to give his gifts of wisdom, understanding, knowledge, and fortitude to the leaders in our justice system.

---

blasphemy ➤ Speaking, acting, or thinking about God, Jesus Christ, the Virgin Mary, or the saints in a way that is irreverent, mocking, or offensive. It is a sin against the Second Commandment.

A time when we publicly use God's name in a reverential manner is when someone takes an oath promising to uphold the law or to tell the truth in court and ends by saying, "So help me, God." This oath is a sacred promise because it is asking God to be a witness to the truth of a person's commitment or testimony. A false oath calls on God to be witness to a lie. That is why the crime of **perjury**, lying under oath, is a serious sin against the Lord, who is always faithful to his promises. If we can't trust individuals who swear to tell the truth, then the law and order of our community is threatened.

People have a deep desire to be connected to the sacred, to the holiness that is God. Yet so much of popular culture seems to poke fun at anything that is sacred and often belittles people who treasure God and holy things. The Second Commandment is all about keeping holy things holy. Keeping the Second Commandment requires a conscious effort not to give in to the many subtle ways God's name and holy symbols are dishonored. God wants us to use his name only for good purposes: to bless, praise, and glorify it. ✳

HMMMMM. . .   When have you questioned whether someone claiming to speak in the name of God was really doing so?

---

perjury ➤ The sin of lying while under an oath to tell the truth. It is a sin against the Second and Eighth Commandments.

1. What does it mean to say that something is sacred? How do we show respect for the sacredness of God?

2. How did people in biblical times understand the importance of names?

3. Why did ancient people make oaths and covenants in the name of their god(s)?

4. Name some of the ways we continue to make sacred vows today.

5. Define *blasphemy.*

6. Why is perjury a serious sin?

Sins against the Second Commandment

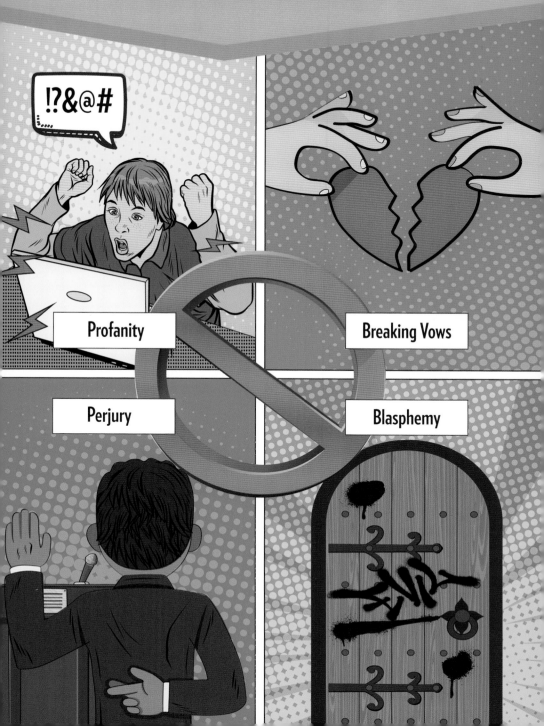

Profanity

Breaking Vows

Perjury

Blasphemy

CHAPTER 6
The Third Commandment: Preserving Holiness

WHY SHOULD SUNDAY BE DIFFERENT FROM ANY OTHER DAY?

SNAPSHOT

Article 21

Sabbath in the Old Testament

Ask your grandparents sometime to tell you what Sundays were like when they were children. It is quite possible they'll tell you that on Sundays most stores and businesses were closed, and people worked at essential jobs only. There were no professional sports games on Sundays, let alone high school games and practices. Just about every Christian attended church and spent the rest of the day visiting family, enjoying a special meal, maybe playing games. Sunday, a day reserved for prayer and rest, was noticeably different from the other six days of the week.

Today, Sundays differ dramatically. Most stores and businesses are open, many people have to work, and many do not attend a religious service. You and your peers may have sporting events to play in or practices or meetings that cut into family time and time for rest and prayer. These changes make some people wonder if we have completely lost our understanding of the Third

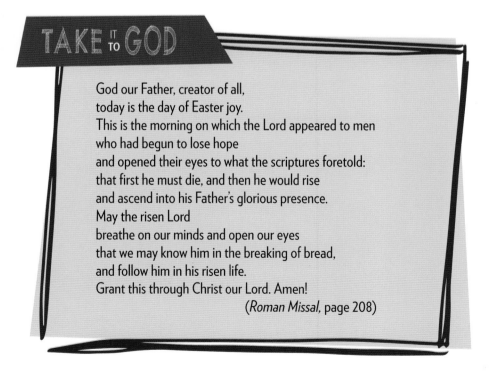

TAKE IT TO GOD

God our Father, creator of all,
today is the day of Easter joy.
This is the morning on which the Lord appeared to men
who had begun to lose hope
and opened their eyes to what the scriptures foretold:
that first he must die, and then he would rise
and ascend into his Father's glorious presence.
May the risen Lord
breathe on our minds and open our eyes
that we may know him in the breaking of bread,
and follow him in his risen life.
Grant this through Christ our Lord. Amen!
(Roman Missal, page 208)

Commandment: "Remember to keep holy the Sabbath Day." The **Sabbath**, which Christians fulfill with the observance of the Lord's Day on Sunday, is a day God set aside for rest and for worship of him. It is God's will that we keep the Lord's Day holy.

Keeping the Lord's Day

A family was invited to talk about how they started taking the Third Commandment more seriously with their daughter's religion class. "It just seemed like our lives were rush, rush, rush," said the mother. "Even on Sundays. Sure, we went to Mass, but then afterward we would go grocery shopping, do the laundry, maybe one of us would go into work for a while. By the time we went to work on Monday, we were exhausted. We hardly saw the kids because after Mass they would head upstairs to do homework or go over to a friend's house for the afternoon."

"One day we just said to ourselves, 'This is crazy,'" continued the husband. "So we talked about it and made an agreement as a family to do a better job at keeping the Lord's Day. We decided to go to the later Mass on Sunday morning so we could sleep in or read, and so I could fix breakfast for everyone. We committed to limiting our activities as much as possible after Mass so that we could focus on being together and doing things as a family. After Mass, we would all stay home for the afternoon unless we planned to visit friends or relatives together. We would not do any shopping or home chores."

© Monkey Business Images / Shutterstock.com

Sabbath ➤ In the Old Testament, the "seventh day" on which God rested after the work of Creation was completed. In the Old Law, the weekly day of rest to remember God's work through private prayer and communal worship. Christians fulfill the Sabbath observance on the Lord's Day, celebrated on Sunday, the day on which Jesus was raised, which Catholics also observe with participation in the Eucharist.

The daughter chimed in. "We would play games as a family, go to the park, pray for our family and friends, visit relatives, or even take naps. Cell phones and computers stayed off until after dinner. We would all eat a nice home-cooked dinner together, and it wasn't until after dinner that we would spend time with our friends, get on the computer, or do homework."

"After a few weeks, I couldn't believe what a difference it made," said the wife. "Of course, there were some sacrifices, but we all felt more relaxed, more in touch with God, even during the rest of the week. I think even the kids would secretly say that they appreciated having a reason to tell their friends that they would be offline for most of Sunday. I don't think God intended us to live at the pace we were living without a break."

UNIT 2

The Origin of the Sabbath

The Bible traces the origin of the Sabbath back to the creation of the world:

> On the seventh day God completed the work he had been doing; he rested on the seventh day from all the work he had undertaken. God blessed the seventh day and made it holy, because on it he rested from all the work he had done in creation. (Genesis 2:2–3)

Of course, this doesn't mean that God got physically or mentally tired and had to rest. Rather, it indicates that he was setting an example of a balanced life. Human beings were not created just for work. We need the Sabbath to refresh and renew ourselves. We need the Sabbath to strengthen our relationship with God through prayer and worship. We need the Sabbath to remind ourselves that there is something more important than making another dollar. Jesus affirms that we have been given the Sabbath for our physical and spiritual well-being when he tells the Pharisees, "The sabbath was made for man, not man for the sabbath" (Mark 2:27).

Keeping the Sabbath is a reminder of God's saving power. The Israelites were commanded to keep the Sabbath in remembrance of their liberation from slavery in Egypt: "Remember that you too were once slaves in the land of Egypt, and the LORD, your God, brought you out from there with a strong hand and outstretched arm. That is why the LORD, your God, has commanded you to observe the Sabbath day" (Deuteronomy 5:15). Jesus intentionally healed people on the Sabbath, angering some of the Pharisees who considered this breaking the law against working on the Sabbath. But Jesus wanted to show that in addition to being a day of rest, the Sabbath was also a time for doing God's work, including healing. He even declared, "That is why the Son of Man is lord even of the Sabbath" (Mark 2:28), connecting saving work with the keeping of the Sabbath.

Keeping the Sabbath is also a reminder of the sacred covenant. Because the commandment to keep the Sabbath is part of the Law of the Old Covenant, keeping the Sabbath is a regular reminder of the covenant and God's faithfulness. God says to the Israelites, "Keep my Sabbaths, for that is to be the sign between you and me throughout the generations, to show that it is I, the Lord, who make you holy" (Exodus 31:13).

© ungvar / Shutterstock.com

This is the braided bread and wine that are blessed and eaten at the Jewish family meal to begin the Sabbath on Friday evening.

To sum up: God is the origin of the Sabbath, giving it to us for our well-being. When we keep the Sabbath, we remind ourselves of God's saving love and his covenantal faithfulness. Our natural response is to praise and thank God in prayer and worship.

Applications of the Sabbath in Scripture	
The Bible applies the concept of the Sabbath as a day of renewal to a variety of practices. Here are a few.	
Practice	**Passage**
Work	"But the seventh day is a sabbath to the LORD your God; you shall not do any work—you, your son or your daughter, your male or female slave, your livestock, or the alien resident in your towns." (Exodus 20:10, *NRSV*)
Rest for the Land	"When you enter the land that I am giving you, the land shall observe a sabbath for the LORD. Six years you shall sow your field, and six years you shall prune your vineyard, and gather in their yield; but in the seventh year there shall be a sabbath of complete rest for the land, a sabbath for the LORD: you shall not sow your field or prune your vineyard." (Leviticus 25:2–4, *NRSV*)
Jubilee Year	"You shall count off seven weeks of years, seven times seven years, so that the period of seven weeks of years gives forty-nine years. . . . And you shall hallow the fiftieth year and you shall proclaim liberty throughout the land to all its inhabitants. It shall be a jubilee for you: you shall return, every one of you, to your property and every one of you to your family." (Leviticus 25:8,10, *NRSV*)

Observing the Sabbath

The Pharisees of Jesus' time had restrictive rules for observing the Sabbath and even challenged Jesus and his disciples for breaking some of these rules. Jesus challenged them for focusing on the letter of the law rather than on the commandment's true, intended meaning (see Matthew 12:1–13). This same challenge holds true for us today. The Church provides for us basic laws for keeping the Sabbath holy, but we must determine how to follow these laws in our circumstances.

Here is a summary of the basic laws:

- Every Catholic is expected to keep the Lord's Day by attending Mass on Sundays and other holy days of obligation. This is one of the Precepts of the Church and is a serious obligation.

UNIT 2

- We are to abstain from working on Sundays and other holy days of obligation, especially work that would keep us from attending Mass or work that keeps us from the relaxation and enjoyment the Sabbath is meant to provide.
- We should devote time on Sundays to rest and leisure, to works of service and charity, to spending quality time with our families, and to spiritual reading, silence, and prayer.

Attending church is an important part of keeping the Lord's Day. What are the best reasons you've heard for attending Sunday services?

Remember, failing to attend Mass on Sundays and other holy days of obligation is an offense against the Third Commandment. Never taking time to pray is also an offense against the Third Commandment. How can we be in a loving relationship with God without the very thing that maintains and nurtures that relationship? Try to keep holy the Lord's Day by abstaining from work if possible and using the time for rest, prayer, and works of charity. ✻

HMMMMM... Why do you think it is so difficult for people to keep the Lord's Day as a day of rest, prayer, and family time?

Article 22

The Lord's Day in the New Testament

People familiar with both the Jewish and the Christian faiths know that the celebration of the Sabbath and the celebration of the Lord's Day fall on two different days of the week—Saturday for Jews and Sunday for Christians. In fact, even the wording of the Third Commandment is different for the two religions, "Remember to keep holy the Sabbath day" for Jews, versus "Remember to keep holy the Lord's Day" for Christians. So how did this shift in names and days of the week come about? You probably would not be surprised to know that the reason is the glorious triumph of Christ's Resurrection.

UNIT 2

Observance of the Sabbath

Jewish observance of the Sabbath begins at sundown on Friday and continues through sundown on Saturday. In their religious observances, Jews follow the practice that the day begins and ends at sundown because the first account of Creation says, "Evening came, and morning followed—the first day" (Genesis 1:5), implying that a day begins in the evening.

The first account of Creation also determines the day on which the Sabbath is celebrated. "On the seventh day God completed the work he had been doing; he rested on the seventh day from all the work he had undertaken. God blessed the seventh day and made it holy, because on it he rested from all the work he had done in creation" (Genesis 2:2–3). Following God's lead, the

Christians also sometimes call Sunday the "eighth day," a practice that started with early Christian theologians. Saint Justin Martyr (c. 100–165) said, "It is possible for us to show how the eighth day possessed a certain mysterious import, which the seventh day did not possess." Now don't try to do the math; it won't work out. There are still only seven days in a week. Calling Sunday the eighth day is a symbolic way of saying that after Christ's Resurrection, everything had changed; the world would never be the same. Sundays are no longer just the first day of the week. They now recall a new beginning in the history of salvation.

Sabbath falls on the last day of the week—Saturday for both Christians and Jews. The Jewish Sabbath is typically celebrated with a special meal on Friday night, Sabbath services at a synagogue on Friday night and Saturday morning, and Torah study and leisure activities with family and friends during the day on Saturday.

The Beginning of the Lord's Day

As faithful Jews, Jesus and his disciples would have carefully observed the Sabbath. Even after Christ's Resurrection and Ascension, his disciples continued to keep the Sabbath and worship in the synagogues for a time—with one important difference. They now also gathered with other believers in Christ to celebrate the Eucharist. The early Christians' life together in Jerusalem is described in Acts of the Apostles 2:42–47. Here are two key verses:

> Every day they devoted themselves to meeting together in the temple area and to breaking bread in their homes. They ate their meals with exultation and sincerity of heart, praising God and enjoying favor with all the people. And every day the Lord added to their number those who were being saved. (Verses 46–47)

Notice that "meeting in the temple area" refers to their continued practice of their Jewish faith. However, "breaking bread in their homes" is the celebration of the Eucharist, the practice of their Christian faith. They did this because Christ had commanded them to do this, on the night before his death. Saint Paul explains this practice in his First Letter to the Corinthians.

© Private Collection / Bridgeman Images

Jesus commanded the Apostles—and us—to continue celebrating the Eucharist in memory of him.

CATHOLICS **MAKING** A **DIFFERENCE**

For over 140 years, the Franciscan Sisters of Perpetual Adoration have had members of their community praying 24/7 before the Blessed Sacrament in their motherhouse in La Crosse, Wisconsin. This practice is called **perpetual adoration**. Besides faithfully praying in the presence of Jesus, these sisters also established schools, colleges, and hospitals, working as educators, social workers, justice advocates, spiritual directors, and missionaries. They join the thousands of other Catholics across the world who are strengthened by spending time with Jesus in Eucharistic adoration.

UNIT 2

> For I received from the Lord what I also handed on to you, that the Lord Jesus, on the night he was handed over, took bread, and, after he had given thanks, broke it and said, "This is my body that is for you. Do this in remembrance of me." In the same way also the cup, after supper, saying, "This cup is the new covenant in my blood. Do this, as often as you drink it, in remembrance of me." For as often as you eat this bread and drink the cup, you proclaim the death of the Lord until he comes. (11:23–26)

Very quickly, these first Christians began to celebrate the Lord's Supper on Sunday, the first day of the week. Again, we see this practice identified in the Acts of the Apostles: "On the first day of the week when we gathered to break bread, Paul spoke to them because he was going to leave on the next day" (20:7). Why did they begin to observe the Eucharist on Sunday? The reason is Jesus Christ's Resurrection. The Gospels carefully record that the Resurrection occurred sometime after the Sabbath day ended and by dawn on Sunday: "After the Sabbath, as the first day of the week was dawning, Mary Magdalene and the other Mary came to see the tomb" (Matthew 28:1).

perpetual adoration ➤ The practice of people committing to pray before the Blessed Sacrament in a designated location so that someone is always in the presence of Christ, twenty-four hours a day, 365 days a year.

Christians have moved the celebration of the Sabbath to Sunday, the Lord's Day, in honor of the Resurrection of Jesus Christ.

Because of Christ's Resurrection, Jesus' followers came to see Sunday not only as the first day of God's creation of the world but also as the symbolic "first day" of the new creation that begins with Christ's Resurrection. They began meeting on Sundays to celebrate the Eucharist in honor of Christ's command to "do this in memory of me." Ultimately, Christians moved the observance of the Sabbath from Saturday, the last day of the week, to Sunday, the day of the Resurrection, the first day of the new creation, and began calling Sunday the Lord's Day in honor of our Lord and Savior, Jesus Christ. ✳

HMMMMMM...
Which term, the *Sabbath* or the *Lord's Day*, best describes what Sunday is for you? Why?

Article 23

Keeping Sunday Holy

Mrs. Perez sighed in frustration as her two teenage children gave her grief about going to Mass again. "Why do we have to go every Sunday?" complained Sofia. "God still sees us if we're praying at home." "We'll be the only kids there," added Mateo. "And I have soccer practice and tons of homework to do."

"That's enough," said Mr. Perez. "It isn't enough for Christians to pray just by themselves. God wants us to support one another in prayer, gathered together to recall all the wonderful gifts he's given us and to receive him in the Eucharist. And if you give this time to God, you will be more centered for all the other things you need to do. As Christians, we are committed to putting God first, and it's best when we do that as a family."

As the Sabbath evolved into the Lord's Day, Christians preserved God's original command to us: "Remember to keep holy the Lord's Day." We keep holy the Lord's Day by celebrating the Eucharist, performing works of service and charity, and taking time for relaxation and prayer. This article looks more closely at specific ways we can do these things.

Attending Mass

You might ask, "Why is missing Mass on Sundays a sin?" One reason is that the practice dates back to the days of the Apostles. The Letter to the Hebrews reminds the faithful to "not stay away from our assembly" (10:25). A few centuries later, Saint John Chrysostom was asked, "Why not just pray in the privacy of our home or in some other place that is sacred to us?" He replied:

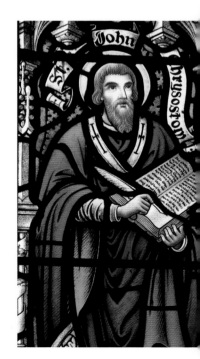

> You cannot pray at home as at church, where there is a great multitude, where exclamations are cried out to God as from one great heart, and where there is something more: the union of minds, the accord of souls, the bond of charity, the prayers of the priests.[1] (*Catechism of the Catholic Church [CCC]*, number 2179)

UNIT 2

Saint John's language may seem dated, and yet the reasons he gives make sense today. You can and should still pray in the privacy of your home, outside in nature, or in some special place that helps you to communicate with God. But the Sunday Eucharist (also celebrated on Saturday evening) is the opportunity to praise God through song, prayer, and Scripture, and to receive the Body and Blood of Christ with the whole community on the day of rest that God set aside for us.

Another reason to participate in the Mass on Sunday is that it is important to gather with other members of the Church on a regular basis. God insists that his people set aside Sunday so that nothing else gets in the way of that date with one another and with God. We should arrange the rest of our lives—our work, study, leisure, and business—so we can be available for Mass and for time to properly relax our minds and bodies.

The most important reason for attending Mass on Sunday, however, is because the Eucharist is the ultimate source of our spiritual nourishment. In the Eucharist, Jesus feeds our heart and soul with his sacred Word and with his holy Body and Blood. Jesus' sacrifice is made present for us as we celebrate the Paschal Mystery. Fed by the Eucharist, we are strengthened to be Christ for others in the week ahead.

Works of Service and Charity

We can certainly perform works of service and charity on other days besides Sunday. But when we keep Sunday free of work and unnecessary commitments, we have time for other people that we do not have during the rest of the week. You could use this time to do activities like these:

© Lisa F. Young / Shutterstock.com

- Take someone to church who needs a ride or who needs a friend to go with them.
- Visit an elderly family member, friend, or neighbor. If you cannot visit in person, make a phone call.
- Volunteer to help serve a meal to those in need, or invite someone who is lonely to share a meal with your family.

CHEW ON THIS

What, then, is rest according to this commandment? It is the moment of contemplation, it is the moment of praise, not that of escapism. It is the time to look at reality and say: how beautiful life is! Contrary to rest as an escape from reality, the Decalogue proposes rest as the blessing of reality. For us Christians, the center of the Lord's day, Sunday, is the Eucharist, which means "thanksgiving." It is the day to say to God: thank you Lord for life, for your mercy, for all your gifts. Sunday is not the day to forget the other days but to remember them, bless them and make peace with life. How many people there are who have many opportunities to amuse themselves, who are not at peace with life! Sunday is the day to make peace with life, saying: life is precious; it is not easy, sometimes it is painful, but it is precious. (Pope Francis, "General Audience," September 5, 2018)

- Visit someone who is in the hospital or a nursing home. Sunday afternoons are a good time to visit.
- Write emails to your legislators encouraging them to take a strong moral stance on a social concern.

These might seem like obvious things, but they are important and we often do not make time for them. You do not have to look far from home to find these works of service. Start by looking at the needs in your own family and neighborhood.

Sunday Rest

We should not forget that the original primary obligation of the Third Commandment is to rest from the week's work. The Old Law saw this as more than just a suggestion; it was an obligation:

> Therefore, you must keep the Sabbath for it is holiness for you. Whoever desecrates it shall be put to death. If anyone does work on that day, that person must be cut off from the people. Six days there are for doing work, but the seventh day is the Sabbath of complete rest, holy to the LORD. (Exodus 31:14–15)

UNIT 2

Jill and Anna felt like they were caught in the middle. They had joined a traveling soccer league and almost all the practices, games, and tournaments were on the weekends, including Sunday mornings. They really hadn't thought much about missing church until their grandma confronted them.

"You two are really okay with missing Mass for the next three months? I'm not okay with that. We need to keep Sunday holy!"

"But, Gramms," Jill replied, "it's a big deal to get on this league. It's really important to us, and the team is counting on us."

"I understand that," said Gramms, "but you can't tell me there isn't a way you can work it out. Talk to your coaches. Go to a Saturday night Mass or even the Sunday night Mass at the Cathedral. Soccer is great, but we need to remember our commitment to God, the most important commitment there is." How would you advise Jill and Anna?

How can you respond to the challenges you face in keeping the Lord's Day holy?

Christians no longer follow the Old Law with its severe penalties, of course. But the seriousness of the moral obligation not to work on the Lord's Day should give us pause, especially if we have not questioned the need to work on Sundays. If you have a job that absolutely requires you to work on Sundays, be creative. See if you can work reduced hours. If that doesn't work, try keeping your Sabbath on another day of the week, like Saturday, or even start looking for a different job.

You can rest and renew yourself in many ways on Sundays. Some people take an afternoon nap. Others use the time for spiritual and recreational reading. Watching an uplifting movie or playing games or taking a walk alone or with family and friends can be fun and relaxing. Just be sure it is something positive and uplifting.

As Christians, we should pause and think of ways we can change the way we do business. We should never make demands on others that would keep them from observing the Lord's Day. When stores and restaurants are open around the clock, including Sundays, it is easy to lose respect for the Third Commandment. Although it is rare, some store owners intentionally close their stores on Sunday, giving their workers the day off to worship and be with their families.

An element of **eschatology**, that is, a life-after-death dimension, is connected to the Third Commandment. The Sabbath rest, the worship of God, and the peace and joy that we experience on Sundays is a foreshadowing of the eternal rest and joy that we will know in Heaven.

© Syda Productions / Shutterstock.com

How can you relax and renew yourself?

UNIT 2

Pope Saint John Paul II explained this in one of his homilies in the Holy Land:

> The Resurrection of Jesus is the definitive seal of all God's promises, the birth-place of a new, risen humanity, the pledge of a history marked by the Messianic gifts of peace and spiritual joy. At the dawn of a new millennium, Christians can and ought to look to the future with steadfast trust in the glorious power of the Risen One to make all things new (see Revelation 21:5). He is the One who frees all creation from its bondage to futility (see Romans 8:20). By his Resurrection he opens the way to the great Sabbath rest, the Eighth Day, when mankind's pilgrimage will come to its end and God will be all in all (1 Corinthians 15:28). ("Mass in the Church of the Holy Sepulchre," number 4)

Reclaiming Sunday as the Lord's Day by participating in the celebration of the Eucharist and taking the time for rest and recreation helps us to remember God's original blessing in creation and to look forward to the wonderful blessings of Heaven. We need to "recreate," so we can be the people God calls us to be. We know this is a blessing—something that is good for us. It is one of those laws written on our hearts and minds, as well as in stone. ✳

HMMMMMM. . .
What is the most important reason for you to keep Sunday holy?

---

eschatology ➤ The area of Christian faith having to do with the last things: the Last Judgment, the particular judgment, the resurrection of the body, Heaven, Hell, and Purgatory.

1. What is the Old Testament basis for keeping the Sabbath Day holy?

2. What are three principal ways Christians are called to observe the Sabbath?

3. Why did the keeping of the Third Commandment move from being observed on Saturday to being observed on Sunday?

4. Why is Sunday sometimes called the Lord's Day?

5. Give three reasons that it is important to attend Mass on Sundays and holy days of obligation.

6. What are some good ways to seek rest and personal renewal on Sundays?

What time are we getting together tomorrow?

I already told u, it's my Sunday family time.

😮

Might seem boring, but we have a good time. 😊

Really? Come on, let's hang out.

Hey, we play games, visit our neighbors, cook a nice meal. Makes me feel good.

Okay, keep your phone close by, I'll text.

Good luck with that. We all shut off our phones for the afternoon!

U crazy? Can't live w/o my phone.

That's what I thought at first.

Message

KEEPING THE LORD'S DAY HOLY
TEXT EXCHANGE

UNIT 2 HIGHLIGHTS

CHAPTER 4   The First Commandment:
Faith, Not Idolatry

Faith:
Accepting all
the truths
of faith

Living
the

First
Commandment

Love:
Loving God completely;
not falling into
indifference or
ingratitude

Hope:
Expecting God's
blessing in this life
and in Heaven

Idolatry: Ancient and Modern

Ancient

Modern

UNIT 2

versus

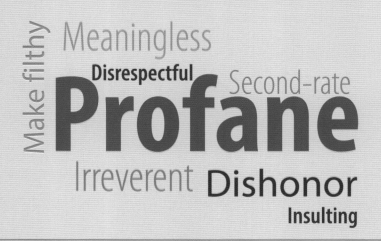

Living the Second Commandment

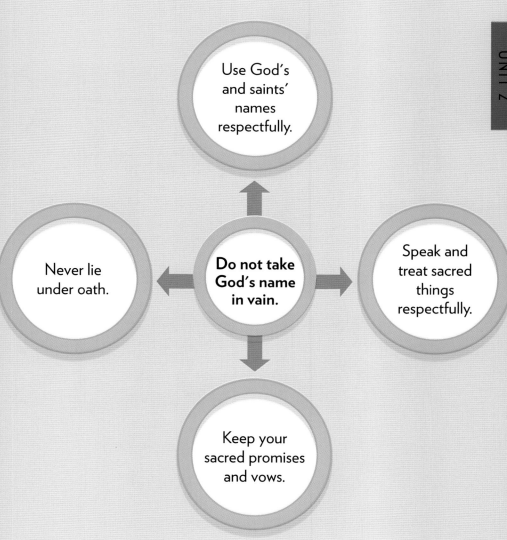

Use God's and saints' names respectfully.

Never lie under oath.

Do not take God's name in vain.

Speak and treat sacred things respectfully.

Keep your sacred promises and vows.

CHAPTER 6   The Third Commandment:
Preserving Holiness

Sabbath in the Bible

**God rested on
the seventh day.**

**Remember you were
slaves and God rescued you.**

**Jesus cured on
the Sabbath.**

**Keep holy the
Lord's Day.**

**"The Sabbath was
made for man."**

UNIT 2

BRING IT HOME

DOES IT REALLY MATTER HOW I THINK ABOUT GOD?

FOCUS QUESTIONS

DEMETRIOS
Our Lady of the Hills College
Preparatory School

The first three commandments are especially helpful in how we think about God. They help us understand the very gravity of God's being. The First Commandment reminds us that allowing anything to take our focus off God does not nourish a healthy relationship with God. If we don't have our focus on God, are we really following him? The Second Commandment helps us recognize the importance of God's name. To use any of God's titles frivolously, or even that of someone else, would be to slander them. The Third Commandment also helps orient our thinking towards God. Going to Mass and honoring the Sabbath may seem like restrictions, but they are really God's way of allowing us to find our rest and comfort in him and all he has created for us.

UNIT 2

REFLECT

Take some time to read and reflect on the unit and chapter focus questions listed on the facing page.

- What question or section did you identify most closely with?

- What did you find within the unit that was comforting or challenging?

UNIT 3
Obedience, Honesty, and Justice

WHY SHOULD I WORRY ABOUT HOW MY CHOICES AFFECT OTHER PEOPLE?

LOOKING AHEAD

UNIT 3

I should be worried about how my choices affect other people because everyone is dealing with something, and those things can hurt them. Many people are always hurting, and they won't show it. When you make a bad choice that injures people, their pain and suffering grow, and they get sadder. On the positive side, when you do something nice for someone, it can make them feel better and take away some of the hurt and sadness.

KARLA
Seton Catholic Preparatory School

CHAPTER 7
The Fourth Commandment: Respecting Authority

WHEN IS IT IMPORTANT TO OBEY OTHER PEOPLE?

SNAPSHOT

Article 24

Families in the Bible

Beginning with this unit, we make the transition from the first three commandments with their focus on the love of God to the final seven commandments with their emphasis on the love of our neighbor. The Fourth Commandment is the first in this group, and it is focused on those closest to us, our family. Unlike the last six commandments, the Fourth Commandment is a positive commandment; it tells us what *to* do rather than what *not to* do.

As is true with all the commandments, the scope of the Fourth Commandment is broader than it first appears. It isn't limited to just the relationship between children and parents. It applies to our relationships with all authorities: teachers, coaches, law officers, civil authorities, and so on. By focusing on the responsibilities and duties that family members have toward one another, the Fourth Commandment teaches us how we are to act toward all people. Jesus taught us that all people are children of his heavenly Father and so, in a spiritual sense, are our brothers and sisters. Therefore, the Fourth Commandment acts like a bridge between the love of God taught in the first three commandments and the love of neighbor taught in the final six commandments.

UNIT 3

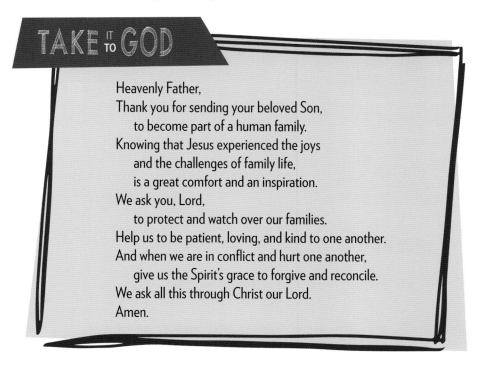

TAKE IT TO GOD

Heavenly Father,
Thank you for sending your beloved Son,
    to become part of a human family.
Knowing that Jesus experienced the joys
    and the challenges of family life,
    is a great comfort and an inspiration.
We ask you, Lord,
    to protect and watch over our families.
Help us to be patient, loving, and kind to one another.
And when we are in conflict and hurt one another,
    give us the Spirit's grace to forgive and reconcile.
We ask all this through Christ our Lord.
Amen.

Families are the most basic building block of communal life. In God's plan, human communities should reflect the love and harmony present in the communion of the Holy Trinity. Families should be the first place where children come to know God's love through the love of parents and grandparents, brothers and sisters, aunts and uncles, and anyone else who is part of their extended family. Think about the things you have learned from your family. Have you have learned what it is like to be loved for who you are, even when you haven't been your best self? Have you learned about responsibility, respect, and forgiveness? Have you learned how to respect differences and play fair?

© Catherine Yeulet / iStockphoto.com

No family will teach and practice these things perfectly. You may be familiar with examples of parents who struggle or who fail to properly love and care for their children. Rather than make us lose hope, this reality helps us understand why God's plan for families is so important and inspires us to do all we can to make our families the loving and supporting communities God intends them to be.

Biblical Views on the Family

In biblical times, the extended family was the central social institution. Unlike many modern Western families, several generations lived together: a father, mother, and children lived with their grandparents, aunts, uncles, cousins, and all these people's spouses and children. Three or four generations would live in close proximity (adjoining tents or houses) if not in the same household.

Within the hierarchical structure of the extended family, each person had a clearly defined social role. The father earned a living for the family through herding, farming, fishing, or some other trade. He was the head of the family. The mother managed the household. Children obeyed their parents. Fathers and mothers passed on the teachings of the Covenant and the Law. Sons were expected to help with their father's trade, and daughters were expected to help their mothers with household chores from a young age. Sons most often inherited the father's trade. It was based on this custom that Jesus followed Joseph, his earthly father, as a stonemason and woodworker.

Besides faithfulness to God, respect for and loyalty to one's family was the strongest value in biblical cultures. A primary way people practiced this value was by honoring their parents. This is a constant theme in the Old Testament, as seen in the biblical version of the Fourth Commandment: "Honor your father and your mother, that you may have a long life in the land the LORD your God is giving you" (Exodus 20:12). God emphasized the importance of respect for one's family by connecting it to one of the promises of the Sinai Covenant, the promise of land. Later on, the Israelites were given severe punishments for failures to keep this commandment: "Whoever strikes father or mother shall be put to death. . . . Whoever curses father or mother shall be put to death" (Exodus 21:15,17).

UNIT 3

Other Old Testament Passages on Honoring Parents	
Proverbs 19:26 (NRSV)	"Those who do violence to their father and chase away their mother, are children who cause shame and bring reproach."
Proverbs 30:17 (NRSV)	"The eye that mocks a father, or scorns to obey a mother, will be pecked out by the ravens of the valley and eaten by the vultures."
Sirach 3:2–6 (NRSV)	"For the Lord honors a father above his children, and he confirms a mother's right over her children. Those who honor their father atone for sins, and those who respect their mother are like those who lay up treasure. Those who honor their father will have joy in their own children, and when they pray they will be heard. Those who respect their father will have long life, and those who honor their mother obey the Lord."

Jesus on the True Meaning of Family

Jesus was a loving and obedient son who honored Mary, his mother, and Joseph, his earthly father. But he shocked his contemporaries with his new and radical understanding of the Fourth Commandment. To start, he left the family trade and therefore his extended family to preach about the Kingdom of God. Leaving one's family for any reason was considered questionable behavior. At one point, his confused neighbors said: "Is this not Jesus, the son of Joseph? Do we not know his father and mother? Then how can he say, 'I have come down from heaven'?" (John 6:42). In Mark 3:20–35, Jesus' relatives come to find him and forcibly take him home saying, "He is out of his mind" (verse 21). Hearing this, Jesus shocks everyone by saying:

> "Who are my mother and (my) brothers?" And looking around at those seated in the circle he said, "Here are my mother and my brothers. [For] whoever does the will of God is my brother and sister and mother." (Verses 33-35)

Part of Jesus' mission was to form a new family, a spiritual family, who would become his Body, the Church. Jesus insisted that loyalty to God and this new family was a higher value than unquestioned loyalty to blood relatives. If there was conflict between loyalty to God and loyalty to one's birth family, loyalty to God was more important. He taught that his followers formed a spiritual family, based not on blood and marriage relations, but on a common

Paolo Veronese / Public domain

Christ extends the meaning of family beyond blood relatives. Who is part of your spiritual family?

UNIT 3

Why are the members of the Church sometimes called the family of God? How is the Church like a family?

belief. The New Law taught by Jesus does not take away from the importance of the Fourth Commandment but helps us to understand its true meaning. We do not obey the Fourth Commandment because of custom or blind obedience; rather, the New Law calls us to respect and honor our parents and other family members because we are all part of the family of God. ✳

HMMMMM. . .

How does loyalty to your family rank in your life priorities?

Article 25

Parent and Child Responsibilities

Chin was complaining again to his best friend. "No matter what I do, it isn't good enough for my dad. If I get a 99 on a test, he asks, 'Why wasn't it a 100?' He wants me to honor and respect him, but I don't feel any of the same from him." Haro was at a loss for what to tell his friend. His experience was almost the exact opposite. His parents praised him for just about everything he tried. "That must make you feel really hurt and angry," Haro replied. "I don't think that's the way families are supposed to be. I think you just have to love and forgive your dad and hope that someday he'll change. Until then, keep visiting my house. My parents will think a 99 is amazing!"

The most basic meaning of the Fourth Commandment, "Honor your father and your mother," is clear to the casual reader. It commands children to respect and honor their parents. By logical extension, it also requires us to respect and obey other people God has placed in authority over us for our good. Jesus' New Law extends the meaning of the commandment even further. The Law of Love requires all family members to love one another with the same love God has for us.

The Fourth Commandment calls children and parents to love and respect each other. What are some responsibilities that children have toward their parents?

The New Law teaches that in addition to children loving and honoring their parents, parents also have a responsibility to love and respect their children. The Letter to the Colossians is an early teaching identifying different roles in the family and how they are rooted in the love of God: "Children, obey your parents in everything, for this is pleasing to the Lord. Fathers, do not provoke your children, so they may not become discouraged. . . . Whatever you do, do from the heart, as for the Lord and not for others" (3:20–21,23; see also Ephesians 5:21–6:4). This passage reveals that parents and children have responsibilities toward each other. Because parents and children have different roles in the family, their specific responsibilities toward each other are also different. Most important, however, is that the letter tells us this obedience should come from the heart, out of our love for one another. When we fulfill our roles within our families, we are allowing God's love to flow through us to each member of the family.

Honoring Parents

What does it mean to honor parents? Instead of a typical list of obligations, the Church defines the duties of this commandment as *attitudes* that lead to specific actions. The Church teaches that the attitudes children owe parents are respect, gratitude, obedience, and assistance. Showing respect to parents brings harmony to family life.

Respect is the foundation of any healthy relationship. Respect comes naturally for children when they experience the love and respect a parent has for them. When children are young, this usually happens pretty easily because they look up to their parents and believe that their mother or father can do no wrong. However, as children get a little older and develop their own desires and beliefs, they may challenge their parents' values and push against the boundaries their parents have set. This is a natural and even necessary dynamic, but it means that mutual respect can become more challenging. Even so, the Fourth Commandment requires that we listen to our parents with an open and patient attitude, doing our best to try to understand their point of view.

Another requirement of children is to show gratitude toward parents. Many parents sacrifice a great deal for their children, giving them their time, attention, and financial help. It takes a lot of money to raise a child from infancy through college. And then there are the hours taking children to and from school and extracurricular activities. Of course, these are parents' responsibilities, but parents occasionally need to know that their children appreciate it! We shouldn't wait until Mother's Day or Father's Day to say thanks. We should find opportunities to express our appreciation to our parents for providing us with what we need in order to grow physically, mentally, and spiritually.

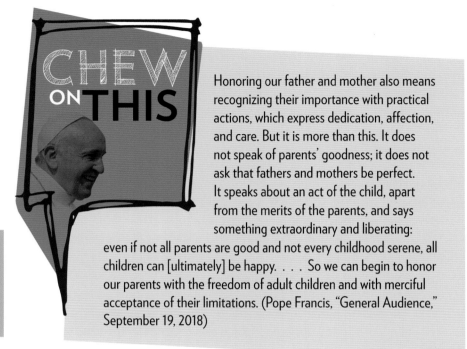

CHEW ON THIS

Honoring our father and mother also means recognizing their importance with practical actions, which express dedication, affection, and care. But it is more than this. It does not speak of parents' goodness; it does not ask that fathers and mothers be perfect. It speaks about an act of the child, apart from the merits of the parents, and says something extraordinary and liberating: even if not all parents are good and not every childhood serene, all children can [ultimately] be happy. . . . So we can begin to honor our parents with the freedom of adult children and with merciful acceptance of their limitations. (Pope Francis, "General Audience," September 19, 2018)

Then there is the duty of obedience. That is a word most people really do not like to hear. Most children generally don't have a problem doing what their parents ask, yet for some, it is a constant challenge to follow their parents' requests. They may protest, bargain, and delay just to make sure their parents really meant what they said. The commandment to honor our mother and father should help to provide the motivation we need to trust our parents' judgment, even when we don't agree with the importance or the reason behind their request. The only exception to the obedience requirement is if a parent, teacher, or someone else in authority asks us to do something we know is wrong. For example, if an overzealous parent or coach suggests cheating to gain an advantage, God's Law requires us to not follow that suggestion.

Let's be clear about this important exception to obedience. No child or teen should ever have to endure abusive parents and unsafe family situations. No one has to obey a parent who is trying to make them keep secrets about abusive or illegal behavior. In these situations, a child or teen's safety is of utmost importance, and the proper authorities must be notified and appropriate actions taken.

Last in the list of duties for children is the responsibility they have to assist their parents. Assistance may come in the form of doing regular chores or just helping out when needed to babysit, carry in groceries, help make dinner, or

How do you show your honor for the people God has put in authority over you: parents, teachers, and coaches, for example?

UNIT 3

do yardwork. As we grow older, we will discover that the commandment goes deeper than that. It also means that grown children must care for their parents in their old age, giving them the moral and material support they need, especially when they are ill, lonely, or in crisis.

Parents' Responsibility for Children

We don't always like to hear "This is for your own good," a statement parents often make to their children, but parents are supposed to know better than we do what is truly good for us. As infants, many of us received vaccinations that our parents knew were painful, but the discomfort was necessary to prevent dangerous childhood diseases. Our parents winced as we protested those needles, but they knew what was good for us. In a similar way, our parents have the responsibility to teach us about God and the moral life and to make rules for our safety—even if it means telling us things we would rather not hear. Believe it or not, parents do not enjoy telling their children no. In fact, it would be much easier just to let children do whatever they want—but then what kind of parents would such people be?

Not only must parents provide for the physical, emotional, and spiritual needs of their children, but they must also be their children's first educators, especially when it comes to their faith life. The family should also be the first place where we learn how to love God and one another as Jesus Christ taught

MAKE IT SO

You and Olivia have been friends for the past year. Olivia moved to town to live with new foster parents. You know the family and they seem like kind, generous people. But Olivia is having a hard time adjusting. She is constantly breaking curfew, complains about chores she's expected to help with, and often puts down her foster mom. She has shared bits and pieces of her childhood with you, and she's been through some hard times. Still, you believe that her life would be easier if she would try harder to appreciate and obey her foster parents. From what she's told you, there isn't anything wrong with how her foster parents have treated her; it seems more likely that she just isn't used to being part of a stable family unit. Lately, Olivia's even been talking about just leaving them and trying to live on her own. What could you say to Olivia to help her understand the importance of family—even if it isn't the family she was born into?

us to love. Parents need to create a home in which love, respect, caring, forgiveness, service of others, and faith are the normal values practiced by everyone in the family. Ideally, parents should start instilling these values at an early age, by praying with their children at meals and bedtime and doing service together as a family, starting with simple things and taking on more difficult challenges as children grow older. By making sure their children attend Mass and are prepared for the sacraments, parents teach their children to have faith in God and to develop a relationship with him.

Ideally, our parents are our first **catechists**, teaching us the truths revealed by God for our salvation. For this reason, the family home is called the domestic church. However, some parents are not ready for this responsibility or are overwhelmed by other demands. It is never too late to work on these things together. There are many examples of families who started praying together, attending Church together, and serving others together for the first time when their children were teens. We need to work with our parents to make our family a community of grace and prayer and the primary place where we learn and practice human virtues and Christian charity.

---

catechist ➤ Catechesis is the process by which Christians of all ages are taught the essentials of Christian doctrine and are formed as disciples of Christ. Catechists are the ministers of catechesis.

Parents are responsible for helping children learn to love God and grow in faith.

As we grow older, the natural progression that God created requires that parents give us more freedom as we make our own choices. This can be difficult for some parents. We are all familiar with stories of parents who pushed their son or daughter to be a doctor, even though the child's talents and interests were more artistic or mechanical. Even Mary and Joseph had difficulty letting go when Jesus started to become more independent. When they found him in the Temple after he'd been missing for three days, they didn't understand his explanation of being about his Father's business. The Gospel tells us that Mary had to ponder his words in her heart, seriously considering what Jesus was saying about his life's work (see Luke 2:41–51).

Figuring out our **vocation** is something we have to do for ourselves; a parent's responsibility is to encourage and support us in whatever vocation we choose. Of course, the most important thing a parent can do is teach us from an early age that our first calling is to follow Jesus.

---

vocation ➤ A call from God to all members of the Church to embrace a life of holiness. Specifically, it refers to a call to live the holy life as an ordained minister, as a vowed religious (sister or brother), or in a Christian marriage. Single life that involves a personal consecration or commitment to a permanent, celibate gift of self to God and one's neighbor is also a vocational state.

Advice on Honoring Parents

Showing honor to parents is a sensitive topic for teens. For one thing, it is natural for teens and their parents to be in occasional power struggles over curfews, car privileges, future plans, and so on. Another challenge is that all parents are different; this can cause teens to wish their parents acted more like someone else's parents. Given these and other challenges, here is some good advice to follow.

- **Spend time with your parents.** Teens and parents have busy lives with school, work, friends, church commitments, and so on. Because of this, teens and parents need to be intentional about spending time together. How can you have a relationship with your parents if you don't spend time with them? How do they know how important they are to you if it seems like you are avoiding them?

- **Remember that your parents are people too.** Parents are usually doing their best at parenting even if it isn't perfect. A teen told a story about how she was always complaining about her mother's cooking. Then she spent several months away from home. During that time, she realized how much work it takes to cook every day and to please everyone with your cooking. When she returned home, she tried not to complain about her mother's cooking again.

- **Do not misplace your emotions.** When you are upset with friends or disappointed by something at school, it is easy to let angry or sad feelings spill over into family life. But being angry with your parents when you are really angry with a friend or even angry with yourself isn't dealing with the real problem—and it is not very respectful to Mom and Dad.

- **Remember that God has given your parents authority over you.** Parents have the responsibility to create family rules that keep their children safe and guide them in living moral lives. One young adult put it this way, "When I show respect for my parents' authority, I feel like I am also respecting God's authority." ✳

HMMMMM. . . Which attitude is the most difficult for you to have toward your parents or guardians: respect, gratitude, obedience, or assistance?

Article 26
Respect for Public Life

Pattie was fuming after reading through her social media posts. "I don't get how anyone can criticize our president! God put him in charge, and that means we must all support him. If you don't agree, keep your opinions to yourself!"

"Hold on," replied Charles. "We live in a democracy. That means people have a right to speak up if they don't agree with the policies of any person in government. Our faith calls us to judge our government's policies according to the values of Jesus. I agree we should always respect our leaders, but I don't think we should always assume they are morally right on every issue."

Discussing the Church's involvement in politics can be a touchy subject. In some families, people cannot even talk about religion and politics without it turning into a shouting match. Some people have strong beliefs that faith should not have anything to do with our public life. But they could not be more wrong.

Our faith should strongly influence our public life. This book uses the phrase "public life" instead of "political life" to be as expansive as possible. Most people associate politics with local, state, and national governments.

Service organizations like Big Brothers Big Sisters clearly contribute to the common good, but all public groups should be committed to the common good.

UNIT 3

Although the Fourth Commandment applies to our relationship with these authorities, it includes other public groups and organizations also, such as schools, scouting organizations, clubs of all kinds, sports teams, and service organizations. Take a moment to think about how many different groups and organizations you belong to. Have you thought about how the Fourth Commandment applies to your relationship with them?

New Testament Teaching on Obedience to Civil Authorities

Saint Paul teaches about the respect and obedience we owe **civil authorities** in his Letter to the Romans, chapter 13. At the beginning of the chapter, he teaches that public institutions should reflect God's will: "Let every person be subordinate to the higher authorities, for there is no authority except from God, and those that exist have been established by God" (verse 1). Later he emphasizes the importance of obedience to legitimate authority: "Pay to

Anonymous/Unknown author / Public domain

I DIDN'T KNOW THAT!

There have been times in history, especially in Europe in the Middle Ages, when Church authority and political authority almost completely overlapped. In countries such as Italy, France, and Germany, popes and bishops crowned kings, and kings influenced the appointment of popes. This led to situations in which some Church leaders became too caught up in political ambition and palace politics and failed to call for needed societal reform. This is why canon law generally forbids priests and bishops from holding political office. The *Catechism* calls for a clear separation of political and religious authority: "The Church, because of her commission and competence, is not to be confused in any way with the political community. She is both the sign and the safeguard of the transcendent character of the human person" (CCC, number 2245).

---

civil authorities ➤ Leaders of public groups that are not religious institutions, particularly government leaders.

all their dues, taxes to whom taxes are due, toll to whom toll is due, respect to whom respect is due, honor to whom honor is due" (verse 7). Finally, he emphasizes that God's Law is based in love and that love is the fundamental principle that undergirds all of our public relationships: "Love does no evil to the neighbor; hence, love is the fulfillment of the law" (verse 10).

These passages could seem to suggest that Paul is teaching us to obey civil authorities in every situation. However, in the Acts of the Apostles, we find Peter and Paul getting into trouble with civil authorities on several occasions (see 5:17–42, 16:16–23, 21:27–36). Peter and Paul do not directly try to cause these situations, but they do not back away from them. In defense of his actions, Peter simply tells his accusers, "We must obey God rather than men" (Acts 5:29). (Tradition says that both Paul and Peter were executed in Rome for crimes against the Roman government, most likely their refusal to worship the emperor.) These and other New Testament passages teach us that all human authority is rooted in God, and because of that we owe our obedience to civil authority except when it becomes clear that such obedience is in conflict with God's moral law.

The True Role and Nature of Public Groups

Saint Paul's teaching about God's Eternal Law reminds us that every person and every human society can come to know that law through creation and the use of human reason—in other words, natural law. The natural law established by God should be the basis for all public groups, Christian and non-Christian, including all civil authorities. All public groups and organizations are called by God to respect his moral order through their understanding of natural law. He calls public leaders to safeguard the fundamental rights of the human person and to respect and promote human freedom. He calls them to be committed to the common good of society and to work toward this good by morally acceptable means.

The Holy Trinity calls Christians to be part of public life. The Father sent his Son to teach us how to live the Beatitudes and to be models for other people for living a life in communion with God. The Father and the Son send the Holy Spirit to empower us with his supernatural gifts to live that life of faith and holiness. Although it is true that God calls some individuals to remove themselves from public life to live as hermits or in cloistered communities, even these people still participate in society by praying for the common good.

No public group or government perfectly reflects God's will or perfectly follows his moral law. This should not prevent Christians from participating in these groups and witnessing to the moral law. Our participation in public life is obedience to the second Great Commandment: love your neighbor as

yourself. By respecting each person's God-given dignity and safeguarding the rights that flow from that dignity, we help the organizations we are part of better reflect the moral law. We also do this through our respect for the leaders of our groups and political communities and through our obedience to their legitimate orders and requests.

To better understand this important concept, let's apply these ideas to being a member of a sports team. A sports team exists to help people be physically active, to develop their physical skills, to build positive relationships with other people, and to provide entertainment for others. These things are all consistent with God's will, even though the sports team has nothing directly to do with practicing religion. Further, each member of the team has a responsibility to respect the other team members, to help them grow in their skills, and to follow the coach's directions. When everyone on the team fulfills these responsibilities—even when they are challenging—it makes the team members feel happy and fulfilled. What happens if the team loses sight of its real purpose, or if the team members don't respect one another? What happens if the team members are selfish, or if they don't follow the coach's directions? Being on a team like that is most likely not going to be a happy experience. When any public group or political community is not in line with God's Eternal Law, it cannot fulfill its role in his plan of salvation.

Being *in* the World, Not *of* the World

So far the discussion about the role of public groups and civil authorities in God's plan might seem quite optimistic, perhaps too optimistic for those familiar with history. It is easy to point out times and places where governments are guilty of creating sinful laws and participating in actions directly contrary to the moral law. Fighting unjust wars, allowing slavery, and denying freedom of religion and freedom of the press are just a few examples of the ways societies have failed to follow the moral law. On a lesser scale, some public groups allow and encourage favoritism, prejudice, greed, and misinformation. Some groups discourage or even forbid any mention or outward practice of religious faith.

When faced with these situations, it can be helpful to remember that Christians are called to be in the world, not of the world. This means that we are called to give witness to our faith and to God's moral law in all that we say and do. This will happen only if we Christians associate with people who do not always share our values, which is why we must be *in* the world. And this will happen only if we challenge values that are contrary to God's values, which is why we must not be *of* the world. Saint Paul summed this up in a brilliant verse in his Letter to the Romans: "Do not conform yourself to this age but be transformed by the renewal of your mind, that you may discern what is the will of God, what is good and pleasing and perfect" (12:2).

Being *in* the world but not *of* the world can be a challenging task. It may mean making uncomfortable choices that make us stand out, such as getting up early to go to Church on a school trip. It may mean making the extra effort to speak to a leader privately about something we disagree with. It may mean choosing not to be a part of some groups or associations because their core values directly contradict God's Law. However hard these things might be though, when we do them we will know the peace and joy that the Holy Spirit gives to those who trust in him. ✳

UNIT 3

What is the difference between blind obedience to your country and obedience that is informed by your conscience?

Article 27
Faithful Citizenship

This time it was Charles's turn to vent. "I keep hearing in class that it is our religious obligation to vote. But I don't see the point. No matter which party gets elected, nothing really changes. And when there are changes, they don't seem to help those who most need change."

"I know," Pattie responded. "But what's the alternative? to just give up? That seems pretty hopeless."

In this article, we consider the implications of the Fourth Commandment for governments and for our role as citizens. This is an important topic for teens who are close to voting age. It is a well-known statistic that voter turnout for national and state elections is significantly less for people ages eighteen to twenty-nine than for any other age-group. Typically, less than a third of this age-group turns out to vote. If the number of young adults voting doubled, they could easily determine the final election results. Participation as a young adult citizen does make a difference!

The bishops of the United States used the phrase "faithful citizenship" in their teaching on this topic. The phrase is clever because it has a dual meaning. On the one hand, it indicates that Catholics are to strive to be faithful citizens of their country, obeying its just laws and being active participants in the political process. On the other hand, it also can be read to mean that Catholics must first be faithful to God in their role as citizens. Our role as citizens must be informed by our faith as we work to make the laws and policies of our country better reflect God's moral law.

The US bishops provide many resources to help citizens bring their faith to bear on important public issues.

The Role of the State

A basic moral principle is that the state exists for the good of its citizens, not the other way around. The state exists to defend and promote the common good of society. Therefore, all states have important responsibilities in regard to their citizens. The most basic of these obligations is to ensure that the primary physical needs of all the state's citizens are, needs such as food, water, housing, and emergency medical care. But to meet these needs, societies must also promote the exercise of virtue and support the spiritual life of their people. In fact, in order to enable people to reach their God-given potential, societies must give priority to spiritual values.

Making sure that all people are cared for requires patience, sacrifice, and solidarity—in other words, a society that embraces the concept of the common good. If a society does not live out these higher values—the values taught by Christ—then it will inevitably degenerate into a society of the rich and the poor, a totalitarian society in which a minority rule through violence and by restricting the freedoms of its citizens.

UNIT 3

CATHOLICS **MAKING** A DIFFERENCE

Many Catholics in the United States do not know that almost every state has a Catholic organization that is devoted to following that state's political issues on behalf of the Catholic bishops in that state. They are typically called Catholic Conferences, and their responsibilities include the following:

- working with political and community leaders on behalf of the bishops to shape laws that serve human dignity and the common good
- educating Catholics in the state on how to apply their faith to political issues and the political process
- providing resources to help Catholics make informed decisions on voting during election times

It would be well worth your time to go to the website of your state's Catholic Conference to see how it can assist you in being a faithful citizen.

---

solidarity ➤ Union of one's heart and mind with those who are poor or powerless or who face an injustice. It is an act of Christian charity.

As human communities have developed over the centuries and different forms of government have emerged in history, the Church has been active in promoting the values required to create just and peaceful nations. This list summarizes some of the most important values that states must practice in fulfilling their duties to their citizens:

- States must protect citizens' basic freedoms, especially the freedom of speech and the freedom to choose and practice their religious beliefs.
- States must provide for the education of their citizens. Civic leaders must not purposely keep citizens ignorant to more easily manipulate them.

© Illhoward / iStockphoto.com

The Church and the state have unique and complementary roles in protecting and promoting the common good.

- States must allow and promote the formation of associations and groups through which citizens can meet in solidarity to work for social justice and to obtain what is their due—groups such as political parties, labor unions, justice education institutes, and so on.
- States must provide the stability and just order that results in a secure and peaceful society. This typically requires laws protecting individuals and their property and some kind of police force to enforce those laws. But these laws and their enforcement must be moral themselves.
- With the growth of worldwide transportation, communication, and commerce, it is more and more necessary to develop international laws and organizations to protect the common good of all people. Nations must not exploit citizens of another country for the benefit of their own citizens.

What has become increasingly evident in the last century is how important the Christian virtue of solidarity is in creating a just and peaceful world. People are interconnected through technology, through business and financial practices, and through environmental practices. When one nation pollutes the oceans, many nations are affected. When one nation suffers an economic decline, people all over the world can be affected. Living in solidarity requires us to share food and other material goods and to live in a way that doesn't deprive others, near and far, of what they need to live. It also requires us to show a spiritual solidarity, a commitment to the principle that every person is a child of God—our spiritual brother and sister—no matter where in the world he or she lives. This kind of solidarity will grow only if Christians, empowered by the Holy Spirit, share the spiritual goods of faith that our heavenly Father has so graciously shared with us through his Son, Jesus Christ.

The Role of Citizens

The Fourth Commandment requires that we fulfill the obligations we have as citizens. Governments and other civic institutions are part of God's plan to create human communities that are committed to the common good. Our civic communities require the active cooperation and participation of all citizens in order to work effectively. By obeying civic laws, paying taxes, voting, and giving our opinion on public policies and issues, we help to build a society based on truth, justice, solidarity, and freedom.

UNIT 3

Like some children who find it difficult to obey their parents, some people think that traffic laws, tax laws, or fire safety laws do not apply to them. But think about the consequences if that were actually true. Increased accidents, the loss of money to build roads and fund schools, and increased fatalities and property damage in accidental fires would most likely result. Unless a law is truly unjust, we are obligated to follow it. In democratic countries, such as the United States, most laws protect the common good and therefore deserve our respect and obedience. However, there are cases of unjust laws being passed, even laws that were attempting to protect the common good.

What if a law is truly morally wrong, or what if obeying a law actually works against the common good? If we have properly formed our conscience and believe that a particular law is morally wrong, we are obliged not to follow it. Disobeying the immoral demands of a civil authority or refusing to follow an immoral law is called **civil disobedience**. Examples of civil disobedience throughout history are many. During World War II, courageous people in Nazi-occupied European countries hid Jewish people from the Nazis when the laws required Jews to be turned in. In the struggle for civil rights in the United States, Martin Luther King Jr. and other civil rights activists were arrested for refusing to honor laws that were racially prejudiced. Soldiers have refused to fight in wars that do not meet the requirements of a just war.

© Suzanne Tucker / Shutterstock.com

These teens are marching to end gun violence. How can you influence public policy to help the improve common good?

---

civil disobedience ➤ Deliberate refusal to obey or an immoral civil law or an immoral demand from civil authority.

The privilege of living in a democratic society is that we do not have to wait for unjust laws to pass before doing anything about them. We can work to prevent them before they become law. This requires being involved in the political process. We must encourage and vote for political candidates who respect natural law and the common good. We must educate ourselves about political issues. We must influence our lawmakers to vote for laws that increase the common good, and we must vote against laws that are immoral or that decrease the common good. Christians are called to live as responsible citizens and to ensure that our civil law reflects God's moral law. ❋

How have you seen your family members and members of your faith community practice their duty as faithful citizens?

UNIT 3

1. Besides faithfulness to God, what was the strongest value among biblical peoples? How was this value practiced?

2. How did Jesus' teaching on the meaning of family challenge the people of his time?

3. What attitudes toward their parents does the Fourth Commandment require children to have?

4. What responsibilities do parents have for their children in obedience to the Fourth Commandment?

5. What is the role of public groups and civic communities in God's plan?

6. Explain what it means to be *in* the world, not *of* the world.

7. What responsibilities does the state have for its citizens?

8. What obligations do we have as faithful citizens?

Jesus, Mary, and Joseph—the Holy Family—have always been a model of family love, devotion, and unity.

1. How does the artist portray love, unity, and devotion in this image?

2. How is human love as participation in the love of the Trinity symbolized in this image?

CHAPTER 8
The Eighth Commandment: Reality versus Illusion

WHAT HARM IS THERE IN TELLING A LITTLE LIE?

SNAPSHOT

Article 28

Honesty: The Key to Being Real

The Eighth Commandment, "You shall not bear false witness against your neighbor," teaches us the virtue of truthfulness, or honesty. Given that God is the source of all truth, it should make perfect sense that if we wish to live in communion with God, we must live in the truth. Yet the Eighth Commandment is probably the most frequently violated commandment of all the Ten Commandments. Why? Because when we break one of the other nine commandments, we usually end up lying to ourselves or someone else.

We lie to ourselves to convince ourselves that something wrong is okay. We tell ourselves things like, "There's no harm in having this drink" or "Everyone else is cheating, so it can't be wrong." We sometimes lie to other people to hide our guilt. We tell them things like, "Mom, I'm not on the phone; I've been doing my homework" or "That wasn't me you saw; it had to have been someone else." Many of the messages we hear through the media today don't help us; they communicate lies too. We see and hear false messages like, "Use this program and you can easily lose 20 pounds in two weeks" or "Sex before marriage is no big deal between two consenting people."

UNIT 3

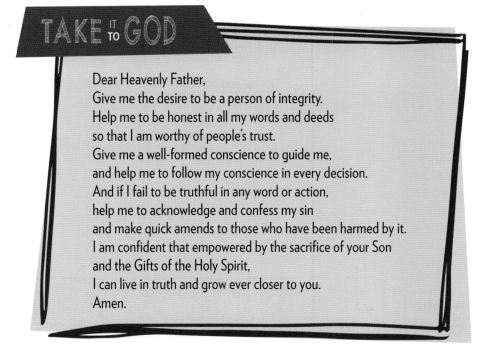

TAKE IT TO GOD

Dear Heavenly Father,
Give me the desire to be a person of integrity.
Help me to be honest in all my words and deeds
so that I am worthy of people's trust.
Give me a well-formed conscience to guide me,
and help me to follow my conscience in every decision.
And if I fail to be truthful in any word or action,
help me to acknowledge and confess my sin
and make quick amends to those who have been harmed by it.
I am confident that empowered by the sacrifice of your Son
and the Gifts of the Holy Spirit,
I can live in truth and grow ever closer to you.
Amen.

Lies Have Consequences

The danger of lies is that the more we tell them, the less we live in reality and the more we live an illusion—in a false world created by our dishonesty. Illusions, however, almost always break apart, exposing the stark reality we have been trying to avoid, often with disastrous consequences. And there is one more problem with illusions: we cannot find God in them.

This is a sad but true story. A woman was at a party with friends and, against their advice, she left to go to another party with a man she had just met. She later returned to the original party, where her friends were furious at her for leaving and accepting a joy ride from a stranger. So, she made up a story that the man had attacked her after they had left, hoping to gain her friends' sympathy. To make a long story short, the man was arrested and then put on trial. Out of shame and fear, the woman persisted in the lie through the trial. The man had a long record of violent crimes, and she had no previous record. The jury believed her, and the man ended up spending several years in prison.

This story is an extreme example of a simple but profound truth: lies hurt. The Eighth Commandment instructs, "You shall not bear false witness against your neighbor" for very good reason. Not only do lies destroy trust and may lead to other crimes, but they also directly affect our relationship with God. Lies are a direct contradiction of the truth and therefore a direct contradiction of God. He is the ultimate truth, the ultimate reality. When we are dishonest, we create false reality, an illusion that denies him.

God Is Truth

Let's use some basic logic to better understand the connection between God and truth. First proposition: What is true is also real. Second proposition: Creation is real. Third proposition: God is the Creator of all reality, or to put it another way, all reality has its origin in God. Conclusion: If God is the origin of all reality, then he is also the origin or the basis of all truth. This is why Jesus Christ, the Second Person of the Trinity, says, "I am the way and the truth and the life" (John 14:6). The whole of God's truth has been made evident in him. Other passages in Scripture attest to this too, such as these verses from Psalm 119:

> Through all generations your [God's] truth endures;
> fixed to stand firm like the earth.
>
> By your judgments they stand firm to this day,
> for all things are your servants.

(Verses 90–91)

This may seem a little philosophical, but it helps us to understand that when we tell lies or deny the truth, we are denying God. Most people don't think of this when they tell a little lie to save themselves some minor embarrassment. Lies not only affect our relationships with other people, but they also affect our relationship with God, even when we think they are private, hidden, or unimportant.

"The light shines in the darkness, / and the darkness has not overcome it" (John 1:5).

UNIT 3

The **Johannine writings** use the symbolism of darkness and light to symbolize this spiritual truth: "Now this is the message that we have heard from him and proclaim to you: God is light, and in him there is no darkness at all. If we say, 'We have fellowship with him,' while we continue to walk in darkness, we lie and do not act in truth" (1 John 1:5–6). In the Gospel of John, Jesus says, "I am the light of the world" (8:12). The author of the Gospel makes this connection between the light (Jesus) and truth:

> And this is the verdict, that the light came into the world, but people preferred darkness to light, because their works were evil. For everyone who does wicked things hates the light and does not come toward the light, so that his works might not be exposed. But whoever lives the truth comes to the light, so that his works may be clearly seen as done in God. (John 3:19–21)

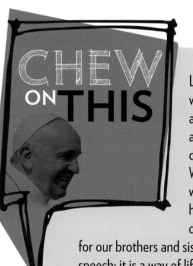

UNIT 3

CHEW ON THIS

Let us ask ourselves: to what truths do our— we Christians'—deeds, our words, our choices attest? Everyone can ask themselves: am I a witness of truth, or am I more or less a liar disguised as true? Everyone ask themselves. We Christians are not exceptional men and women. However, we are children of the heavenly Father, who is good and does not disappoint us, and instills in our hearts love for our brothers and sisters. This truth is not expressed so much in speech; it is a way of life, a way of living, and is seen in every single action (cf. Jas 2:18). This man is a true man, that woman is a true woman: one can see it. But how, if they do not open their mouths. But they behave like true men and women. They tell the truth, they act with truth. It is a good way for us to live. (Pope Francis, "General Audience," November 14, 2018)

Johannine writings ▶ The Gospel of John and the three Letters of John.

God calls us to live in the light of truth and not in the darkness of lies, duplicity, and hypocrisy. We exercise the virtue of truth through the honesty of our actions and the truthfulness of our words. By living in the light of reality—that is, God's truth—we grow in our union with God. By living in the darkness of lies, we grow away from him.

Live in Reality, Not in Illusion

It is not a compliment to be told that you are a good liar. Well-practiced liars can create their own version of reality. Their illusion might go like this: "I'm just doing my best, but people are out to get me, so I'll tell whatever lies are necessary to protect myself." Or, "No one understands the stress I'm under, which is why I have to lie about the things I do to relieve my stress." Some teens are good at keeping an illusion alive with regard to their relationship with their parents: "My parents just don't understand my needs, and I don't want them to be hurt, so I just have to lie to them about some of the things I do with my friends."

Lies are sins, and they endanger both our earthly happiness and our eternal destiny. The danger is that we can begin to believe the lies ourselves. We lose the ability to distinguish between reality and illusion. We cannot find God in the darkness of an illusion. Jesus goes so far as to say that the origin of lies and deception is the Devil: "When he [the Devil] tells a lie, he speaks in character, because he is a liar and the father of lies" (John 8:44). When we tell too many lies, we begin to lose our true identity and our eternal reward. We know our true identity only when we are in right relationship with God.

Christians must be committed to the truth and always on guard against lies and the illusions these lies create. We are, of course, responsible for the lies that begin with us, but we are also responsible to some degree for accepting the lies and illusions of others, especially if we do not make efforts to seek the truth.

Witnessing to the Truth of the Gospel

All truth is important, but the truth the Father revealed for our salvation must have the highest priority in our lives. God sent his Son into the world to reveal this truth, so that all humanity might be saved from sin and death. As Christ's disciples, we are called to participate in his mission by testifying to his Father's plan of salvation. Truly there can be no greater honor for us than to help other people to know the saving love of the Father, Son, and Holy Spirit.

UNIT 3

UNIT 3

How can you witness to the Gospel by serving others in truth and love?

Throughout the centuries, Christians have made great sacrifices to help all people know the love of Christ. Missionaries have left their homes to spend their lives preaching the Gospel in foreign lands. Young people volunteer a week, a year, or even several years in programs that serve those in need. People make regular commitments of their time to serve in food programs, immigrant outreach programs, and homeless shelters, witnessing by both their actions and their words to the love of Christ and inviting those they serve to be part of the Body of Christ.

Should you need inspiration for your own Gospel witness, consider the many martyrs who have given their lives in testimony to the love of God. This is the supreme witness to the truth of faith. The martyrs follow the footsteps of Christ, following him into death with complete confidence that they will share in his resurrected life. There are many stories of martyrs in the lives of the saints; consider making them part of your spiritual reading.

Twentieth-Century Martyrs

Every year, Christians around the world die because of their witness to the truth. By some estimates, there have been more martyrs in the last century than in any other century since the Resurrection of Christ! Here is just a sampling of some of the thousands of people who have been officially recognized as martyrs in the last century.

Martyrs	Reason for Martyrdom
Blessed Martyrs of Nowogródek	Eleven Sisters of the Holy Family of Nazareth were killed by the Nazis in 1943 for protesting the arrest and murder of Polish Jews.
Saints of the Cristero War	A group of twenty-five Mexican martyrs, primarily priests, were executed for carrying out their ministry during the persecution of Catholics from 1926 to 1929.
498 Spanish Martyrs	During the Spanish Civil War (1936–1939), hundreds of Catholics were killed for their faith, especially bishops, priests, and religious sisters and brothers.
Seven Blessed Martyrs of Songkhon (Thailand)	Seven people, including three teenagers, were executed by local police in 1940 because they would not deny the Catholic faith.

UNIT 3

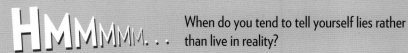

HMMMMMMM. . .

When do you tend to tell yourself lies rather than live in reality?

Article 29

Becoming a Person of Integrity

The woman who had falsely accused a man of a serious crime (see article 28) was living with enormous guilt. She couldn't sleep at night. She desperately wanted the man to be freed from prison but was too afraid to tell the police the truth. She decided to confess her sin to a priest in the Sacrament of Penance and Reconciliation. She was hoping to relieve her guilty **conscience** and didn't plan on going to the police. But the grace of the sacrament caused her to realize that she needed to make **reparation** for her lie. With the encouragement and support of the priest, she met with a lawyer who helped her contact the authorities. Soon the falsely accused man was freed from prison.

Of the many gifts God has given to us, one of the greatest is the gift of conscience. Every person has an inner voice attuned to the moral law, a God-given internal sense of what is morally right and wrong. Our conscience continually calls us to integrity—to make our words and actions consistent with the natural law God has placed in every human heart. When we violate the moral law, our conscience cries out, calling us to recover our integrity, to do what we can to repair the harm we have caused.

Honesty Builds Trust

When teenagers list the important characteristics of good relationships, particularly friendships, the word that surfaces most often is *trust*. We want to be able to trust other people and have them trust us. Without trust, any relationship has a hard time surviving. How long would a friendship last if someone discovered a friend was spreading gossip about them? How long would a dating relationship last if a person found out that the person they were dating was lying about their feelings? How hard is it for marriages to survive if one spouse finds out that the other is secretly seeing another person?

All these situations have one thing in common: one of the people involved is not acting with integrity. Their words or actions are deceitful or dishonest in some way. Honesty builds personal integrity, and integrity builds trust. To be

---

conscience ➤ The "inner voice," guided by human reason and Divine Law, that enables us to judge the moral quality of a specific action that has been made, is being made, or will be made. This judgment enables us to distinguish good from evil, in order to accomplish good and avoid evil. To make good judgments, one needs to have a well-formed conscience.

reparation ➤ The act of making amends for something one did wrong that caused physical, emotional, or material harm to another person.

worthy of another person's trust, we must be truthful in all our words and deeds. We cannot be dishonest and hope to be trusted.

Fortunately, God is constantly at work encouraging us to be people worthy of trust. The natural law inclines us toward living truthfully. Our conscience call us to be people of integrity. When we follow these God-given guides, we will know the true happiness he desires for us.

The Effects of Lying

Human beings have a natural orientation to tell the truth and therefore have to be motivated to tell a lie. Some people lie to cover up something they did wrong, some lie to avoid punishment, and others lie to make themselves appear more important. Well-meaning people sometimes lie to avoid confronting someone with an unpleasant truth. But any of these reasons for saying something false and deceiving someone does not make it morally right. The lie is still a sin against the Eighth Commandment.

Because someone lied about a crime, an innocent man was sent to prison. What are some other effects of lies you have experienced or heard about?

UNIT 3

We have already discussed that when lies and deception are discovered, trust and relationships are damaged or even destroyed. What if lies and deception are not discovered? A lie can still hurt and wound others, even if they never discover the lie. Consider the following scenario: Javier and Sofia are dating. They have a mutual understanding that their relationship is exclusive—that is, they don't date anyone else. But when Sofia goes out of town one weekend, Javier goes out with a girl he met a few weeks earlier. The two believe that what Sofia doesn't know won't hurt her. Are they correct in that assumption? Has the relationship between Sofia and Javier been hurt in some way, even if Sofia never finds out that her boyfriend broke the trust? Yes, their relationship has been hurt because Javier's guilty conscience will change the way he relates to Sofia in small and subtle ways. Their relationship should be built on trust and honesty. But now Javier has been dishonest with Sofia. If that dishonesty continues, it will weaken the relationship and most probably destroy it over time.

Or consider another form of deception—cheating on homework, quizzes, tests, or projects. Is it possible that the teacher or other students could be affected by this decision? Does this have anything to do with them? Or what about the person who is doing the cheating? Is this really a big deal? The quick answer to all of these questions is yes.

How does cheating hurt others? How does it harm the person cheating?

When we fail to be honest, at the very minimum we damage our own personal integrity. We think less of ourselves and find it harder to love ourselves. But because every sin has social implications, the web of deceit often gets larger without our even realizing it. Sir Walter Scott's statement, "Oh, what a tangled web we weave when first we practice to deceive," is as true today as it was when God asked Cain where his brother was. Cain had murdered Abel but tried to deceive God by answering: "I do not know. Am I my brother's keeper?" (Genesis 4:9). We must remember that just as God saw through Cain's deception, he will see through our lies and deceptions.

Making Reparation

The Gospel calls us to make reparation, or amends, for our sins, including sins against the truth. Owning up to our lies is often more difficult than telling the truth in the first place. However, whether the damage was great or small, we must try to undo the harm we have caused by deceit and dishonesty.

Take this true story as an example. A high school cheating scandal began with two students finding copies of a final exam. They made multiple copies for their friends, who in turn made copies for their friends, so that more than a hundred students saw at least some part of the exam. Some students who felt strongly about integrity came forward to tell authorities. A few of the students who had cheated turned themselves in. Others turned their friends in. The consequences were many: lower grades; expulsions from school, sports teams, and honor societies; and broken friendships. The scandal made the local paper, embarrassing the school, its administration, and its alumni. Despite the damage, the students who made reparation by coming forward, confessing, and accepting the consequences helped the school and their classmates to regain needed trust and integrity.

UNIT 3

In the Sacrament of Penance and Reconciliation, the priest will often assign some prayers after we confess our sins. You might think, "What is the point of five Our Fathers and three Hail Marys if I lied to my mom and my school about being sick?" This is a very good question. The praying the priest might ask us to do is your penance, a concrete gesture to take responsibility for our sins. Our penance is a kind of reparation, or healing, that we offer in response for the damage caused by our sins. Saying prayers might not be a direct amends for the damage we have caused, but in prayer we focus our attention on God and God's will for our life. Prayer should remind us that following God's will leads to our ultimate happiness. And sometimes in addition to prayers, a priest will assign a penance directly related to a sin, such as apologizing in person or returning something we might have stolen.

The duty to make reparation is binding on our conscience, which means we will not be free from responsibility and the pangs of guilt until we have made the best efforts possible to repair any damage caused by our dishonesty. If it would cause additional harm to make public reparation—for example, exposing a victim to additional embarrassment—then we must do it privately. If we cannot directly pay back the person we have harmed, then we must do some other act of charity, and the effort we make should in some way be equal to the harm we have caused. In the Sacrament of Penance and Reconciliation, the priest can help us make decisions about appropriate reparations.

Secrets

There are a number of situations in which keeping secrets could be sinful, such as when the secret is covering up some type of sinful behavior or withholding information that is necessary for the public good. A good example is a corporation keeping secret the harmful effects of its products.

However, friends often tell each other things they want kept confidential, such as a problem they are struggling with, a budding love relationship they are in, or some feelings they are processing. These are things we tell our friends when asking for advice, sharing a joy, or seeking support. It is important to honor these requests for privacy and not reveal this information to others. In some circumstances, it is appropriate to take care when deciding what

© Prostock-studio / Shutterstock.com

When is it morally permissible to reveal a secret or break a confidence?

UNIT 3

truthful information should or should not be known to others. For example, there are ways you might speak about another person's faults or mistakes that harms their reputation. Even if the information is true, if there is no serious need to share, it is best to protect the reputation of others. Another time it is important to keep a secret is if your job requires confidentiality. Keeping professional secrets is important, as long as it does not harm the common good.

However, sometimes it is morally permissible—even morally necessary—to reveal something that someone has asked us not to share with others. This situation occurs when not sharing something means that someone might experience serious harm. For example, if your friend tells you he is thinking about suicide, it is important for you to go to an adult trained to help in these situations—a teacher, counselor, coach, or youth minister—and tell that person about your friend's plan, even if you promised your friend you wouldn't tell a soul. Your friend may be angry with you at first, but it's better to lose the friendship for a while than to lose the friend forever. Some other situations when you might need to share what others have asked you to keep to yourself include the following:

- if someone reveals that they have committed a serious crime and refuses your advice to confess it to the authorities
- if someone reveals that they intend to cause serious physical or emotional harm to themselves or another person
- if someone reveals that they are in an emotionally, physically, or sexually abusive situation
- if for some reason keeping the confidence puts you in danger or could make you a criminal accomplice ✳

HMMMMMM. . . . Where have you seen lies that were private or unknown hurt other people?

UNIT 3

Article 30
Other Sins against Honesty

The story of the woman who falsely accused a man of a serious crime (see articles 28 and 29) concludes with her being found guilty of perjury and sentenced to several years in prison. Perjury is a sin against the Second and the Fourth Commandments, but it is also a federal crime. As part of her reparation, the woman was ultimately willing to accept the criminal consequences for her crime. People will disagree about whether her punishment was too lenient or too harsh, but everyone should agree that she took the steps necessary to begin the process of forgiveness and reconciliation with God, with the person she harmed, and with society.

Telling a lie is the most direct offense against the Eighth Commandment, but we can sin against it in other ways, perjury being just one of those ways. Even telling the truth can be a sin against the Eighth Commandment in certain circumstances. In this article, we discuss some of these other sins against honesty.

Public lies can have serious consequences.

Public Lies

In public communication, lies and misinformation take on even greater seriousness because they potentially affect a greater number of people. Unfortunately, examples of public lies and misinformation abound, from pharmaceutical companies not revealing all the effects of their drugs, to public officials giving inaccurate information about the cost of school renovations. Keep in mind that failing to give relevant information is just as morally wrong as giving false information. Public speakers and writers have a responsibility to present information completely and accurately.

Telling the truth in a public hearing or court of law, where often the common good or another person's reputation and freedom are at stake, is an especially serious obligation. A lie told in these circumstances is called false witness. A lie told while under oath is called perjury. Perjury was also discussed in article 20, because most oaths are taken using the name of God.

Sins against Reputation

Another category of sins against the Eighth Commandment is when words are used intentionally to hurt or do violence to another person. A good example of this is telling people about someone's faults and failures without any valid or necessary reason. Even if the information is true, when we pass it on unnecessarily, we injure someone's reputation. This sin is called gossip, or **detraction**, because it detracts from another person's good name. Saint John Vianney (1786–1859) gave some excellent advice about gossip: "If something uncharitable is said [about another person] in your presence, either speak in favor of the absent person, or withdraw, or if possible, stop the conversation."

Even worse is telling a false story about someone to hurt their reputation. This kind of sin is called **calumny**, or slander.

A final sin to be careful of in this category is called rash judgment. Rash judgment is assuming the worst about something a person says or does without knowing all the facts. For example, let's say you see a teammate leaving practice 20 minutes early every day. Rash judgment would be thinking, "If they were really committed to the team they'd stay to the end of practice." However, by asking, you might find out that the teammate is leaving early to care for an elderly grandparent until their mom or dad come home from work.

---

detraction ➤ Unnecessarily revealing something about another person that is true but is harmful to his or her reputation. It is a sin against the Eighth Commandment.

calumny ➤ Ruining the reputation of another person by lying or spreading rumors. It is also called slander and is a sin against the Eighth Commandment.

UNIT 3

Putting ourselves in the place of the other person is a good way to avoid the moral pitfalls of gossip, slander, and rash judgment. Think about how it would feel if people gossiped about you. Then you can empathize with how that person might feel about your gossip. True empathy for other people can break the vicious cycle of gossip and rumors.

When you are tempted to pass along rumors about someone else, put yourself in the place of that person.

Flattery and Boasting

Some sins, like detraction, may not be so much about lying as they are about misusing the truth. One example of this is the misuse of flattery, or **adulation**. It is a good thing to give people honest compliments and affirmations about a job well done or about the progress they've made on a difficult project or challenge, but praising someone for something that you know isn't true is wrong. Praising someone for doing or saying something wrong can even make you an accomplice in that person's sin. For example, let's say your underage friend got drunk at a party and acted outrageously. It would be wrong for you to say to your friend the next day, "The way you acted last night was awesome!" Sometimes people offer false flattery to be nice, to fit in, or to seek some advantage in a situation, but none of these make it moral.

---

adulation ➤ Excessive flattery, praise, or admiration for another person.

Boasting or bragging is another sin that often involves a misuse of the truth. It is certainly moral to share our accomplishments and successes with other people. But if we exaggerate those things to make them seem more praiseworthy, or if we share our accomplishments in a way that draws attention to ourselves at the expense of others, it is morally wrong. For example, someone shouldn't say, "If it wasn't for me, we would have lost the game," knowing that that other team members also played critical roles. We must remember that we are called to follow the example of Christ's humility. If any person had reason to boast, it would certainly be Jesus Christ. Yet "he humbled himself, / becoming obedient to death, / even death on a cross" (Philippians 2:8).

Finally, another sin that is a misuse of the truth is making fun of another person to humiliate them and hurt their feelings. This sin is prevalent among teenagers, as some teens attempt to raise their own social status by putting other people down. Unfortunately, such behavior can also be especially damaging during adolescence, when many teens are forming their values and identity and, as a result, have a fragile self-image. Some people may think they are just being funny by pointing out a flaw in someone's physical appearance or by exaggerating someone's behavior, but those actions and words can deeply wound that person's ego.

MAKE IT SO

At the start of your junior year, your family had to move to a new city and you had to start attending a new school. After a month of feeling like an outsider, you finally feel like you are making some new friends. You've started to hang out with a group of choir members who share your love of music. They seem like a lot of fun, but there's just one problem—almost every time you get together, they start talking about other people, and not always in the kindest way. All the gossip makes you uncomfortable, and you have doubts that most of it is even true. Even worse, sometimes you feel tempted to join in so you can fit in. What can you do to fight this temptation? How can you steer the group in a different direction when the gossip starts?

UNIT 3

Sometimes Truth Must Remain Private

Sometimes it is inappropriate to reveal the truth to someone who asks for it. The welfare and safety of others, respect for privacy, and the common good are sufficient reasons for being silent or discreet about the truth. You are not morally bound to tell the truth to someone who will use it to harm another person. For example, if you have a friend who is staying at your house because she is being harassed or abused by an ex-boyfriend, you have a duty to protect her. If the boyfriend calls and wants to know if she is with you, it is morally permissible to withhold your knowledge of her whereabouts to protect her from further harm.

Sometimes professional confidentiality requires secrecy. Religious leaders, counselors, public officials, lawyers, therapists, and doctors must not reveal confidential information given under the seal of secrecy, except in extreme situations when keeping the secret might cause serious harm to someone. Even if it is not a matter of professional confidentiality, private information that could lead to prejudice against a person must be kept confidential unless a serious reason exists to tell it.

The one place where everyone's secrets are completely safe is in the Sacrament of Penance and Reconciliation. The seal of confession is so sacred that a priest can never tell anyone what he has heard in someone's confession, even in the most serious circumstances. A priest is expected to go to jail, and some have even chosen death, rather than reveal what is said under the seal of confession. ✳

One place where everyone's secrets are completely safe is the Sacrament of Penance and Reconciliation.

UNIT 3

HMMMMM. . . Which do you see committed most often among young people: gossip, slander, rash judgment, flattery, or boasting?

Article 31

Calling Society to Integrity

Lucia shook her head in disbelief. She was reading an article for religion class on immigration. Her parents were immigrants, so she was naturally very interested in the topic. The article was well done and made the case that the Bible's teaching calls Christians to be supportive of immigrants and their needs. But it was the comments after the article that were so shocking. People were saying immigrants were lazy and even calling them thieves and rapists. They were being nasty to other people leaving comments they disagreed with, calling each other horrible names. And this was on a supposedly religious website!

© RoBird / Shutterstock.com

UNIT 3

What can you do to ensure that your social media posts are positive and uplifting?

We live in changing times. Not too many years ago, the media were controlled by relatively few people without any access by ordinary people. But the development of the internet and the technology to access it has given public voice to many more people. Even the comments sections in social networking sites could be considered a form of public media. The Eighth Commandment has an important social dimension that should guide the creation and use of all public media.

CATHOLICS **MAKING** A DIFFERENCE

© Luis Pizarro Ruiz / Shutterstock.com

Saint Francis de Sales (1567–1622) was a person devoted to the truth. He lived during the turbulent later years of the Protestant Reformation when many people in Europe were leaving the Catholic Church. Francis sought to bring people back to the Catholic Church by reaching out to non-Catholics and explaining the true Catholic faith. When people refused to listen to him face-to-face, he wrote and distributed little pamphlets correcting misunderstandings of Catholic doctrine—very possibly the first Catholic to do so. Francis was so gentle, loving, and wise that through his efforts many people came back to the Church.

Many people also sought spiritual direction from Francis de Sales. His duties as bishop kept him from seeing most of these people face-to-face, so he spent most of his evenings writing letters to the people seeking his spiritual wisdom. And during a time when many people thought true holiness could only be achieved by priests and religious, Francis emphasized the holiness of the laity. He even wrote a book that is still popular today, *Introduction to the Devout Life*, instructing laypeople how to live a holy life. Because of his devotion to the truth, Saint Francis de Sales is named the patron saint of journalists and adult education.

Truth in the Media

In modern societies, media sources (which include but are not limited to radio, television, movies, newspapers, magazines, and the internet) are the primary sources of information about our local communities, our nation, and the world. In many ways, media sources have the same responsibilities for the common good as nations do. God's will is that media outlets be sources of truth and moral entertainment. This means, for example, that news outlets should present the news accurately, making sure their sources are reliable and their facts are correct. On controversial issues, they should present perspectives from both sides. Reporters should question the people they interview carefully and expose when people are telling lies or half-truths. Commentators should not present personal opinions as facts. These fundamental principles for trustworthy reporting are sometimes violated in today's ratings-driven media.

Society has the right to information based in truth that promotes human freedom and that calls society to act justly. Society also has the responsibility to see that the media provide such information. The media, especially the news media, must be held accountable for providing information that is balanced, fair, and disciplined in presenting the truth.

What about Art?

Art is a form of social media too. Art can inspire, entertain, educate, and cause us to question and wonder. It is a uniquely human form of expression that many consider a kind of spiritual task. The ability to create art is a gift from God, and in some way the creation of a unique piece of art is a sharing in God's creative power.

A society must protect an artist's basic freedom of expression. But even in countries that accept this moral principle, artists should use their skills to create art in keeping with God's will. The fine arts should portray life, beauty, and truth. Art that is dark and disturbing may also be moral if it is clearly a warning to society about things that threaten beauty, truth, and life.

UNIT 3

UNIT 3

© Hazlan Abdul Hakim / iStockphoto.com

The creation of sacred art has a long history. Sacred art can teach us about Revelation, can inspire us to live holy lives, and can evoke awe and wonder, which leads to praise of God.

The Church encourages the creation of **sacred art**, art that evokes and glorifies the mystery of God. Sacred art reflects the beauty of truth and love visible in Christ. It frequently illustrates themes from Scripture, Tradition, and the lives of the saints. It draws us to adoration, to prayer, and to the love of the Holy Trinity.

---

sacred art ➤ Art that evokes faith by turning our minds to the mystery of God, primarily through the artistic depiction of Scripture, Tradition, and the lives of Jesus, Mary, and the saints.

Using Media Critically

The average person is exposed to hours of media every day. This exposure has the potential to affect our attitudes and values, even unconsciously, which is why we must be discerning in our use of media. Here are some suggestions for critically using the media:

- Evaluate the moral message of the songs, TV shows, movies, books, and games you listen to, watch, read, and play. Does the message support the values of God's moral law, or does it undermine the values of the moral law?
- Seek reliable sources to evaluate the moral messages in media and to help you choose which media you will use. For example, you might visit the United States Conference of Catholic Bishops' website for movie reviews.
- If, for example, a particular artist, TV series, or radio station consistently promotes values and actions that are contrary to God's moral law, stop watching or listening. Don't make yourself an accomplice to an immoral media source.
- Consider going one step further if you find a particular media source consistently promoting sinful actions and values. Contact the organization or person in charge of the media source and let them know of your disapproval. ✳

UNIT 3

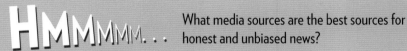

HMMMM... What media sources are the best sources for honest and unbiased news?

1. How are the Johannine symbols of light and darkness connected to the Eighth Commandment?

2. What kind of truth should have the highest priority in a Christian's life? How can you witness to this truth?

3. Explain how honesty is related to trust and integrity.

4. What is reparation?

5. Name and explain three sins against a person's reputation.

6. Is it ever inappropriate to reveal the truth, and if so, when?

7. What responsibility do social media have for safeguarding the truth?

8. Describe three ways you can be responsible in your use of media.

UNIT 3

 STUDY

1. Why do you think that speaking the truth is revolutionary in our society today?

2. How are truth and democracy related?

3. What elements of this photograph (subject, lighting, background, focus) impact your thoughts about truth and society today?

CHAPTER 9

The Seventh and Tenth Commandments: Justice versus Injustice

WHAT IS THE CONNECTION BETWEEN STEALING AND INJUSTICE?

SNAPSHOT

Article 32

Biblical Teaching on Possessions

The Seventh Commandment, "You shall not steal," seemed so simple when we were children; it just meant that you didn't take other children's toys. As we grow older though, this simple commandment becomes far more complex. We come to understand that there are many ways of stealing—laziness at work, tax fraud, corporate espionage, and misleading product advertising—that do not involve taking someone else's physical property.

The Tenth Commandment, "You shall not covet your neighbor's goods," addresses the sinful attitudes of envy and greed that are often at the root of stealing from others. We open ourselves up to committing many other sins when envy and greed control our heart's desires. God's grace helps us to embrace the poverty of spirit that is necessary, especially in our materialistic culture, to avoid the unholy influence of envy and greed.

UNIT 3

TAKE IT TO GOD

Just and loving God,
You are the Father of all people, making us all brothers and sisters.
Give me a vision of the world as you would have it,
  a world in which the weak are protected, and no one is poor
    or hungry,
  a world in which the riches of your creation are shared by all,
  a world in which all races and cultures live in harmony and
    mutual respect,
  a world in which the earth and all its creatures are protected
    and cared for,
  a world in which peace is built on justice, and justice is guided
    by love.
Help me to follow your Son by speaking out for those in need
  and calling society to justice.
And empower me with the Gifts of the Holy Spirit
  to be faithful in following your call even when I do not see success.
Amen.

Material Possessions and God's Plan

Both the Seventh and Tenth Commandments give witness to a basic moral truth that is related to the common good: God has given the Earth and all its resources to the whole human race to take care of and enjoy. When we take care of the Earth and distribute its resources equitably, no person needs to live in poverty or hunger. Unfortunately, the world's history is marked by the unjust distribution of wealth and a division between the rich and the poor. The prophets and Jesus repeatedly warn us against the dangers of failing to take care of the needs of the poor, and the Church continues to give society moral guidance through its social teaching on issues of justice and peace.

God intends that the Earth's resources be used for the good of all human beings. How well do you think this is being done in the world today?

Back when your parents were teenagers, there was a popular bumper sticker that said, "He who dies with the most toys wins." It expresses an attitude for acquiring possessions, an attitude that many still live by today. The human race has struggled with the moral issues of private property, material wealth, and the just use of the Earth's resources since the beginning of human history. As a response to this struggle, Christ's interpretation of the Seventh and Tenth Commandments provides a clear path for putting material possessions in their proper perspective. A hint: The one who dies with the most toys doesn't necessarily win in God's plan for our salvation.

The Old Law on Possessions

The Old Testament account of Creation reveals this foundational principle about material possessions: God has given the Earth and all its resources to the whole human race to care for and enjoy. He tells the first man and woman: "Fill the earth and subdue it. Have dominion over the fish of the sea, the birds of the air, and all the living things that crawl on the earth. . . . See, I give you every seed-bearing plant . . . to be your food" (Genesis 1:28–29). Adam and Eve stand for all humankind, and God's command to them to care for the Earth and his promise to provide them food extends to every human being. Passages such as this one, from Psalm 8, affirm this:

> What is a man that you are mindful of him,
>> and a son of man that you care for him?
>
> Yet you have made him little less than a god,
>> crowned him with glory and honor.
>
> You have given him rule over the works of your hands,
>> put all things at his feet;
>
> All sheep and oxen,
>> even the beasts of the field,
>
> The birds of the air, the fish of the sea,
>> and whatever swims the paths of the seas.
>
> (Verses 5-9)

The fact that the Earth's resources are meant to be shared by all people does not negate the principle of private property though. Revelation and reason teach us that in just societies, families and individuals need certain material possessions to survive: clothing, shelter, tools, food, and so on. In the Books of Exodus and Leviticus, the moral laws that accompany the Sinai Covenant recognize the right to personal possessions through specific laws dealing with property damage, theft, and lending (see Exodus 21:33–22:14 and Leviticus 25:23–55).

The most fundamental law regarding personal possessions is given in the Ten Commandments: "You shall not steal" (Exodus 20:15). Outside of some exceptional circumstances, we cannot take someone else's property without their permission. This includes borrowing someone's property and not giving it back, finding a lost object and not returning it to its owner, willfully

UNIT 3

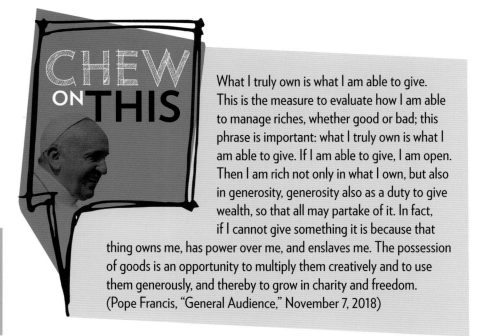

CHEW ON THIS

What I truly own is what I am able to give. This is the measure to evaluate how I am able to manage riches, whether good or bad; this phrase is important: what I truly own is what I am able to give. If I am able to give, I am open. Then I am rich not only in what I own, but also in generosity, generosity also as a duty to give wealth, so that all may partake of it. In fact, if I cannot give something it is because that thing owns me, has power over me, and enslaves me. The possession of goods is an opportunity to multiply them creatively and to use them generously, and thereby to grow in charity and freedom. (Pope Francis, "General Audience," November 7, 2018)

destroying someone's property, following dishonest business practices, break-ing a personal or business contract, or paying unjust wages to your employees if you own a business. The only exceptions outlined by the *Catechism* are if the owner's consent can be presumed or if the owner's refusal "is contrary to reason and the universal destination of goods"[1] (*CCC*, number 2408). Theft brings chaos and injustice, upsetting the order and fairness that societies need to thrive.

However, the right to private property is not absolute, even in the Old Testament. The right to private property is subordinate to the just distribution of the Earth's resources and the common good. The Jubilee Laws in Leviticus, chapter 25, attest to God's concern for the needs of the poor. After the Lord led the Israelites into the Holy Land, he required that every fifty years the people celebrate a Jubilee year, a holy year of rest and restoration, celebrating liberty in the land. Part of the Jubilee Laws relate to the buying and selling of land. God reminds his people that the land he gave them ultimately belongs to him: "The land shall not be sold irrevocably; for the land is mine, and you are but resident aliens and under my authority" (verse 23).

The year of Jubilee was a time to return purchased land to the original owner. If someone had fallen into poverty and had to sell their land, in the Jubilee year they received the land back, even if they had not been able to raise enough money to purchase it back in the years before. This account in

Scripture reminds us that we should consider the goods we have to ultimately belong to God and to be used to grow the Kingdom of God, including fairly distributing the Earth's limited resources.

The New Law on Possessions

Christ had a lot to say on material possessions and wealth; it was one of the topics he taught about most frequently. Let's begin by looking at the Sermon on the Mount, the summary of the New Law. In the first beatitude, Christ says, "Blessed are the poor in spirit, for theirs is the kingdom of heaven" (Matthew 5:3). The version in Luke is more direct:

> Blessed are you who are poor,
>> for the kingdom of God is yours.
>
> Blessed are you who are now hungry,
>> or you will be satisfied.
>
> (6:20–21)

In Luke, Jesus also pairs this beatitude with a warning:

> But woe to you who are rich,
>> for you have received your consolation.
>
> But woe to you who are filled now,
>> for you will be hungry.
>
> (6:24–25)

Most of Jesus' hearers would have been shocked at this teaching. The common belief at the time was that wealth was a sign of God's favor and blessings. Jesus seemed to be saying the exact opposite. Or more precisely, he was saying that detachment from wealth is necessary for entering the Kingdom of God. He makes this point even more clearly in later sections of the Sermon on the Mount and the Sermon on the Plain:

> Do not store up for yourselves treasures on earth, where moth and decay destroy, and thieves break in and steal. But store up treasures in heaven, where neither moth nor decay destroys, nor thieves break in and steal. For where your treasure is, there also will your heart be. (Matthew 6:19–21)

No one can serve two masters. He will either hate one and love the other, or be devoted to one and despise the other. You cannot serve God and **mammon**. (Matthew 6:24)

If you lend money to those from whom you expect repayment, what credit [is] that to you? Even sinners lend to sinners, and get back the same amount. But rather, love your enemies and do good to them, and lend expecting nothing back; then your reward will be great and you will be children of the Most High. (Luke 6:34–35)

In these teachings, Jesus makes clear at least four things. First, poverty is not a sign that God is displeased with someone. Second, God has a preferential concern for those who experience poverty. Third, lust for wealth is a danger to our spiritual welfare; it causes us to trust in money and material possessions for our happiness rather than trusting in God. Fourth, wealth is to be shared with others, especially those in need. God wants us to take responsibility for sharing the bounty of creation fairly and justly and to not hoard our wealth.

Jesus continues to make these points in his encounters with people and in the **parables** he uses to teach about the Kingdom of God. Let us look at two encounters that Jesus had with wealthy people,

Meister des Codex Aureus Epternacensis / Public domain

Using parables such as the Rich Man and Lazarus (see Luke 16:19–31), Jesus teaches us the proper use of wealth.

---

mammon ➤ An Aramic word meaning wealth or property.

parable ➤ Generally a short story that uses everyday images to communicate religious messages. Jesus used parables frequently in his teaching as a way of presenting the Good News of salvation.

UNIT 3

the rich young man and Zacchaeus. The account of the rich young man is told in all three synoptic Gospels (Matthew 19:16–30, Mark 10:17–31, and Luke 18:18–30). In this encounter, a rich young man approaches Jesus and asks what he must do to have eternal life. The young man had kept the Ten Commandments all his life. Jesus tells him he must do one thing more: sell what he has and give the money to the poor so that he will have treasure in Heaven. This is a significant challenge for him to make, and we are told that the young man "went away sad, for he had many possessions" (Matthew 19:22). Mark adds the detail that Jesus looked at the young man with love (see 10:21), a reminder that God loves both the rich and the poor.

Parables That Use Images Related to Wealth

The parables on this list teach about the Kingdom of God, using images related to wealth and money. Some of them relate to love for the poor and the dangers of hoarding wealth, and some use images related to money to show the radical generosity of God's love and forgiveness that we are also called to share with one another.

Love for the Poor and the Dangers of Hoarding Wealth	
The Dishonest Manager	Luke 16:1–8
The Great Dinner	Luke 14:12–24
Lazarus and the Rich Man	Luke 16:19–31
The Rich Fool	Luke 12:16–21
The Radical Generosity of God's Love and Forgiveness	
Canceled Debts	Luke 7:41–43
Laborers in the Vineyard	Matthew 20:1–16
The Unforgiving Servant	Matthew 18:23–35

Although we do not know what the rich young man ultimately did with his wealth, we do know Zacchaeus's decision (see Luke 19:1–10). Zacchaeus, a wealthy tax collector, announces without any prompting from Jesus, "Behold, half of my possessions, Lord, I shall give to the poor, and if I have extorted anything from anyone I shall repay it four times over" (verse 8). Jesus replies, "Today salvation has come to this house" (verse 9). Jesus commends Zacchaeus's faith, a faith which is testified to by his willingness to correct any dishonesty he may have committed. Zacchaeus commits to reparation, a requirement

© Evgeny Shkolenko / iStockphoto.com

How will you honor the biblical teaching that God wants our wealth shared with others, especially those in greatest need?

for repairing the harm caused by unjustly taking someone's property or money. This is an example of **commutative justice**, which requires that we return what we have stolen in the same condition it was when we stole it, or its equivalent.

In summary, the New Law of Christ helps us to see the deeper meanings of the Seventh and Tenth Commandments. Besides teaching that stealing is wrong, the Seventh Commandment teaches us that we are personally responsible for how we use the goods of the Earth and the wealth that comes from human labor. When we have embraced the poverty of spirit called for by the beatitude "Blessed are the poor in spirit," we no longer cling to material possessions. We understand that no person should have more than they need while other people go without basic necessities. The Tenth Commandment teaches us that envy for our neighbor's material goods results in greed, one of the capital sins. Greed is the passion for wealth and the power that comes from it, a passion that takes over the place that God should have in our lives. ✳

HMMMMMM. . .   Where do you see Jesus' teaching challenging our culture's approach to wealth and possessions?

---

commutative justice ➤ This type of justice calls for fairness in agreements and contracts between individuals. It is an equal exchange of goods, money, or services.

Article 33
Called to Be Just

Yolanda heard her father talking once again about the latest papal teaching. "Why does the Pope keep talking about economics?" he complained. "The Church has no business talking about politics or economics. Their only focus should be on people's souls."

"Dad, we've been learning about the Church's social justice teaching in religion class. What Jesus taught matters for politics and economics," Yolanda responded. "Besides, Jesus talked a lot about loving the poor and taking care of people in need. Seems to me that it isn't an either-or thing. How can we care about saving people's souls and not also care about their material needs? We have to do both—at least that's what Jesus taught."

The human person is composed of both body and soul, so upholding the dignity of the human person means being concerned for not only the salvation of souls but also for people's material needs. We must grow in our loving communion with God, which begins in this life and will be fulfilled in Heaven, and we must grow in the love of our neighbor, which means desiring their salvation and working for a just society in this life even though it will only reach perfection in Heaven. From this, we can see that the Church's mission is different from the mission of political authorities; the Church's concern for our earthly needs is an extension of her ultimate goal of leading our souls to Heaven. The Church has a responsibility to make judgments about social issues that affect

UNIT 3

© Saint Mary's Press

The Church has given direction on social issues over the last two thousand years, in keeping with the Gospel call.

the fundamental rights of the person or the salvation of souls and, when necessary, to be prophetic in calling society to greater justice.

Especially in the last century, the Church has provided clear and consistent teaching on issues of economic justice, war and violence, respect for life, and environmental justice. The teaching of the Church on these and other social issues is sometimes called the social doctrine of the Church. In this article, we consider the basic social doctrine themes. In future articles, we consider specific social issues in light of this doctrine.

Basic Social Doctrine Themes

The Church's **social doctrine** has been taught in the last century by a rich treasure of **conciliar**, papal, and bishops' documents. These documents are readily available online on the official Vatican website and the websites of national and regional conferences of Catholic bishops. Only by reading these documents directly can you learn the full scope of this tradition and the nuanced and reasoned judgments on particular social issues. However, the bishops of the United States have highlighted these seven key themes that are at the heart of all Catholic social doctrine.

The Life and Dignity of the Human Person

A just society is based on the principle that human life is sacred and that every individual has an innate, God-given dignity. This means that people are always more important than things. Society must protect human life and dignity from the beginning of life at conception until its natural end. Attacks on the life and dignity of the human person come from evils such as abortion, euthanasia, cloning, poverty, hunger, war, torture, the death penalty, and terrorist attacks. The equal dignity of human persons calls society to ensure that the goods of the Earth are distributed in just and charitable ways to every person in the world, to eliminate sinful inequalities.

The Call to Family, Community, and Participation

Human beings are social creatures, created by God to live in loving and caring communities. Marriage and family is the fundamental human community that forms the foundation of all other social institutions. Thus, marriage and the family must be supported and strengthened by society, not undermined by it.

---

social doctrine ➤ The teaching of the Church on the truth of Revelation about human dignity, human solidarity, and the principles of justice and peace; and on the moral judgments about economic and social matters required by such truths.

conciliar ➤ Something connected with an official council of the Church, normally an Ecumenical Council such as the Second Vatican Council.

As members of communities, all people have both a right and a responsibility to work together for the common good and well-being of all, especially those who are poor and vulnerable.

Rights and Responsibilities

Human life and human dignity can be protected only if society safeguards basic rights, such as food, clothing, shelter, education, dignified work, health care, religious freedom, and freedom of speech. The most fundamental right is the right to life, which must be protected from conception to natural death. Every person shares in the responsibility to support and protect these rights.

The Option for the Poor and Vulnerable

A basic test of any just society or state is how its most vulnerable members are treated. Christ's teaching and example are clear that we are to love both those who are rich and those who are poor but that we have a special obligation to put the needs of those who are poor and vulnerable first, even above our own comforts and wants. Societies that are marked by sharp division between the rich and the poor must work to reduce those inequalities and provide for a more just distribution of the goods of the Earth.

UNIT 3

CATHOLICS MAKING A DIFFERENCE

In 1998, corporate attorney Mark Bilott was approached by a farmer from his hometown in West Virginia. The farmers' cattle were being poisoned by a chemical in the local water supply. The chemical came from industrial waste improperly discarded by the DuPont chemical company. Eventually it came to light that the chemical, PFOA, was also poisoning human beings, and DuPont knew about it. Mark Bilott represented the farmer and the local people, suing the very kind of corporation he previously had defended. He faced many obstacles and difficulties including being shunned by his colleagues, being personally attacked, dealing with family struggles, and experiencing health issues caused by the stress. But Bilott continued the fight, sustained by his faith and compassion for the victims. The court cases have gone on for over twenty years, but in 2017 Bilott won a huge settlement for thousands of people whose health has been affected by the chemical pollution. Bilott's work is far from over, and he continues his fight for justice.

The Dignity of Work and the Rights of Workers

A fundamental theme in the Church's social doctrine is that economies exist to serve people; people do not exist to serve economies. All people have a right to dignified work by which they can contribute to society and support themselves and their families. For this to happen, the basic rights of workers must be respected, such as the right to fair wages, the right to organize and join labor unions, and the right to take economic initiatives to start new businesses and industries.

Solidarity

As members of a global family, we are all connected by an intricate web of life, regardless of our national, racial, ethnic, economic, and ideological differences. This interconnectedness requires us to live together, united as brothers and sisters, in relationships that are marked by peace, love, and reconciliation instead of war, hatred, and mistrust.

Care for God's Creation

At the beginning of Genesis, God calls Adam and his descendants to be stewards and caretakers of the Earth. Human beings are called to live in right relationship with all of God's creation, protecting both people and the planet. Modern life and technology have created serious environmental challenges that must be addressed in solidarity. Failure to do so imperils future generations.

Catholic social doctrine emphasizes the theme of solidarity, which is the principle that all people are connected by an intricate web of life. We are all beloved children of God and must treat one another with love and respect.

UNIT 3

The Two Feet of Social Action

Our response to social injustice can be thought of as having two components. On the one hand, we must try to alleviate immediate needs by giving food to the hungry, clothing to the naked, comfort to the sick and imprisoned, and so on. This is sometimes called the work of service, or charity, and is often summarized in the **Corporal Works of Mercy**. On the other hand, we must also work to change the structures of society that keep people hungry or poor or that motivate them to commit crimes. This is called the work of justice. Charity and justice are like two feet that walk together in our faith.

Both service and justice are needed as part of our response to social injustice. Works of service are more immediate, and often the results are easier to see. Works of justice are more long term, more complex to deal with, and the results may never come. But Christ calls us to be faithful—though not necessarily successful—and he will strengthen and guide us in this work. ✳

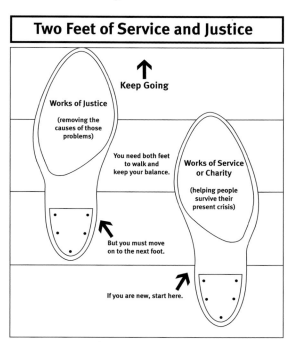

Two Feet of Service and Justice

Keep Going

Works of Justice
(removing the causes of those problems)

You need both feet to walk and keep your balance.

Works of Service or Charity
(helping people survive their present crisis)

But you must move on to the next foot.

If you are new, start here.

UNIT 3

HMMMMM. . .

Which of the seven themes of Catholic social teaching do we most need to pay attention to in today's world?

Corporal Works of Mercy ➤ Charitable actions that respond to people's physical needs and show respect for human dignity. The traditional list of seven works includes feeding the hungry, giving drink to the thirsty, clothing the naked, sheltering the homeless, visiting the sick, visiting prisoners, and burying the dead.

Article 34

Calling Society to Justice

A principle at the heart of the social doctrine of the Church is this: "Man is himself the author, center, and goal of all economic and social life. The decisive point of the social question is that goods created by God for everyone should in fact reach everyone in accordance with justice and with the help of charity" (*Catechism of the Catholic Church*, number 2459). This article applies this principle to three contemporary social issues: labor issues, environmental issues, and international issues.

Labor Issues

As a young person, your primary work is to be a student and to study and learn. You are probably still discerning what your future vocation will be. Whatever it ends up being, you will probably have several different occupations throughout your life. Remember that the primary value of all work is to benefit ourselves and society. By contributing our talents to society, we participate in the divine work of creation. Even more, when we work in such a way that our labor reflects Christ's teachings and values, we share in Christ's saving mission, our ultimate vocation in life.

© mangostock / Shutterstock.com

What are some of the rights that all workers have in light of the Seventh Commandment? What responsibilities do workers have toward their employers?

In light of the Seventh Commandment, "You shall not steal," workers have important responsibilities to their employers and to society. People need to give their best to the work they do. Coming in late, slacking off at work, or not getting enough sleep to do your best work is, in a sense, stealing from the company. More important, workers need to keep a humble and positive attitude toward their work and their fellow workers. Following instructions carefully and cheerfully, being willing to learn from other employees, being willing to assist other employees, and taking initiatives to improve personal work performance are all ways workers reflect the values of Christ in their workplace.

Companies and employers also have responsibilities in light of the Seventh Commandment. First and foremost, they have the responsibility to make sure the goods and services they provide contribute to the good of society and not to its harm. They must be sure that their manufacturing processes do not harm their workers or the environment. They have a responsibility to provide their employees with fair and just wages and benefits. They must not practice discrimination in their hiring practices. They must not ask their employees to do anything immoral or illegal.

The Church recognizes that there may be times when the interests of the worker and the interests of the employer come into conflict. In these cases, efforts at negotiation that respect the rights and duties of both employee and

UNIT 3

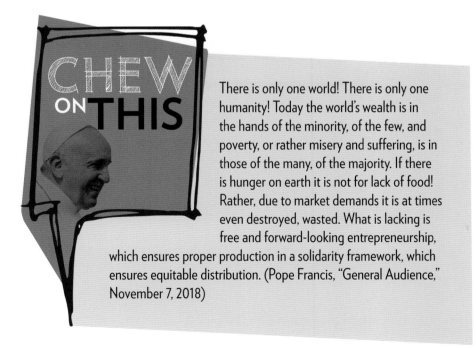

CHEW ON THIS

There is only one world! There is only one humanity! Today the world's wealth is in the hands of the minority, of the few, and poverty, or rather misery and suffering, is in those of the many, of the majority. If there is hunger on earth it is not for lack of food! Rather, due to market demands it is at times even destroyed, wasted. What is lacking is free and forward-looking entrepreneurship, which ensures proper production in a solidarity framework, which ensures equitable distribution. (Pope Francis, "General Audience," November 7, 2018)

employer must be made. The Church affirms the rights of workers to form trade and labor unions that speak and negotiate for the rights of workers. Recourse to labor strikes should be a last resort after all other attempts at negotiation fail. Workers and employers should never resort to violence in labor disputes.

When it comes to work and workers, we should be aware of one more social justice issue—slavery and human trafficking. Slavery still exists today, particularly in the form of human trafficking. It exists because it provides some people with an economic advantage. Estimates are that every year, millions of people are forced into slavery across the globe. This human trafficking takes many forms. For example, people are forced into **prostitution** or are lured into another country and forced to work in prisonlike conditions or under the control of totalitarian governments that severely limit personal freedoms. The moral law condemns any act that leads to the enslavement of human beings—people bought, sold, or exchanged like merchandise.

© guentermanaus / Shutterstock.com

The consequences of not caring for the Earth have been made clear in recent environmental disasters, such as the destruction of the Amazon rainforest. In order to prevent future catastrophes, every person will need to do their part to protect the environment.

---

prostitution ➤ The act of providing sexual services in exchange for money, drugs, or other goods. It is a serious social evil and is a sin against the Sixth Commandment.

Environmental Issues

Today, almost all people recognize that caring for the environment is an important moral issue. Environmental pollution, overgrazing, overplanting, overfishing, the destruction of the rainforests, the destruction of plant and animal species, and global climate change are all issues we hear about regularly. It took decades for human beings to recognize the damage that modern manufacturing, modern agriculture, and rampant consumerism were causing to the environment, and the Church was one of the early voices in recognizing care for the environment as a moral issue.

In 2015, Pope Francis released the encyclical "On Care for Our Common Home" *("Laudato Si")*. At the beginning of the encyclical, Pope Francis says:

> This sister [Mother Earth] now cries out to us because of the harm we have inflicted on her by our irresponsible use and abuse of the goods with which God has endowed her. We have come to see ourselves as her lords and masters, entitled to plunder her at will. The violence present in our hearts, wounded by sin, is also reflected in the symptoms of sickness evident in the soil, in the water, in the air and in all forms of life. (Number 2)

Pope Francis issues an urgent call to all the people of the world to change the way we treat God's creation, saying that if we don't do this soon, the consequences will be devastating. Here are a few of the points he makes in the encyclical:

- Human beings are primarily responsible for the destruction of the environment and the misuse of the Earth's resources, most often in the service of business interests and consumerism—the "throwaway" culture.
- The Earth does not belong to us. It was here before us, and God has given it to us to care for. Instead, we have largely exploited it.
- The people who suffer the most from climate change are the poorest among us. Addressing climate change and caring for the Earth is also a social justice issue.
- Although there have been many positive responses to environmental degradation, so far they have been inadequate.
- Human beings need to change. We need to change our priorities to care for creation. We must reject consumerism. We must learn to cooperate rather than compete.

International Issues

It is an interesting exercise to look at the labels on the things you own and the things you eat and see what country they came from. Chances are that the majority of these things came from outside the United States. The reality that ordinary people routinely buy goods manufactured in other countries and create goods that will be sold in other countries is a sign that we live in a truly global economy. The moral law requires that our global economy must be just; nations must treat one another—and the people that live in those nations—with respect and fairness.

Working for international justice is most needed to overcome the gap between the world's richest and poorest nations. According to the Pew Research Center, 15 percent of the world's families are poor, living on less than $2 a day and another 56 percent are low income, living on less than $10 a day (2015 statistics). The richest 16 percent (including the US) live on more than $50 a day. The causes for this gap are many: poor national leadership and planning, the lack of natural resources, natural disasters, corrupt government officials, and warfare are some examples. Whatever the causes, rich nations must not exploit poor nations through practices like forcing poor nations into high interest international loans, supporting corrupt government officials, selling weapons to governments that oppress their people, or buying goods from companies that abuse their workers or do not pay their workers just wages.

Justice must also be practiced in relations between nations. People in wealthy nations must not take advantage of the workers in other nations by paying low wages for inexpensive goods.

UNIT 3

Nations have a responsibility to help one another's economic and social development. The good news is that the percentage of the world's poorest families has been declining since the beginning of the century. By helping individual nations to develop just and fair economic systems and to develop government systems that support human rights, the entire international community grows stronger. True development does more than just increase a nation's wealth or economic productivity; it is concerned with the whole person and helps to increase each person's ability to respond to God's call and live out their vocation.

The Church is a strong advocate for international justice and cooperation. Although it is not the role of the clergy of the Church to get directly involved with national or international politics, the Church's leaders do speak out in support of just economic development and against unjust economic and political systems. They call the laity to take initiative in addressing the causes of poverty and to bring greater justice to economic and political systems. The members of the Church, the living Body of Christ, take seriously their responsibility to be agents of justice and peace in the world. ✳

UNIT 3

HMMMMMM. . .   How are the three justice issues discussed in this article related?

Article 35

Envy and Greed

"Did you see Damon's new car?" Tim asked Shauna. "I'm so jealous! My parents would never get something like that for me.

"I know," replied Shauna. "And did you see Lucas's new phone? It's the newest one that just came out last week, and I've still got this hand-me-down from four years ago. It's not fair!"

So far we have focused on sins that are primarily against the Seventh Commandment. But **envy** and **greed**, the two primary sins against the Tenth Commandment, usually precede sins against the Seventh Commandment. The desire to have more than we need, and the desire to have something that someone else has, can lead us to sins of fraud, theft, and injustice. In this article, we look more closely at envy and greed and how to combat their influence in our lives.

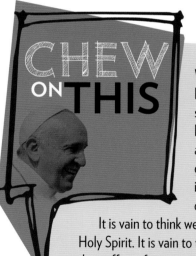

CHEW ON THIS

We must instead allow ourselves to be unmasked by these Commandments on desire, so they may show us our poverty, in order to lead us to a holy humiliation. Each of us can ask ourselves: which awful desires do I most often feel? Envy, greed, gossip? All these things that come to me from inside. We each can ask ourselves this and it will do us good.

It is vain to think we can correct ourselves without the gift of the Holy Spirit. It is vain to think we can purify our heart through a tremendous effort of our own will: this is not possible. We must open ourselves to the relationship with God, in truth and in freedom: only in this way can our efforts bear fruit, because the Holy Spirit is there to carry us forward. (Pope Francis, "General Audience," November 21, 2018)

---

envy ➤ Resentment that we direct at others who have some success, thing, or privilege that we want for ourselves. It is one of the capital sins and contrary to the Tenth Commandment.

greed ➤ The desire to accumulate earthly goods beyond what we need. It is one of the capital sins and contrary to the Tenth Commandment.

Controlled by Envy or Greed

Have you ever been controlled by envy—that feeling that grows in you when you see other people with something that you want too? Before envy takes control, we are usually content with things we have. Then we notice a friend, acquaintance, or maybe just someone in an advertisement with something we don't have. That person seems so happy, and we start to think that we'd be happier if we just had this thing too. We forget that true happiness comes from being in right relationship with God. Saint Thomas More (1478–1535) once said, "If we were to . . . value everything according to its true nature, rather than according to people's false opinion, then we would never see any reason to envy any person!"

We start to feel sad for ourselves because we can't afford it, or maybe we would be embarrassed to be seen with it. We start to imagine ways we could get it, and it occupies more and more of our thoughts. We even start thinking of ways to steal it or secretly buy it. Before we know it, we are no longer controlled by our own conscience and reason; our envy is now fully in charge.

Greed is the cousin of envy. When we are under the control of greed, there is no limit to our desire for something: money, stocks, gold, power, fame—just about anything can be the object of greed. Like envy, greed also leaves us feeling dissatisfied and sad, for no matter how much we have of the thing we desire, there is always an empty place in us that wants more. The greedy heart has a thirst that is never quenched.

UNIT 3

© MMPhotography / iStockphoto.com

Our culture's focus on having lots of things makes it easy to be envious of the things other people have. When are you most tempted to feel envious of other people?

Envy and greed are two of the seven capital sins. This means that they are often at the root of many other sins, such as cheating, theft, lying, and even violence against other people. Saint Ephrem of Syria (c. 306–373) put it this way: "Whenever you envy your neighbor, you give demons a place to rest." Envy and greed are also disorders of the natural appetites that we have for food, drink, comfort, and protection from the elements. These desires are good in themselves, but when they become exaggerated and control our thoughts and behavior they are no longer good, but are sinful instead.

Envy and greed can lead to a type of sin that is a particular temptation to students. The sin of **plagiarism**—copying someone else's words or ideas without permission or without giving proper credit—has existed for centuries. But it has become far easier to commit plagiarism because of the vast amount of information on the internet. All you have to do is search, copy, and paste. This form of stealing is also cheating, and people who are caught doing it can face severe penalties.

Pirating music, video, and software is a relatively new form of stealing. Pirating music and video was much harder when music was distributed on vinyl records and when you could see movies only at the theater or as a TV broadcast. Now digital recordings make it much easier to do. If people download an illegal copy of a song or movie, they are stealing from hundreds of people—not only the artists who created it but also the technical crew, the support staff, and the local store owners who depend on your purchase to make their living.

Combating Envy and Greed

Feelings of envy and greed are not sins in themselves. These negative feelings creep into our hearts unbidden; they are the result of concupiscence, the traces of Original Sin in our lives. However, once we recognize those feelings, we have a choice to make. We can choose to hold on to them, dwell on them, and let them grow in our heart and mind, and thus let sin begin.

© Jason Stitt / Shutterstock.com

Why are greed and envy capital sins? How do you combat envy and greed?

---

plagiarism ➤ Copying someone else's words or ideas without permission or giving proper credit to the person.

Or we can choose to banish them and replace them by exercising the virtues of goodwill toward others, personal humility, and trust in the providence of God. Our practice of these virtues will combat our feelings of envy and greed, making them less and less an influence in our lives. Here are some suggestions for cultivating these three virtues in your life:

- To have goodwill toward others is to desire what is best for other people and to take joy in their happiness. Goodwill requires that you take your mind's focus off your needs and wants and turn it toward the needs of the other person. In this way, goodwill is the opposite of envy. A good way to cultivate goodwill when you start feeling envious of someone else is to say a simple prayer like this: "Father, I pray for [person's name] happiness. Help me to rejoice that you have blessed her [or him]."

- Envy often comes from pride, the belief that we deserve special treatment or are more important than others in some way. It happens when we think something like this: "Why does he have that and I don't? I'm just as good as he is." The antidote to pride is personal humility, which is the recognition that God already loves us completely and blesses us, and that there is nothing we can do to earn more of his love. We recognize that material possessions are not a sign of God's love for us. This helps to free us from envying other people's situations and material things.

- Greed is a sign that we really don't trust in God. It is based in the fear that we will not have enough of something to meet our needs. But Jesus tells us that this fear is without basis: "Look at the birds in the sky; they do not sow or reap, they gather nothing into barns, yet your heavenly Father feeds them. Are not you more important than they?" (Matthew 6:26). Develop your trust in the **providence** of God by praying something like this every day: "Father, help me to trust that you will provide everything I need today. Help me to understand that you are the source of true happiness. Do not let me succumb to the belief that I need more of anything than you give me."

UNIT 3

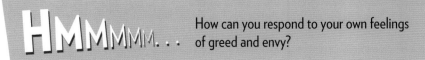

HMMMMMM. . . How can you respond to your own feelings of greed and envy?

---

providence ➤ God's divine care and protection.

Article 36
Living Simply So Others May Simply Live

Money can be a touchy subject. Our culture places a great deal of importance on having it. We often measure our worth by how much we have. We get stressed when we think we don't have enough—which for some people is most of the time. We sometimes compromise our values and even our physical and emotional well-being to get more money. But there is a simple Gospel solution to this trap. It's called *living simply so that others can simply live.* To put it another way, it means resisting the culture of **consumerism**.

Besides avoiding the sins of greed and envy, there is also a justice reason for simple living. Reason and science are making it clear that the Earth has limited resources. Our God-given stewardship over the Earth's resources cannot be separated from our moral obligation to use these resources wisely and justly. God has provided us with enough resources so that when they are shared fairly among all the people of the Earth, everyone can live without hunger and poverty. But when some people accumulate too much money and material goods, it often means that other people have less and sometimes so much less that people are kept poor and hungry.

Christ provides the example of simple living for us to follow. He embraced a lifestyle of voluntary poverty. Let's look first at Christ's example and then at the challenge of living a simple lifestyle.

This painting by Rembrandt depicts the man from the Parable of the Rich Fool counting his money. If Rembrandt were painting this today, in what setting might he depict the rich fool?

© bpk Bildagentur / Gemaeldegalerie, Staatliche Museen, Berlin, Germany / Jörg P. Anders / Art Resource, NY

---

consumerism ➤ The preoccupation with buying and having more material things.

Christ's Example

Jesus' life and teaching revealed that **poverty of heart** (sometimes called spiritual poverty) is necessary for us to be in communion with God. People who have poverty of heart recognize their need for God. This is why Jesus says, "Blessed are the poor in spirit" (Matthew 5:3). Without God, we are truly empty and alone; no amount of material wealth can fill that void. In fact, material wealth often gets in the way of our recognizing our need for God.

There is a powerful passage in the Gospel of Mark on this topic. Take a minute to read Mark 10:17–31. This passage begins with the story of the rich young man. He wanted to follow Jesus and had followed the Ten Commandments since his youth. But then Jesus gave him this challenge: "You are lacking in one thing. Go, sell what you have, and give to [the] poor and you will have treasure in heaven; then come, follow me" (verse 21). We don't know what this young man's final decision was, but the Gospel tells us that he went away sad, for he had many possessions. To drive the point home, Jesus warns his disciples that material wealth can be dangerous to our salvation: "How hard it is for those who have wealth to enter the kingdom of God!" (verse 23).

UNIT 3

MAKE IT SO

You and your cousin decide to go shopping for some clothes for the new school year. Your idea is to visit thrift stores and second-hand stores, but your cousin wants to shop for only new clothes at boutique clothing stores. She tells you how envious she was last year when several of her friends showed up with new clothes in the latest colors and styles. "It took a lot of convincing, but I finally wore my parents down so they would give me money for the latest outfits," she says with pride. You recognize that your cousin's focus might be too much on status and material goods and, perhaps, not in line with the call of the Gospel. What can you say to her about your desire to shop more simply? How do you fight the effects of envy and greed and the pull of the consumerist culture?

---

poverty of heart ➤ The recognition of our deep need for God and the commitment to put God above everything else in life, particularly above the accumulation of material wealth.

The disciples were amazed at his words because they were raised in a culture that believed material wealth was a sign of God's blessings! They asked themselves, "Then who can be saved?" (verse 26). Jesus reminds them that we cannot save ourselves with our own efforts, "For human beings it is impossible, but not for God. All things are possible for God" (verse 27). In other words, material blessings can be a trap. They can lead us to believe that we can "save" ourselves from the unpleasantness of life—even make us forget that there is a life after death. We must take the step of faith to renounce any belief that owning and having things can truly make us whole and happy. Remembering what Jesus says to Peter can help us: "We have given up everything and followed you." Jesus replies, "Amen, I say to you, there is no one who has given up house . . . or lands for my sake and for the sake of the gospel who will not receive a hundred times more now in this present age . . . and eternal life in the age to come" (verses 28–30).

I DIDN'T KNOW THAT!

Many saints had clever sayings about poverty of heart:

- "The love of worldly possessions is a sort of birdlime (a sticky substance to trap birds), which entangles the soul, and prevents it flying to God." (Saint Augustine of Hippo, 354–430)
- "As riches are the instruments of all vices, because they render us capable of putting even our worst desires into execution, so a renunciation of riches is the origin and preserver of virtues." (Saint Ambrose of Milan, c. 340–397)
- "The less we have here, the more shall we enjoy in God's Kingdom, where the mansion of each is proportioned to the love with which they shall have imitated Jesus Christ." (Saint Teresa of Ávila, 1515–1582)

Gospel Teaching on Poverty of Heart

In many places in the four Gospels, Jesus teaches about the importance of poverty of heart, which is the basis for living simply.

Gospel Passage	Summary
Mark 12:41–44	the widow's mite
Matthew 13:44–46	Parable of the Treasure Buried in the Field, The Pearl of Great Price
Luke 12:15–21	Parable of the Rich Fool
Luke 12:22–32	"Do not worry about your life and what you will eat, or about your body and what you will wear" (verse 32).
Luke 12:33–34	"Where your treasure is, there also will your heart be" (verse 34).
Matthew 6:19–21,24	"Store up treasures in heaven" (verse 20) and "no one can serve two masters" (verse 24).

Christ's actions reflected his words. During the three years of his active ministry, he did not own a home or any material possessions beyond the clothes on his back. When a scribe approached Jesus to become one of his followers, Jesus responded, "Foxes have dens and birds of the sky have nests, but the Son of Man has nowhere to rest his head" (Matthew 8:20), indicating his lack of possessions. He depended entirely on the generosity of others to finance his mission (see Luke 8:3). He traveled everywhere by foot, the transportation method of poor people (except for his triumphal entry into Jerusalem before his Passion).

These two small coins are mites, which were used in the ancient Roman Empire. The Parable of the Widow's Mite teaches that even the poorest person can have a truly generous heart.

The Challenge of a Simple Lifestyle

Living a simple lifestyle or choosing voluntary poverty is a challenging and complex topic. First of all, God does not call every Christian to a vow of poverty, especially the radical poverty of Jesus. Second, people will have different definitions of what a simple lifestyle is depending on their country, their culture, and their current economic status. Third, people's situations may limit their economic choices; this is especially true for teenagers who are usually not in control of their own economic situation.

These challenges should not deter us from taking Jesus' call to live a simple lifestyle seriously. Here are some ideas to get you started, suggested by other teens:

- Shop at thrift stores and secondhand clothing stores. "I bought a whole season's wardrobe for ten dollars," said one student, "and I kept those clothes from going into the dump." Other options are trading clothes with friends or using your school's clothing exchange for clothes that fit the school dress code.
- Skip the car, and ride your bike wherever you need to go. Public transportation and ride sharing are other ways to keep it simple and to be environmentally responsible.

Living a simple lifestyle can be as simple as shopping in a thrift store instead of always buying new clothes.

UNIT 3

- There is no need to spend lots of money for leisure activities. Watch movies at home with friends and save on the expensive movie tickets. Go without electricity altogether and instead play board games by candlelight and spend time outside.

If you are already making choices like these to live simply, congratulations, and keep working at it. If you have never seriously considered this call, spend some time praying about it, and ask God to point out one way you can make your life simpler. This is an important topic for families to discuss too. If your family hasn't talked about it recently, maybe you can bring it up for a family discussion.

Living simply often leads to less consumption of the Earth's resources. For example, you and your family might decide that rather than having multiple TVs in your home, one will be enough. This decision leads to lower energy use, a reduction in the use of materials used in the manufacturing of televisions, and even reduced use of landfill space when the televisions become old or malfunction and need to be disposed of. When you use less of the world's resources, you allow a more equitable share for people in greater need. In choosing to live simply, money saved might be used for **almsgiving**, which is making monetary contributions to help people who are poor and needy. This is a work of justice that is pleasing to God. As a teenager, you might not feel wealthy, but do not neglect this important practice of giving to those in need, even if what you can give is very little (remember the story of the widow's mite?). Almsgiving should be a lifelong habit, one that will be easier if you begin now. ✳

UNIT 3

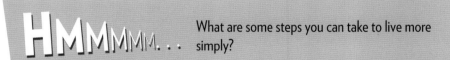

HMMMMM. . . What are some steps you can take to live more simply?

---

almsgiving ➤ Freely giving money or material goods to a person who is needy, often by giving to a group or organization that serves poor people. It may be an act of penance or of Christian charity.

1. Summarize the Old Law's teaching on material possessions.

2. Why did Jesus Christ's teachings on poverty and wealth shock the people of his time?

3. Define the concept of social doctrine.

4. Choose two key principles of the social doctrine of the Church and explain their significance.

5. What responsibilities do employers have in regard to their workers?

6. What responsibilities do rich nations have toward poor nations according to the social doctrine of the Church?

7. Why does envy or greed leave us feeling sad and dissatisfied?

8. What are some ways you can combat envy and greed?

9. What is poverty of heart, and how is it taught in the Gospels?

10. How did Christ provide us with an example of living simply, and how does he call us to do likewise?

UNIT 3

ART STUDY

This art piece is called *Seven Days of Garbage* and is meant to be a statement on consumerism.

1. What thoughts or questions come to mind as you reflect on this art?

2. What do you think the artist is saying about our culture of consumerism?

3. How is this art a statement on the sins of envy and greed?

UNIT 3 HIGHLIGHTS

CHAPTER 7   The Fourth Commandment:
Respecting Authority

Biblical Meaning of Family: Old Testament

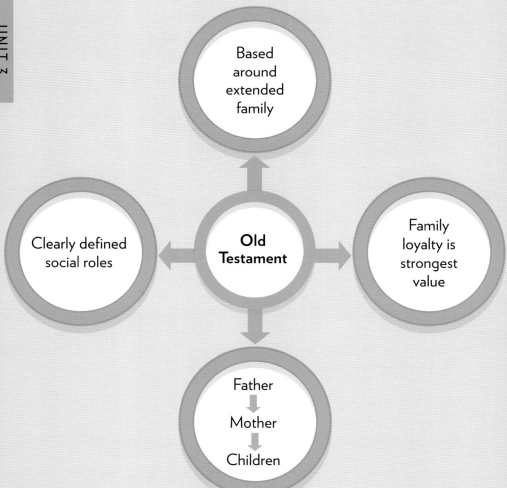

Biblical Meaning of Family: New Testament

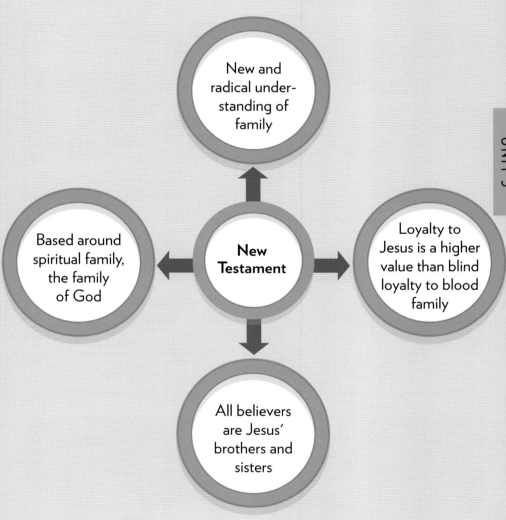

Fourth Commandment Responsibilities

Children's Responsibilities for Parents	Parents' Responsibilities for Children

Respect

Provide for Needs

Gratitude

Keep Safe

Assistance

Educate in Faith

Faithful Citizenship

"Pay to all their dues, taxes to whom taxes are due, toll to whom toll is due, respect to whom respect is due, honor to whom honor is due." (Saint Paul)

People of faith must fulfill their civic obligations to promote and build a free and just society.

The state exists to defend and promote the common good of society.

We are called to be in the world but not of the world.

God calls public leaders to safeguard people's fundamental rights.

"We must obey God rather than men." (Saint Peter)

CHAPTER 8

The Eighth Commandment:
Reality versus Illusion

Living the Second Commandment

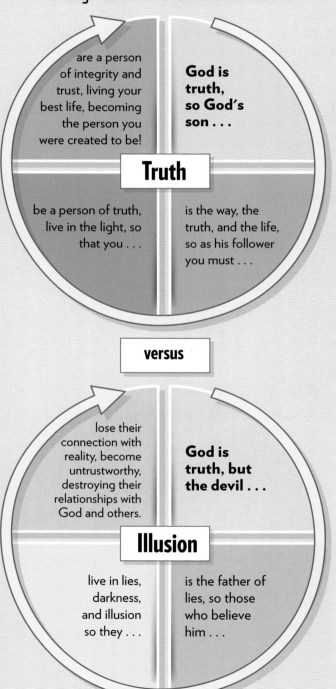

are a person of integrity and trust, living your best life, becoming the person you were created to be!

God is truth, so God's son . . .

Truth

be a person of truth, live in the light, so that you . . .

is the way, the truth, and the life, so as his follower you must . . .

versus

lose their connection with reality, become untrustworthy, destroying their relationships with God and others.

God is truth, but the devil . . .

Illusion

live in lies, darkness, and illusion so they . . .

is the father of lies, so those who believe him . . .

Other Sins against the Second Commandment

CHAPTER 9 The Seventh and Tenth Commandments: Justice versus Injustice

Biblical Teaching on Possessions

We are stewards of Creation.

"You shall not steal."

Just distribution of the Earth's resources

Preferential care for the poor

Detachment from material wealth

Images: Shutterstock.com | © catwalker | Shutterstock.com

The Seven Themes of Catholic Social Teaching

1
God made each person, so every life is important and should be protected.

5
Work is important in God's plan for adults and their families, so jobs and pay should be fair.

2
God made us to be part of communities, families and countries, so all people can share and help each other.

6
God made everyone, so we are all brothers and sisters in God's family wherever we live.

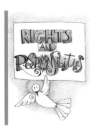

3
God wants us to help make sure everyone is safe and healthy and can have a good life.

7
The world was made by God, so we take care of all creation.

4
God wants us to help people who are poor, who don't have enough food, a safe place to live, or a community.

UNIT 3

Envy

jealousy, resentment, or sadness
because of another's good fortune

one of the capital sins

takes over our thoughts, we are
no longer controlled by conscience

fight this feeling with humility
and goodwill toward others

Greed

the desire to accumulate wealth, power, fame, etc., beyond what we need

one of the capital sins

leaves us feeling dissatisfied and sad, no matter how much we have

fight this feeling with trust in God's providence

UNIT 3
BRING IT HOME

WHY SHOULD I WORRY ABOUT HOW MY CHOICES AFFECT OTHER PEOPLE?

FOCUS QUESTIONS

KARLA
Seton Catholic Preparatory School

UNIT 3

I should worry about how my choices affect people because they might be going through something, and the thing that I do might hurt them even more. Because we never know what is going on in other people's lives, we should be as nice to them as we can. We should not talk bad about people, because we never know what is causing their actions or poor attitude. In this unit, I was reminded that I need to get back to the basics when I think about how I want to treat others. The Ten Commandments guide us with important values for treating others with dignity and respect. We should also remember how Jesus challenges us to go the extra mile through his teachings and actions.

REFLECT

Take some time to read and reflect on the unit and chapter focus questions listed on the facing page.

- What question or section did you identify most closely with?

- What did you find within the unit that was comforting or challenging?

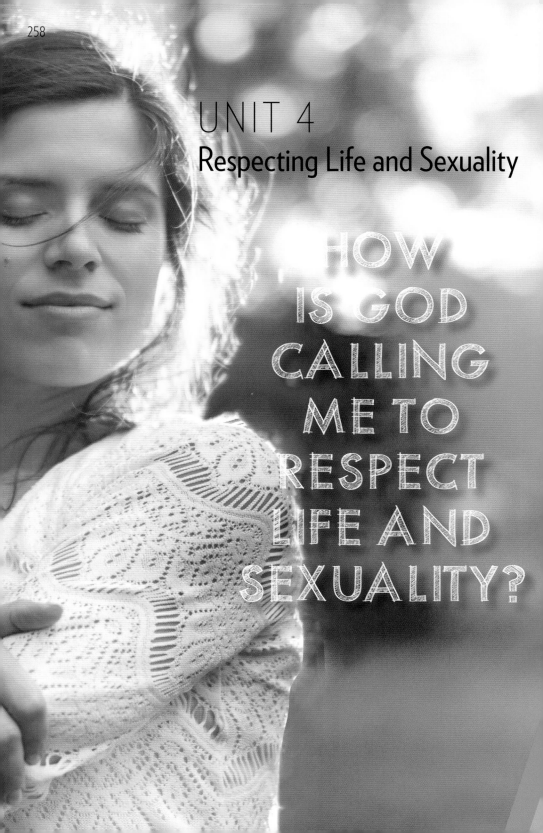

UNIT 4
Respecting Life and Sexuality

HOW IS GOD CALLING ME TO RESPECT LIFE AND SEXUALITY?

LOOKING AHEAD

UNIT 4

I can show respect for others in my life by doing the little things that take little or no extra effort. There are many times when I have an opportunity to show my respect to others. But for me to do this, I must first show respect for myself, including my sexuality. Some ways I can show respect for myself might be working out to maintain a healthy lifestyle, reading to fill my mind with Knowledge, and even going on walks to get away from the daily stress of being a high school student. If you can achieve self-respect, you then will be better able to show respect to others.

MATTIAS
Seton Catholic Preparatory School

CHAPTER 10

The Fifth Commandment: Respecting Life

HOW CAN I SHOW MY RESPECT FOR LIFE?

SNAPSHOT

Article 37
Sacredness of Life in the Bible

What is the one thing every human being must have in order to think, speak, and act? Did "the gift of life" immediately occur to you as the answer to this question? The gift of life is so basic that it is easy to take for granted. Sometimes it is only after witnessing a birth, spending time with someone who is dying, or having a near-death experience that we are reminded that life is a precious gift. Human beings naturally struggle against death. Take a minute to think about that last statement: Human beings naturally struggle against death. Popular culture tends to present death as an unfortunate but natural part of life. But if death is so natural, why do we struggle so hard to prevent it? Our faith gives the answer: God did not create human beings for death but for eternal life. The Fifth Commandment, "You shall not kill," teaches us this important truth.

TAKE IT TO GOD

Lord, God of Abraham, God of the Prophets, God of Love, you created us and you call us to live as brothers and sisters. Give us the strength daily to be instruments of peace; enable us to see everyone who crosses our path as our brother or sister. Make us sensitive to the plea of our citizens who entreat us to turn our weapons of war into implements of peace, our trepidation into confident trust, and our quarreling into forgiveness.

Keep alive within us the flame of hope, so that with patience and perseverance we may opt for dialogue and reconciliation. In this way may peace triumph at last, and may the words "division," "hatred," and "war" be banished from the heart of every man and woman. Lord, defuse the violence of our tongues and our hands. Renew our hearts and minds, so that the word which always brings us together will be "brother," and our way of life will always be that of: Shalom, Peace, Salaam! Amen. (Pope Francis, "Invocation for Peace," June 8, 2014)

The gift of life is God's greatest gift to us. All human life is sacred because God creates human beings in his image. To murder or to intentionally harm yourself or another person is a sin against human dignity and against God's gift of life. These are the minimum requirements of the Fifth Commandment, clearly taught in the Old Law. In the New Law, Christ goes further, teaching us to put away all thoughts of anger and vengeance and even to love our enemies.

Michelangelo's famous painting in the Sistine Chapel shows God sharing the spark of life with Adam and depicts the sacredness of human life.

The Sacredness of Human Life in the Old Testament

In the biblical account of Creation, God blew the breath of life into Adam, the first man (see Genesis 2:7). This action conveys the truth that at the beginning of life God creates our soul, our spiritual principle, and unites it with our physical body, thereby sharing his divine image with us. For this reason, human life is qualitatively different from the life of every other creature. Every human life is sacred from its beginning, at the moment of conception, because every person has been created in the image and likeness of God (see Genesis 1:26). Because of this, human life is uniquely sacred; killing a human being is not the same thing as killing a plant or animal. The murder of a human being is a sin against the sacred dignity of the human person and against the holiness of God.

Murder is also wrong because God alone is the author of life and death. Two Old Testament songs witness to this truth. Moses's song in the Book of Deuteronomy proclaims:

> See now that I, I alone, am he,
>   and there is no god besides me.
> It is I who bring both death and life.
>   (32:39)

In her song, Hannah, the mother of Samuel, proclaims, "The LORD puts to death and gives life, / casts down to Sheol and brings up again" (1 Samuel 2:6). The power of life and death is God's alone, so the murder of another person assumes a power that is not for human beings to claim.

The Sacredness of Human Life in the New Testament

In the New Testament, Christ reveals the core value at the heart of the Fifth Commandment: a radical respect for human life. When we accept this truth, it is easy to see that the Fifth Commandment is about more than murder. In the Sermon on the Mount, Jesus commands us to have a deep and radical respect for the sacredness of the human person.

> You have heard that it was said to your ancestors, "You shall not kill; and whoever kills will be liable to judgment." But I say to you, whoever is angry with his brother will be liable to judgment, and whoever says to his brother, "Raqa," [an abusive word probably meaning "imbecile"] will be answerable to the Sanhedrin, and whoever says, "You fool," will be liable to fiery Gehenna. (Matthew 5:21–22)

> You have heard that it was said, "An eye for an eye and a tooth for a tooth." But I say to you, offer no resistance to one who is evil. When someone strikes you on (your) right cheek, turn the other one to him as well. (5:38–39)

> You have heard that it was said, "You shall love your neighbor and hate your enemy." But I say to you, love your enemies, and pray for those who persecute you, that you may be children of your heavenly Father, for he makes his sun rise on the bad and the good, and causes rain to fall on the just and the unjust. (5:43–45)

UNIT 4

In these passages, Jesus is teaching that respect for human life is about more than just not killing other people. If we truly have respect for human life, we must avoid harm of any kind to another person, physical or otherwise. More than that, we should even respond to hatred and violence with love, to be an example for others of God's love!

What does this mean for us? Hopefully you aren't striking other people, and other people are not hitting you. But what about bullies who mock other people to make themselves feel better? or that person who always must get in the last word to look more important? or those who always get angry and defensive at the smallest thing? How do we react to these people? Do we mock them in response? Do we complain about them behind their backs? Do we get angry and say hurtful things? This is what Jesus is warning us against.

How would driving while texting be a sin against the Fifth Commandment?

Applying Jesus' Teaching on the Sanctity of Life

When we take Jesus' teaching on the sacredness of life to heart, we come to understand that any word or action that causes harm to another person is a sin against the Fifth Commandment. This includes violent assaults, rapes, torture, and acts of terrorism. It includes hazing rituals and name calling. We aren't saying, of course, that all these sins are the same. Some actions are more serious than others. Name calling isn't nearly as serious as a violent assault or rape.

But name calling is still wrong. In fact, your actions must only have the potential to harm someone to be wrong. Reckless or unsafe driving, for example, is a sin against the Fifth Commandment, even if no one gets hurt, as are practical jokes that could accidently cause embarrassment or physical harm to someone.

The Fifth Commandment also includes avoiding harming the spiritual lives of other people. One example of how we harm other people's spiritual lives is through the sin of **scandal**, which is leading another person into sin through our words or actions. For example, offering alcohol to someone who is underage is scandalous behavior. Scandal can also be a sin of omission, such as skipping Mass on Sunday, which sets a bad example for others about their spiritual well-being. Scandal is a grave or mortal sin when we deliberately lead another person to commit a serious sin.

Scandal is particularly wrong when committed by those who are supposed to teach and educate. Remember Jesus' words, "Whoever causes one of these little ones who believe in me to sin, it would be better for him to have a great millstone hung around his neck and to be drowned in the depths of the sea" (Matthew 18:6).

The Fifth Commandment covers business practices and governmental policies as well. It forbids endangering people by selling unsafe products or services. It forbids medical or psychological experimentation on human beings that might seriously endanger their lives or health, even with their consent. It forbids business practices or legal policies that take advantage of poor people or poor nations, possibly leading to starvation and disease. It is a sin to put profit above peoples' health and safety.

The Fifth Commandment reminds us that every person on Earth is made in the image of God and is precious to him. There are no exceptions. This truth is at the heart of Christian morality. It is the foundation for loving other people and loving ourselves. ✳

UNIT 4

 Where do I see the Fifth Commandment violated by words or actions that hurt or injure other people?

---

scandal ➤ An action or attitude—or the failure to act—that leads another person into sin.

Article 38

Beginning-of-Life Issues

The Fifth Commandment calls individuals and society to respect and protect human life at all stages of development. Most people would agree that it is a serious evil to kill a child, a teenager, or an adult in the prime of life. But opinion changes when talking about the beginning of life or the end of life. These issues can be confusing because the arguments people make supporting abortion and euthanasia can sound very reasonable. They talk about supporting the right to choose and that it is wrong to take away other people's right to choose for themselves. For some things, our culture has made an individual's right to choose a moral absolute.

But let's think about that for a minute. Clearly, you don't have a moral right to choose to run a red light. You don't have a moral right to choose to rob a bank. You don't have a moral right to choose to murder someone. In other words, you do not have a moral right to choose something when the thing you are choosing is wrong or evil. Recall the three elements that determine the morality of any act: the object, the intention, and the circumstances. If the object (the act itself) is wrong, then that moral choice can never be right. Keep this principle in mind as we discuss these life issues. Just because many people have come to accept abortion and euthanasia as acceptable moral choices, that does not make these choices right. This change in public opinion goes directly against God's moral law.

God's Revelation in Scripture and Tradition is clear that human life is sacred and must be protected from its natural beginning to its natural end. The Catholic Church has been a strong moral voice calling society to protect human life from "womb to tomb." This concept is sometimes called "the seamless garment of life," a reference to Christ's seamless garment that the soldiers cast lots for at his Crucifixion (see John 19:23). The seamless garment of life concept emphasizes that all Fifth Commandment issues are interconnected and rooted in the same principle: that all human life is sacred and precious to God. This article looks at Fifth Commandment issues that come up at the beginning of life, and the next article looks at issues that come up at the end of life.

Abortion

Abortion is the deliberate termination of pregnancy by killing the unborn child in the womb. The ability to abort children has existed for a long time, but until recently most societies and religions considered this act a moral evil. In the 1970s, the United States made abortion legal, and many other countries have done the same. But remember that acts that are legal are not always moral. What is legal often becomes commonplace and acceptable, and today abortion has tragically become commonplace.

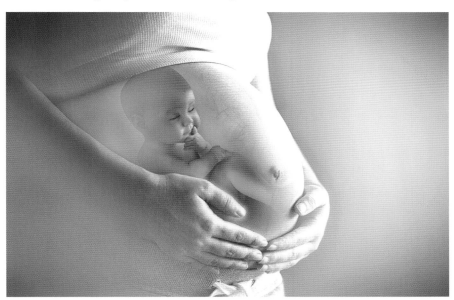

A new human life is created at the moment of conception and must be protected throughout its development.

The Church, however, has never wavered in her complete support for the right to life of unborn children from the moment of their conception (when the egg and sperm unite). Direct abortion—that is, abortion performed to end a pregnancy and the life of an unborn child—is a serious sin and is strongly forbidden by the Law of God. (An example of an indirect abortion is the rare case of a critically ill mother or a mother with an ectopic pregnancy who requires a medical procedure that is not an abortion but that indirectly results in the death of her unborn child. The medical procedure has double effect: saving

---

abortion ➤ The deliberate termination of a pregnancy by killing the unborn child. It is a grave sin and a crime against human life.

the life of the mother and ending the life of the child. The first is intended. The second is not. This tragic situation would be morally tolerated because the death of the child is not directly intended.)

Many of the arguments for abortion may seem reasonable at first glance but do not hold up under scrutiny. Some people argue that in the first weeks or months after conception, the embryo is not a unique human being with its own rights and dignity. But science presents us with the following facts:

- From the moment the sperm and ovum meet, the cell formed has its own unique human DNA, which no other human being has. Left to its natural development, this cell will always develop into an adult human being— not a frog, a dog, or a tree.

CATHOLICS **MAKING** A DIFFERENCE

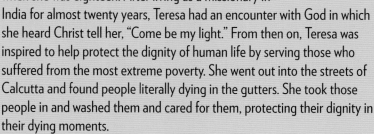

Saint Mother Teresa of Kolkata (Calcutta) (1910–1997) inspired many people to commit themselves to the sanctity of human life from womb to tomb. She was born in Macedonia and joined the Sisters of Loretto when she was eighteen. After living as a missionary in India for almost twenty years, Teresa had an encounter with God in which she heard Christ tell her, "Come be my light." From then on, Teresa was inspired to help protect the dignity of human life by serving those who suffered from the most extreme poverty. She went out into the streets of Calcutta and found people literally dying in the gutters. She took those people in and washed them and cared for them, protecting their dignity in their dying moments.

In 1948, Mother Teresa received permission to leave her convent to start the Missionaries of Charity, a religious order of women who set up hospitals and homes for the dying. By the 1990s, the Missionaries of Charity could be found all over the world, helping homeless people, abused women, and orphans, as well as those suffering from AIDS, drug addiction, and other illnesses. Mother Teresa is recognized around the world for her advocacy for all human life, from the unborn child to those nearing the end of their life. She died in 1997, leaving behind a thriving order of priests, nuns, and laypersons devoted to the service of the neediest people in our world.

- As early as twenty-one days after conception, the embryo's heart begins to beat. At nine weeks, the fetus has fingerprints. At twelve weeks, the fetus sleeps, exercises, curls its toes, and opens and closes its mouth. At eighteen to twenty weeks, the fetus is fully capable of feeling pain.
- The fetus's body is clearly differentiated from its mother's body. Although the mother's body provides oxygen and nourishment, the baby has its own intact and separate body. Its blood is not shared with the mother, and it often even has a different blood type.

These are some of the facts that lead to the conclusion that a unique human life begins at the moment of conception.

People also argue that a pregnant woman has the right to make choices about her own body, including the baby growing inside her womb. It is true that a woman does have the right to make choices about her body, but the baby's right to life is an infinitely greater value than the mother's right to an abortion. Some people also argue that if a baby's father abandons the unborn child and its mother, the woman should not have to carry the burden of having the child by herself. But this doesn't alter the fact that the baby is a person and has rights. The right to life supersedes the fact that having the child might be inconvenient or financially burdensome. Of course, society should continue to work toward making fathers fully accountable for the children they conceive and providing pregnant women with options such as pregnancy support and adoption.

Because abortion is a serious sin against the moral law, society has a responsibility to prevent this tragedy. We must work to change societal acceptance of abortion and to overturn the laws that make it legal. Providing material, emotional, and spiritual help for women facing a crisis pregnancy is a crucial way to help them avoid choosing

© dsc / iStockphoto.com

What are some ways that we can provide support for women facing difficult or unplanned pregnancies?

abortion. Encouraging people to see adoption as a loving alternative to abortion can help to save lives too. And greater respect for the gift of sexuality can go a long way in preventing the situation in the first place.

The Catholic Church stands as a strong voice for those who cannot speak for themselves. Parishes, dioceses, and conferences of bishops, for example, foster respect for life by communicating the gravity of abortion and reminding people about the beauty and purpose of the gift of human sexuality. And even though the canonical penalty for having an abortion is **excommunication**, the Church actively reaches out to women who have had abortions to assist in their healing and reconciliation. If someone you know has had an abortion, only to realize later what a great wrong it was, programs like Project Rachel can help them to find healing and can lead to reconciliation with God and the Church, especially through the Sacrament of Penance and Reconciliation.

Prenatal Testing, Genetic Engineering, and Stem Cell Research

Modern advances in genetics research raise new beginning-of-life moral issues. With the guidance of the Holy Spirit, the Magisterium teaches how to apply the moral law to these issues. One issue is prenatal testing, also called prenatal diagnosis, which is testing the embryo or fetus for diseases or birth defects while it is still in the womb. The Church teaches that prenatal testing is morally permissible as long as it does not harm the fetus and is done for the purposes of safeguarding and healing the developing baby in the womb or after birth. But prenatal testing for the purpose of deciding whether to abort the baby is morally wrong. The Church's 1987 document "Instruction on Respect for Human Life in Its Origin and on the Dignity of Procreation" (*"Donum Vitae"*) explains: "It is gravely opposed to the moral law when this is done with the thought of possibly inducing an abortion, depending upon the results: a diagnosis must not be the equivalent of a death sentence"[1] (*Catechism of the Catholic Church*, number 2274).

Genetic engineering is the manipulation of an ovum or fetus's genetic coding. This could be used to produce a "designer baby," that is, to create a person with predetermined qualities, such as a specific gender, hair color, and so on. Genetic engineering for this purpose is morally wrong because it falsely puts human beings in God's role of determining the uniqueness of every human person. However, certain forms of genetic engineering, called gene treatment

UNIT 4

---

excommunication ➤ A severe penalty that results from grave sin identified in Church law. The penalty is either imposed by a Church official or happens automatically as a result of the offense. An excommunicated person is not permitted to receive Holy Communion or other sacraments until the excommunication has been lifted.

or gene therapy, are used to prevent diseases or physical disabilities. These uses are morally permissible and encouraged as long as there is no significant possibility of harm to the fetus.

Stem cell research has been a controversial political issue. Stem cells are unique cells that have the potential to reproduce themselves as different human tissues and organs. Stem cell therapy is already used for bone marrow transplants and to treat leukemia. Scientists hope that it can be used to treat many other diseases and maybe even to grow new organs. However, one of the main sources for stem cells is fetal tissue, and some stem cell researchers want to use aborted embryos and fetuses for their research. Though stem cell research is not itself immoral, for obvious reasons the Church has condemned stem cell research that uses aborted embryos and fetuses and embryos created through in vitro fertilization. A good intention cannot justify an evil act.

These beginning-of-life issues are clear examples of an important moral principle: Just because human beings have the technology and knowledge to do certain actions doesn't mean those actions are morally right. Remember that we must defend the rights of human beings from conception through all the stages of life. For that reason, we must defend, care for, and heal embryos as we would any other human being. ✳

What arguments have you heard others make in support of keeping abortion legal? How would you answer those arguments?

UNIT 4

End-of-Life Issues

"When I die, I want to choose how I go out," Jeff told Katie. "I'm not going to be in terrible pain or brain dead with only tubes keeping me alive. I have a right to choose when and how I die."

"I used to think the same thing," replied Katie. "And then my great aunt Beth got bone cancer. It's terribly painful, but she never complained. She said the doctors did a good job of controlling the pain. Even near death, she put her complete trust in God's will for her. 'I'll die when God decides it is time to call me home' she told us. We were all grateful for every extra day we had to spend with her. She really inspired me and changed my mind about how I think about suffering and death."

We now turn our attention to moral issues connected with the end of our life on Earth. As we do this, we remember that death is only the end of life for our physical body. Because our compassionate and loving Father sent his only Son for our eternal salvation, our soul lives on, and we will know eternal life in resurrected bodies. In that life "he will wipe every tear from their eyes, and there shall be no more death or mourning, wailing or pain" (Revelation 21:4). If we focus on the promise of this ultimate destiny, we will more easily make the right moral choices—those rooted in respect for the human person and using scientific research that is carried out according to moral criteria—at the end of life.

Euthanasia

The end-of-life issue that we probably hear about most frequently in the news is **euthanasia**, also called mercy killing. Proponents of euthanasia make it an issue of human freedom, saying that people who have a serious physical disability or people who are terminally ill and in severe pain—or their families if the people are incapable of making their own decisions—have a right to choose to end their suffering. This sounds like a good and noble intention, but does it ever make euthanasia right?

Remember the three elements that determine the morality of any human action: the object, the intention, and the circumstances. If either the object or

---

euthanasia ➤ A direct action, or a deliberate lack of action, that causes the death of a person who is disabled, sick, or dying. Euthanasia is a violation of the Fifth Commandment against killing.

© Zetar Infinity / Shutterstock.com

By loving and caring for people who are approaching death, we can help them reach the natural end of their life with dignity.

UNIT 4

the intention is bad, the action is a sin. In the case of euthanasia, the object—that is, the act itself—is a serious violation of God's Law. It violates human dignity and the respect we owe to our Creator, the author of human life. Even the best of intentions—for example, sparing family members the anxiety of watching a loved one go through a long and painful disease or easing a sick person's suffering—do not justify euthanasia. The *Catechism* acknowledges that thinking of euthanasia as moral is an "error of judgment into which one can fall in good faith," but it stresses that this "does not change the nature of this murderous act, which must always be forbidden and excluded" (number 2277).

When discussing euthanasia, it is important to understand the Church's teaching on natural death. Rejecting euthanasia as a moral choice does not mean that we must prolong the life of a person who is near death through extraordinary measures. When a person has come to the end of life and is actively dying, it is legitimate to reject treatments that are considered extraordinary, such as heart pacemakers, special breathing apparatus, and medications that are used only to prolong life. Likewise, the use of painkillers is allowed even if their use risks bringing death more quickly because the direct intention is to relieve the dying person's suffering, not to cause death. The painkillers have a double effect, one that is intended and one that is not.

I DIDN'T KNOW THAT!

The Catholic Church of Our Lady of the Conception of the Capuchins has a crypt—an underground space—that has six rooms decorated with human bones! The bones come from vowed religious brothers of the Capuchin order (no new bones have been added since 1870). After the brothers died and were buried for many years, their bones were dug up and added to the rooms in the crypt. Though this may seem dark and disturbing to us today, it was used as a reminder that our time on Earth is short and that we will all eventually die. So, what will you do with your precious life while on this Earth? The crypt is open to the public, so if you are ever in Rome, you might want to visit!

Rejecting euthanasia is not a lack of compassion for people who are suffering and dying. To the contrary, it rejects the false solution offered by euthanasia in favor of the sometimes harder but morally right response: placing our trust in God until the natural end of our days on Earth. We do this with the help of God's grace and the compassionate support of others. Christians have an outstanding history of caring for people who are sick, disabled, and dying. Through hospice programs, medical advances in relieving pain, and spiritual support, we help one another make that transition from death into new and eternal life with God.

Suicide

Suicide is also a grave offense against the Fifth Commandment. Sacred though life is, for some people it can at times seem overwhelming, and they seek desperate solutions. But the answer is not **suicide**. By committing suicide, a person takes over a decision that is God's alone to make: when and how we die. It is always God's will that we preserve our own lives as well as the lives of others. Suicide is the ultimate rejection of God's gifts of hope and love.

---

suicide ➤ Deliberately taking one's own life. It is a serious violation of the Fifth Commandment, for it is God's will that we preserve our own lives.

It causes devastation to the surviving family and friends, and it also wounds the greater human family, which is prematurely deprived of the gift of the life of the person who commits suicide.

Although suicide is always wrong, the Church recognizes that serious mental illness or suffering can contribute to the decision a person makes to take their own life. If you know someone who is thinking about suicide, it is essential that you do what you can to get the person the medical or psychological help they need, even if it breaks a promise of confidentiality. If you know someone who has committed suicide, you should not presume that they are forever lost to the love of God or condemned to Hell. As the Church, we pray for those who have committed suicide, placing them in God's love and mercy.

In the darkest of times, remember to trust in God's love for you and persevere in seeking help. There are many people you can turn to for help and comfort, including family, friends, pastors, teachers, and counselors.

UNIT 4

The Death Penalty

The moral law, when applied to the death penalty, is complex and nuanced. The Old Law dictated the death penalty for a strikingly large number of offenses (see Exodus, chapter 21, or Leviticus, chapter 20, for some examples). But in the New Law, Christ teaches forgiveness for all sins and love for our enemies. Christ, however, was not applying the moral law to social policy. In the past, many states did not have the means to imprison someone for life. Because of this, the Church allowed that for the common good, states could use the death penalty to defend innocent people from criminals who were proven threats to society and could not be safely locked away.

Times change, however, and the prisons of modern societies keep dangerous criminals safely locked away for life if necessary. During his papacy, Pope Saint John Paul II updated the *Catechism of the Catholic Church* to state that moral reasons for using the death penalty "are very rare, if not practically non-existent"[2] (number 2267). Later, Pope Francis updated the *Catechism* again to state this even more strongly: "The Church teaches, in the light of the

Gospel, that 'the death penalty is inadmissible because it is an attack on the inviolability and dignity of the person,'[3] and she works with determination for its abolition worldwide" (number 2267). Following this teaching of our recent popes, the bishops in the United States and other countries have issued strong statements calling for an end to the death penalty.

Autopsies, Organ Donation, and Cremation

Although it may seem a little morbid, there are moral questions concerning the treatment of dead bodies. Even though the soul has departed the physical body, corpses should be treated with all due reverence out of respect for the person who has died. Burying the dead is one of the Corporal Works of Mercy.

The donation of a dead person's organs for either organ transplants or medical research is morally permissible and even encouraged. These donations must be free gifts, however, and the organs must not be taken without the permission of the person or his or her legal representatives. The donation of organs after death can be a lifesaving gift. Carefully consider this option and make whatever legal preparations are necessary to see that your wishes are carried out.

Similarly, autopsies are morally permissible if necessary, to determine the cause of death or for medical research. Again, the corpse should be treated with care and reverence. Finally, bodies can be either buried or cremated, as long as cremation doesn't signify a denial of faith in the resurrection of the body and the ashes are reverently laid to rest through interment or inurnment. Also, it is important that the Rite of Christian Burial be celebrated. ✳

HMMMMM. . . What are your thoughts about death, especially how you would like your earthly life to end?

UNIT 4

Article 40
Called to Be Peacemakers

War has been one of the greatest threats to the sacredness of life throughout the millennia of human existence. Whether fought with spears and clubs or with nuclear weapons, the loss and devastation to human life has been horrific. It is estimated that between forty and seventy million people died as a direct result of World War II. And it is not just soldiers who die; sometimes more civilians die due to the famines, diseases, and genocides that accompany the evil of war. It is almost impossible to imagine the devastation and death that would be caused by a worldwide war today using nuclear, chemical, and biological weapons.

This is why the beatitude "Blessed are the peacemakers, for they will be called children of God" is more important than ever. God calls people of faith to be ambassadors of peace and reconciliation and to tirelessly work for the creation of just societies. Injustice is the breeding ground for armed conflict; societies built on justice have little need to resort to war.

War is a horror caused by injustice and disregard for human dignity. We are permitted to engage in war only as an act of legitimate self-defense and when specific criteria are followed to ensure a minimum of violence and harm.

UNIT 4

In Scripture, we see a growing awareness that love is incompatible with violence. The early history of the Old Testament has many of stories of war; often these battles are waged in God's name or at his command. Yet even in the Old Testament, glimpses of insight show that God is not a God of violence but of nonviolent love. See Isaiah's prophecies of the Messiah (2:4) and of the suffering servant (52:13–53:12). When Jesus, the prince of peace, breaks into history, he tells us, "Love your enemies, and pray for those who persecute you" (Matthew 5:44). By his own example of accepting humiliation and suffering rather than resorting to violence to protect himself and destroy his enemies, Jesus sets a new standard. We, his disciples, are called to do everything possible to promote peace and convert hardened hearts through nonviolence and love, even sacrificing our own lives if necessary.

And this is what Christians have done throughout the last two thousand years. Starting with Saint Stephen, whose story is told in Acts of the Apostles 6:8–7:60, hundreds of thousands, maybe even millions, of Christians have given their lives as martyrs. The exact number is hard to determine. These Christians chose to die for their faith, loving their enemies instead of turning to violence.

Legitimate Self-Defense

Does the New Law of Christ demand that we never resort to violence to defend ourselves or others? No, it does not. Our love for others, including our enemies, is balanced by our love for ourselves. It is perfectly correct to insist on our own right to life. Thus, when threatened with bodily harm by an unjust aggressor, we have a legitimate right to defend ourselves and others. It can even be a grave duty when you are entrusted with the lives of others, such as someone serving as a police officer or soldier. But harming the aggressor must be a last resort. For example, if a burglar wants to steal from you, it is far better to allow the theft than to kill the thief. If we must fight to protect ourselves, our direct intention must always be to protect our own life, not to hurt or kill the aggressor. However, if a threat to our own life exists and we have no alternative except to kill or be killed, it would be permissible to kill in self-defense. This principle of **legitimate defense** of life is the basis for civil law and the right to self-defense.

Many Christians, past and present, have renounced violence completely, even in legitimate self-defense. Their extraordinary witness has inspired Christians and non-Christians to take more seriously God's call to be peacemakers.

---

legitimate defense ➤ The teaching that you can use the amount of force necessary to defend yourself or your nation from an aggressor if attacked.

War

Moral law requires that all citizens and all nations do everything they can to avoid war. Pope Paul VI, frustrated by modern warfare, affirmed this teaching when he called for "War no more; no more war!" in a speech to the United Nations assembly. Our reason and the Law of Love tell us that it makes more sense to resolve conflicts without using violence in our homes, our communities, and among nations.

The reality, however, is that war still happens, and countries have a moral right and responsibility to defend their citizens. The principles of legitimate self-defense are just as applicable for nations as they are for individuals. War must be a last resort whenever there is a conflict between nations. To help states determine when war is justified, the Church developed criteria that must be met for a war to be morally permissible. States that ignore or violate these criteria are committing crimes against humanity.

Criteria for a Just War	
Just cause	You must have a just cause—that is, you are using war to prevent or correct a grave, public evil.
Comparative justice	The good you achieve through war must far outweigh the resulting loss of life and disruption to society that will occur.
Legitimate authority	Only duly constituted public authority may use deadly force or wage war.
Probability of success	War may not be used in a futile cause or in a case where disproportionate measures—for example, using nuclear or biological weapons resulting in a massive loss of life—are required to achieve success.
Proportionality	The overall destruction expected from the use of force must be outweighed by the good to be achieved. In particular, the loss of civilian life must be avoided at all costs.
Last resort	Force may be used only after all peaceful alternatives have been seriously tried and exhausted.
If any of these conditions are not met, the war cannot be considered just, and believers should not participate in the fighting or support the war through other means.	

UNIT 4

Christians have differing perspectives on the use of the **just war** theory and participation in a just war. Public authorities have the right to call citizens into military service for legitimate self-defense. For some Christians, answering this call and fighting in a just war fulfills a moral duty. However, other Christians take Christ's command to love our enemies so seriously that they cannot in conscience fight in any war. The Church asks all governments not to force these conscientious objectors to serve as soldiers and to provide alternative ways for them to serve the needs of their country. Many Christians witness to nonviolent love by serving in the Peace Corps, participating in long-term Christian service programs, or even serving in the military as medics or chaplains.

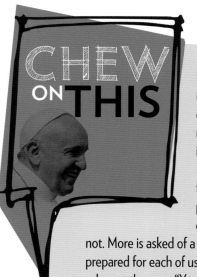

None of us can survive without mercy; we all need forgiveness. Therefore, if to kill means to destroy, terminate, eliminate someone, then not to kill would mean to care for, appreciate, include. And also forgive.

No one can delude him or herself: "I am fine because I do nothing wrong." A mineral or plant has this type of existence, however, man does not. A person—man or woman—does not. More is asked of a man or woman. There is good to be done, prepared for each of us, each his or her own, which makes us ourselves at the core. "You shall not kill" is an appeal to love and mercy; it is a call to live according to the Lord Jesus, who gave his life for us and rose for us. Once, here in the Square, we all repeated together a Saint's expression about this. Perhaps it will help us: "It is good to do no wrong, but it is wrong to do no good." (Pope Francis, "General Audience," October 17, 2018)

---

just war ➤ War involves many evils, no matter the circumstances. A war is only just and permissible when it meets strict criteria in protecting citizens from an unjust aggressor.

The Gospel calls all Christians to be peacemakers. How can you promote peace and support nonviolent conflict resolution in your school and community?

Because one of the criteria for a just war is to avoid harm to noncombatants, many people question whether a just war is possible in modern times. The use of nuclear, biological, and chemical weapons kills soldiers and civilians alike. After war is over, mines and biological contaminants are left behind, infecting, injuring, and killing innocent people, which are most often children. Even without a war, the world's buildup of weapons causes more harm than good. The enormous sums of money spent creating weapons keep us from using those resources to provide basic human rights to the neediest of people. Popes since Paul VI have consistently called for an end to the race to build and stockpile new and more dangerous kinds of weapons. ✳

UNIT 4

HMMMMM... Why is a just society important for preventing wars and other acts of violence?

Article 41
Personal Health

How's your health? Taking care of your health is a moral issue related to the Fifth Commandment, "You shall not kill." This commandment also requires that we not cause harm to ourselves. Here's a short questionnaire to assess how you are doing in this area:

- Do you eat a healthy diet, with lots of fruit and vegetables, and avoid too much fat, sugar, and salt?
- Do you get regular exercise, at least 30 minutes or more a day?
- Do you maintain a healthy weight (being too underweight is just as unhealthy as being too overweight)?
- Do you get enough sleep (at least 8–10 hours a night are needed for most teens)?
- Are you tobacco, alcohol, and drug free?
- Are you a safe driver, obeying speed laws and never talking on your phone or texting while driving?

© Stormcab / iStockphoto.com

Bigger is not always better when it comes to food. What are some other messages in our society that work against maintaining a healthy lifestyle?

If you can honestly answer yes to all of these questions, congratulations! If you have to answer no to two or more, you probably need to take better care of your health, one of the most important gifts God has given you.

Moral Issues Regarding Health

You will not find any explicit revelations in Scripture or Tradition telling you to exercise daily or giving the requirements for a healthy diet. What you will find are teachings about the sacredness of our bodies and the importance of treating our bodies reverently. Psalm 139 praises God for the wonder of our bodies:

UNIT 4

You formed my inmost being;
>   you knit me in my mother's womb.
I praise you, because I am wonderfully made;
>   wonderful are your works!

(Verses 13–14)

The wonderful works the psalmist is talking about are all of us. Saint Paul reinforces the importance of our bodies when he tells the Corinthians, "Do you not know that your body is a temple of the holy Spirit within you, whom you have from God, and that you are not your own?" (1 Corinthians 6:19). And the *Catechism* instructs us: "Life and physical health are precious gifts entrusted to us by God. We must take reasonable care of them, taking into account the needs of others and the common good" (number 2288).

Our motive or intention for taking care of ourselves is important. Some people's primary motive for living a healthy lifestyle is to look attractive. But the primary reason to live a healthy lifestyle is to take good care of the bodies and minds God has given to us. When our focus for eating a healthy diet is simply to look good, it can easily lead to a skewed perspective and even result in eating disorders like bulimia and anorexia. Remember, having the correct intention for acting morally is as important as the act itself.

Behaviors that directly put our health in danger, such as the abusive and illegal use of alcohol, tobacco, or drugs, are a particularly serious moral concern. These behaviors are a temptation many people face, but they are a particularly dangerous temptation for teens. A young person's maturing body and mind is particularly at risk with the use of these substances, making a young person more vulnerable to addiction and poor decision-making. Teens using alcohol and drugs are more likely to be victims of violence, to be sexually active, to have lower grades, and to be victims in car accidents. The best moral decision you can make is to avoid alcohol and drugs completely.

UNIT 4

© Rob Marmion / Shutterstock.com

Living a healthy lifestyle is a spiritual discipline. It requires personal commitment and ongoing discipline, but the benefits to your body, mind, and spirit are well worth it.

A friend you have known for years is living an unhealthy lifestyle. She is only getting three or four hours of sleep a night. She is eating lots of junk food and drinking energy drinks to stay awake. She says she hates exercising. You have noticed that she seems more depressed and anxious lately. When you talk to her, she says she would like to change her life but doesn't know how. How might you help your friend take better care of herself? How can you set an example of taking good care of yourself through a healthy lifestyle?

The Challenge of a Healthy Lifestyle

We all know the importance of caring for our health by eating nutritious foods, leading physically active lifestyles, avoiding health hazards such as cigarettes and alcohol and other drugs, and making moral choices regarding sexuality. Yet it can be a challenge to always choose what is moral and healthy. Many factors in our culture contribute to the challenge of maintaining a healthy lifestyle. Here are a few of those factors:

- We are bombarded with ads for fast food, which is typically high in fat, sugar, and salt.
- Teens are often affirmed and encouraged to fill up their lives with so many activities that their sleep time is affected.
- Some movies and TV shows glamorize lifestyles filled with alcohol, drugs, and dangerous driving, making these unhealthy practices seem attractive.
- The explosion of electronic-based entertainment—television, computers, video games, cell phones, movies—discourages more physically active forms of entertainment.
- We live in a culture that expects instant results, but it takes time for new, healthy habits to show their effects. When people do not see results right away, they tend to go back to their old habits.

UNIT 4

These factors are powerful but do not have to control our choices. Living a healthy lifestyle is a spiritual discipline. Scientific studies have shown a connection between body and mind; for example, people with healthy lifestyles have better cognitive (brain) functioning. Is there a similar connection between a healthy body and a healthy soul? This has turned out to be a difficult question to answer because there is no scientific way to measure the health of a person's soul. So researchers look to external signs that indicate people's religiosity, things like whether they attend religious services and whether they pray or meditate. Researchers have found some interesting correlations, including these:

- Hospitalized people who never attend church have an average stay of three times longer than people who attend regularly.
- Elderly people who never attend church have a stroke rate double that of people who attend regularly.
- In one national study, people who scored high on religious indicators had a 40 percent lower death rate from heart disease and cancer.

These studies tend to be controversial and by themselves cannot prove a direct correlation between people's faith and how physically healthy they are. But they do tend to support a central truth of our faith: Our body and soul are bound together in this life to form a unique human person. It only makes sense that what is good for one is probably good for the other.

If you are having difficulty living a healthy lifestyle, you can start by asking God in prayer to give you the desire to change and to give you the strength you need to persevere. Ask family and friends to support you; we are more able to keep our commitments when we work at these commitments with other people. Finally, if you find yourself slipping back into unhealthy habits, don't give up. You are building a lifestyle for a lifetime, and God will be with you with each new commitment. ✻

UNIT 4

HMMMMM. . . What is the biggest challenge you face in living a healthy lifestyle?

1. Why is human life qualitatively different from the lives of all other creatures?

2. How does Jesus' teaching on the sanctity of human life go beyond just condemning murder?

3. Give two reasons used to justify abortions. Then state the Church's arguments against them.

4. When is genetic engineering morally permissible?

5. Why is euthanasia a serious offense against the Fifth Commandment?

6. Why is suicide wrong?

7. Why are Christians called to be peacemakers?

8. Give four criteria that are necessary for a just war.

9. Why do we have a moral obligation to take care of our physical health?

10. What are some of the challenges people face in maintaining a healthy lifestyle?

Seamless Garment of Life

Protecting the Sanctity of Life
from Conception to Natural Death

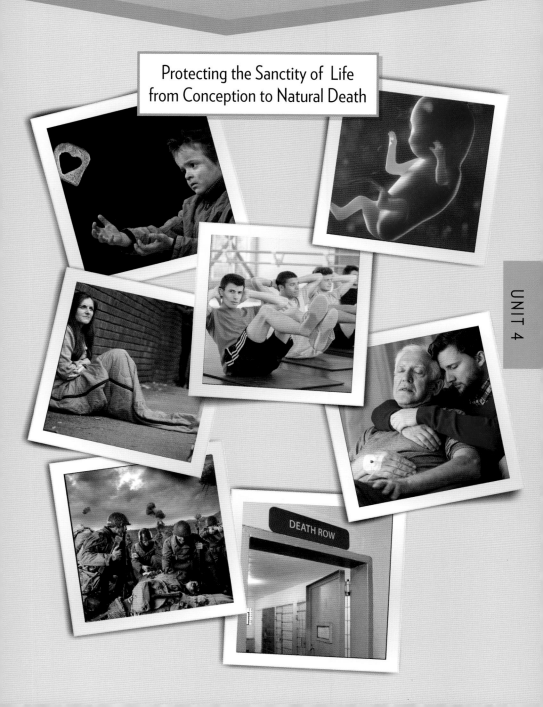

UNIT 4

CHAPTER 11
The Sixth and Ninth Commandments: Respecting Sexuality

WHY IS SEX OKAY IN MARRIAGE ONLY?

SNAPSHOT

Article 42

Sexuality: Sharing in God's Life-Giving Power

Perhaps you have heard these thoughts or have even had them yourself: Why does the Church make such a big deal about sex? Aren't there more important things to be concerned about going on in the world? And who is the Church to tell us how to behave sexually? It's filled with unmarried men who take vows of celibacy, and some of them have even acted inappropriately themselves.

These are all great questions. As you have been learning about in this book, the Church *is* concerned about all that is going on in the world, including issues related to sexuality. Our sexuality is a big deal; it is a wonderful gift, giving human beings the power to bring new life into the world. It also underlies our capacity to enter into loving and caring relationships and calls us to form bonds of friendship with others. For those called to marriage, it provides the power to procreate and bring new life into the world.

When sexuality is used incorrectly, it has great power to harm people and relationships. Two commandments forbid its misuse: the Sixth Commandment, "You shall not commit adultery," and the Ninth Commandment, "You shall not covet your neighbor's wife." These commandments call us to purity of heart by cultivating the virtue of chastity in our lives. By mastering our sexual passions and avoiding sexual sin, we will know the happiness that comes from being in relationships of true love and faithfulness.

UNIT 4

TAKE IT TO GOD

Dear Jesus,
I know that sex and our sexuality are
    a wonderful and powerful gift from you.
It is also a really challenging gift at times.
So many people treat it like it's no big deal,
    but it is a big deal.
Help me to stay chaste,
    to keep my heart pure
    and to focus on true purposes of sexuality.
With your help, I know I will be strengthened
    to deal with all challenges that may come my way.
Amen.

Theology of the Body

In a series of 129 general addresses delivered from September 1979 to November 1984, Pope Saint John Paul II gave the world a wonderful gift: his teaching on sexuality, marriage, and the family. He called this teaching the "theology of the body" because as he stated in one of his addresses: "The body, and it alone, is capable of making visible what is invisible: the spiritual and divine. It was created to transfer into the visible reality of the world the mystery hidden since time immemorial in God, and thus be a sign of it" (February 20, 1980).

Supporting his teaching with truths drawn from Scripture and Tradition, Pope Saint John Paul II shows how our bodies reveal to us the nature of God. He taught that our bodies have a **nuptial** and a **generative** meaning—that is, they reveal that human beings are called to participate in God's love and life. It is precisely with and through our bodies and our sexuality that we participate in God's plan of salvation. This article draws on Saint John Paul II's theology of the body to understand the purpose of the gift of sexuality.

The Image of God

Our sexuality is a sign of God's own nature. This isn't to say that God is a male or female creature like us. But consider the obvious purpose of the two sexes. Men and women are naturally drawn into relationship with each other—a relationship whose deepest expression is the intimate love between a husband and wife. This visible reality—expressed as a physical, emotional, and spiritual union—reveals to us an invisible reality, the nature of God himself. The marital union of man and woman —their total giving of themselves to each other—is an image of the communion of the Father, Son,

© Adam Jan Figel / Shutterstock.com

This famous icon depicts the Three Persons of the Trinity as angelic beings. God the Father is on the left, Jesus Christ in the center, and the Holy Spirit on the right. Notice how their heads are inclined toward each other as a sign of respect and communion.

UNIT 4

---

nuptial ➤ Something related to marriage or a marriage ceremony.

generative ➤ As a theological term, something related to the power of producing new life.

and Holy Spirit, the primary communion of love that all other earthly communions share in. This truth is revealed in the first biblical account of Creation:

> God created mankind in his image;
>> in the image of God he created them;
>
> male and female he created them.
>
> (Genesis 1:27)

Notice the parallelism in this poetic verse. "God created mankind in his image" is the same as "male and female he created them." The two genders, male and female, are necessary parts of being made in God's image. Men and women are both necessary in God's plan, and men and women are both equal in dignity in his sight. He created men and women with the need to be in relationship with each other. Why? God wanted to make it clear that we are not meant to be alone, that we are created to be in loving communion with one another and also with the Holy Trinity.

The second biblical account of Creation emphasizes this truth. In this account, the first man is lonely; he is meant to be in relationship with others, but the animals are not his true companions. So God says: "It is not good for the man to be alone. I will make a helper suited to him" (Genesis 2:18). He makes a woman to be the man's partner, a true soul mate made from the man's own rib, equal to the man but unique in her own right.

UNIT 4

Man and woman were created to be partners and soul mates. How do you see this demonstrated in the married people you know?

The fact that men and women were made to be in relationship with each other does not mean that God calls every person to marriage. Some people are called by God to remain unmarried for the sake of the Kingdom of God (see Jesus' words in Matthew 19:10–12). But whether married or unmarried, all people benefit from healthy relationships with people of the opposite sex. Priests affirm the importance that good friendships with women play in their lives. Religious sisters will say the same about male friends. The important role that sexuality plays in our lives does not require marriage or the physical act of having sex.

Participating in God's Love and Life

The Sacrament of Matrimony and the total self-giving of husband and wife to each other is not just an image of the divine communion of the Holy Trinity; it is also a call to share in God's love and his life-giving power. The theology of the body calls this the nuptial and the generative meanings of the body.

When Pope Saint John Paul II says that our bodies have a nuptial meaning, he is saying that the gift of sexuality orients men and women to give themselves completely, body and soul, to each other in marriage, to "become one body" (Genesis 2:24). In marriage, a man and a woman commit to loving each other completely and without conditions—in essence to love each other as God loves. Whether we are married or not, however, it is right to say that our sexuality is a call to share God's love with others. Through our physical bodies, we share God's love with others through our words, our actions, and our touch.

© Nattakorn_Maneerat / Shutterstock.com

The theology of the body teaches us that our sexuality draws us into loving communion with each other and calls us to support the gift of life.

UNIT 4

When Pope Saint John Paul II says that our bodies have a generative meaning, he is saying that the gift of sexuality is also oriented toward bringing new life into the world. God tells the first man and woman, "Be fertile and multiply; fill the earth and subdue it" (Genesis 1:28). God is the author of all life, but he shares the ability to bring new life into the world with his creatures. In marriage, a man and a woman participate in God's life-giving power by bringing children into the world. Whether or not God calls us to have children of our own, the gift of sexuality calls us to support the gift of life. We can do this by loving and caring for all the children God brings into our lives. And just as important, we can help others to accept God's invitation to eternal life by sharing the Gospel message with them.

To summarize, our sexuality and sexual identity as male or female is a great and wonderful gift, one we must gratefully and happily embrace. Both men and women reflect the image of God, especially when we are in loving relationships with other people. Our sexuality calls us to share God's love with others. It also calls us to share in his life-giving power, whether it is by bringing children into the world or by helping others answer our heavenly Father's invitation to know the fullness of life that comes through faith in his Son, Jesus Christ. ✳

UNIT 4

HMMMMM. . . How would you explain to someone why sexuality is about more than just having sex?

Article 43

Chastity: The Key to Sexual Integrity

"What do you think about the discussion of chastity that we're scheduled to have in religion class tomorrow? Sabina asked her friend Lucinda. "I mean, that's just for uptight, unhappy people, right?"

"Right," replied Lucinda, "because you are so not chaste."

"Wait, what are you talking about?" Sabina asked.

"Well, you are always wearing revealing clothes and making comments about guys all the time on social media," teased Lucinda.

"Wait? What? I don't do that," Sabina replied, getting a little annoyed by her friend. Just then, a smile crept across Sabina's face. "I see what you you're doing. You're actually showing me that I *am* already chaste."

Lucinda smiled, "Yes, I'm just teasing to make a point. Chastity is about respecting yourself and respecting others, and you already do that. And you seem pretty happy!"

When you hear the word **chastity**, what image comes to your mind? Some people think of chastity as something practiced by uptight, unhappy individuals who are afraid of their sexuality. But this is not true chastity. Chaste people deeply appreciate the gift of their sexuality, so they choose to resist temptations to use that gift in ways that demean or hurt themselves or others. And they are often quite serene and happy people because they are using God's gift for the purposes he intended, and they do not have to worry about the harm to body and soul that sexual sin leaves in its wake.

No matter our vocation, we are called to be chaste. What does chastity look like for a priest? a married couple? a consecrated religious? a single person?

chastity ➤ The moral virtue by which people are able to successfully and healthfully integrate their sexuality into their total person, leading to an inner union of body and spirit: recognized as one of the fruits of the Holy Spirit.

UNIT 4

Both the Sixth and Ninth Commandments, "You shall not commit adultery" and "You shall not covet your neighbor's wife," call all people to live chaste lives. Yes, even married people must practice chastity. This article considers the general vocation to chastity that all people are called to.

Integration and Self-Control

Chastity is the moral virtue of living a life of sexual integrity. Integrity comes from the root word *integer*, meaning "whole." To be a person of integrity means that nothing divides you; your inner life and your outer life are united. Thus, a chaste person's thoughts, words, and actions all reflect God's purpose for the gift of sexuality. For example, a chaste man will not flatter a woman who is not his wife with the secret intention of seducing her into having sex with him. A chaste woman will not flirt with a man who is not her husband in

CATHOLICS **MAKING** A **DIFFERENCE**

Saint Maria Goretti (1890–1902) is the patron saint of chastity and purity. Saint Maria was only twelve years old when she died, fatally wounded while fending off a rapist. She was born in Italy to a peasant family that was too poor to send their children to school. After her father's death, she assumed responsibility for keeping house, while her mother and siblings worked in the fields. One day an eighteen-year-old neighbor, Alessandro, made sexual advances. When Maria resisted the attempted rape, the young man stabbed her numerous times. She died at the hospital the next day. As she lay dying in her bed, she forgave Alessandro "for the love of Jesus." After serving twenty-seven years in prison, Alessandro went to Maria's mother and begged for forgiveness. And at Maria's canonization in 1950, Alessandro was among the crowd of 250,000 who gathered to celebrate in Saint Peter's Square. We celebrate Maria for her heroic commitment to the value of chastity and for her forgiveness of Alessandro. This is not meant to imply that women who are violently attacked should resist their attackers until the point of death. But Maria's commitment to defending Christian values serves as an inspiration for courageously following Christ in our lives.

UNIT 4

any way that suggests she is sexually interested in him. Chaste men and women will not dress in ways that are intended to provoke sexual arousal in others. All these actions cause sexual disintegration and can open the doors to sexual sin.

Jesus is our model for living a chaste life. In the Sermon on the Mount, he teaches us this: "You have heard that it was said, 'You shall not commit adultery.' But I say to you, everyone who looks at a woman with lust has already committed adultery with her in his heart" (Matthew 5:27–28). Jesus faithfully followed this teaching on chastity in his own life. The Gospels give witness that he lived a life of sexual integrity. He had deep and loving relationships with both men and women, yet never once did he commit a sexual sin or even hold lust for another person in his heart.

God gives us the help we need to live chaste lives; the Holy Spirit enables us to follow Christ's example through the grace of Baptism. But this takes practice and self-control. We live in a sex-obsessed culture that sends us dozens of messages every day that tell us it is okay to act on our sexual impulses. People of all ages experience pressure to be sexually active outside of marriage, and this pressure can be intense for young adults because of their changing bodies and developing sexuality. To resist these temptations, we must be vigilant in mastering our sexual passions. As any honest adult will tell you, this is a lifelong task, so don't be fooled into thinking that once you are past your teenage years, you will not have any more sexual temptations to face!

Ten Ways to Practice Chastity
1. Pray. Thank God for the gift of sexuality, and ask for the strength to live a life of chastity.
2. Seek out a parent or another trusted adult you can talk to when you have questions about sexuality.
3. Focus on making friends—not romances—with people of the opposite sex.
4. Turn a critical eye toward media messages that use sex to sell products.
5. Remind yourself that your value does not depend on whether and how much you date.
6. Stay away from drugs and alcohol. Impaired judgment on a date can lead to trouble.
7. If you are on a date and your boyfriend or girlfriend starts getting too intimate, tell them to STOP in clear and certain terms.
8. If you have a boyfriend or a girlfriend, communicate openly and set boundaries about touching.
9. Remember that more teenagers are not having sex than are having sex.
10. Make a vow—a nonnegotiable commitment—to avoid intimate sexual activity until you get married.

Purity of Heart

Jesus proclaims in the sixth beatitude, "Blessed are the clean of heart, for they will see God." In this beatitude, he teaches that living the virtue of chastity requires maintaining purity of heart through the practice of modesty. The *Catechism of the Catholic Church (CCC)* refers to the heart as the seat of moral personality. Our heart "enables us to see *according to* God; . . . [Purity of heart] lets us perceive the human body—ours and our neighbor's—as a temple of the Holy Spirit, a manifestation of divine beauty" (number 2519). Having a pure heart is the opposite of having a lustful heart.

Businesses often use human sexuality for advertising purposes in subtle and sometimes not-so-subtle ways. Why does "sex sell"?

The Temple in Jerusalem, described in the Old Testament, was a magnificent structure, but its most sacred room was deep within. Only one person, the high priest, could enter the Holy of Holies—the innermost sacred room. He could do this only after going through ritual purification. Our bodies are magnificent temples also, temples of the Holy Spirit. We too must protect our sacred inner space, our heart, from contamination by impure influences.

The virtue of modesty is one special way we protect our sacred, intimate center. We don't tell just anybody our most private secrets; we should not let just anybody see or touch our sacred places. Modesty requires patience in responding to our sexual desires. It requires that we maintain decency in our words and actions toward others. It requires discretion in what we wear, what we listen to, and what we watch so that we do not unnecessarily arouse our own sexual desires or the sexual desires of other people. Chastity and modesty are both virtues related to the Cardinal Virtue of **temperance**, meaning they are virtues through which we curb our lust to maintain the right balance in using God's gifts.

The Rewards of Avoiding Sin

The best way to avoid sin, especially sexual sin, is to be prepared! Make a plan on how you will respond to sexual situations. For example, you might want to use your parents for an excuse. "My mom says I cannot have guests over in a room with the door shut," or "My dad will be furious if I'm not home on time" have worked for many teens. If you wait until temptation presents itself, you are likely to find yourself at a loss for the right words.

God's Word in Sacred Scripture can be a big help in forming our conscience in order to resist temptation. Let's consider some teachings from the First Letter of John. Chapter 2 starts with this encouragement: "My children, I am writing this to you so that you may not commit sin. But if anyone does sin, we have an Advocate with the Father, Jesus Christ the righteous one" (verse 1). The chapter goes on to give this warning:

> Do not love the world or the things of the world. If anyone loves the world, the love of the Father is not in him. For all that is in the world, sensual lust, enticement for the eyes, and a pretentious life, is not from the Father but is from the world. Yet the world and its enticement are passing away. But whoever does the will of God remains forever. (Verses 15–17)

Even though he is writing about sin, the author is positive and hopeful. Several times he reminds the reader that if we keep Christ's commandments we will conquer evil and live in communion with the Holy Trinity. Here is one example:

temperance ➤ The Cardinal Virtue by which one moderates his or her appetites and passions to achieve balance in the use of created goods.

> Let what you heard from the beginning remain in you. If what you heard
> from the beginning remains in you, then you will remain in the Son and in the
> Father. And this is the promise that he made us: eternal life. (Verses 24–25)

This Scripture passage and many others remind us that the road to chaste living may seem difficult at times, but it is well worth the effort. The kind of discipline required for sexual abstinence before marriage is good practice for the lifelong commitment you will make in whatever vocation God calls you to. Rather than seeing chastity as a burden, consider the freedom it gives: freedom from worry about pregnancy, freedom from disease, and freedom from the emotional wounds that result from sexual sin. Chastity provides the freedom to be sexually healthy and whole, according to God's design. ✳

 **HMMMMM...** What are the challenges that teens face today in living a chaste life?

UNIT 4

Article 44

Sins against Chastity

The Ninth Commandment, "You shall not covet your neighbor's wife," warns us against the dangers of lust and carnal **concupiscence**. Concupiscence is any desire for pleasure or sensual experience that is against reason and the moral law. Concupiscence is one of the consequences of Original Sin, and it makes us more inclined to give in to sinful temptations. Carnal concupiscence is the desire for sexual experiences that are morally wrong. One of the effects of carnal concupiscence is that some people think that sex and love are basically the same thing. That's what someone means when they think or say, "If you really loved me, you'd have sex with me." But this is only a rationalization. Sex and love only go together in the committed relationship of sacramental marriage. In fact, a true sign of someone's love for you is that they would wait to save sex until the two of you are married.

The Sixth and Ninth Commandments teach that sexual intercourse is only morally permissible between a husband and wife. This is because our bodies themselves are visible signs that our sexuality is oriented toward sharing in God's love and in his power of creating life. Sexual intercourse is the ultimate physical expression of our sexuality, the fullest expression of the love that can bring new life into the world. The power of love shared and the potential for new life that can result from sexual intercourse require the commitment of marriage. Because of this, any form of intimate sexual activity outside of marriage is a sin against chastity.

Fornication and Prostitution

The most direct sin against chastity is **fornication**. *Fornication* is a biblical term that refers to having sexual intercourse outside of marriage. This includes living together before marriage. People you know, even friends, may believe that casual sex is no big deal. But it is a serious moral wrong. The physical consequences of fornication can include unwanted pregnancies and sexually transmitted diseases. There are also emotional consequences; premarital sex often leads to broken hearts and feelings of shame and betrayal. Finally, forni-

UNIT 4

cation has serious spiritual consequences. Deep in our conscience we know that sex outside of marriage is wrong, so it leads us to separation and alienation from God. Simply put, fornication leaves people wounded in body and spirit.

Gossip and the media may cause you to think that everybody is sexually active, but the reality is that the majority of teenagers are not having sex. And the number of sexually active teens has been declining over the last thirty years. Perhaps more importantly, studies show that the majority of teens who have had sex say they wish they had waited.

Prostitution, another form of fornication, is a serious societal sin. The prostitute and the person paying for the sex are treating the prostitute's body as a thing to be used rather than as a temple of the Holy Spirit. The evil of prostitution is even greater when it involves children or teens, or when people are forced or sold into prostitution.

Why are pornography and prostitution serious sins against the Sixth and Ninth Commandments? What do these sins imply about the dignity and value of a person and his or her body?

UNIT 4

Masturbation and Pornography

Masturbation, genital activity alone or with another person that does not result in sexual intercourse, is also a sin against chastity. Masturbation is all about self-pleasure without sharing life or real love. So are other forms of genital sexual activity that stop short of sexual intercourse, such as oral sex. They are forms of exploitation and are not appropriate sexual expressions for unmarried people. Like fornication, these activities can also result in disease and emotional wounds that can prevent true intimacy in future relationships.

prostitution ➤ The act of providing sexual services in exchange for money, drugs, or other goods. It is a serious social evil and is a sin against the Sixth Commandment.

masturbation ➤ Self-manipulation of one's sexual organs for the purpose of erotic pleasure or to achieve orgasm. It is a sin because the act cannot result in the creation of new life and because God created sexuality not for self-gratification but to unify a husband and wife in marriage.

© Stenko Vlad / Shutterstock.com

An offense against the Sixth and Ninth Commandments that is growing in our time is **pornography**. The internet has made this evil more accessible to people of all ages. Pornography is dangerous because it violates human dignity. It makes the gift of sexuality an object to be exploited and abused. Even though the models and actors may agree to participate in the creation of pornography, there is nothing right and so many things wrong with viewing pornographic images. The chemistry in people's brains makes them particularly susceptible to the temptation of pornography and can make viewing pornography very addictive. The use of pornography leads to a serious lack of reverence for the gift of sexuality and in some cases has been linked to abusive and even violent sexual acts, especially toward women.

Homosexuality

Homosexuality is an especially challenging sexual issue. For reasons that are still unclear, some people experience a strong sexual attraction toward persons of the same sex. For most of these individuals, this same-sex attraction is deep seated and not freely chosen. Although today there is generally a greater social

---

pornography ➤ A written description or visual portrayal of a person or action that is created or viewed with the intention of stimulating sexual feelings. Creating or using pornography is a sin against the Sixth and Ninth Commandments.

MAKE IT SO

Your friend Rich has been dating Caitlin for a couple of months. They've been spending more and more time together and really seem to get along. One night Rich texts you and says, "Guess what? Caitlin is going to spend the night!" You text back, "That's cool. I'm surprised her parents are okay with that." Rich texts back, "Oh, they think my parents are going to be home and supervising, but they're gone for the weekend!" After a couple of minutes you respond, "Dude, this doesn't seem like you. You sure about this?" "No worries," texts Rich. "Nothing is going to happen that we cannot handle." Actually, you think Rich is in for more than he can handle. How do you respond to help him and Caitlin make a good choice for chastity? How will you maintain your chastity when faced with similar choices?

acceptance of people with a same-sex attraction, this has not always been true; these men and women have been ridiculed, ostracized, and even attacked and killed. The Catholic Church affirms that people who experience exclusive or predominant sexual attraction towards people of the same sex are children of God and must be treated with respect, compassion, and sensitivity. It is a grave moral offense to discriminate, act violently toward, make jokes about, or look down on them.

Although the Church is clear about accepting people with same-sex attraction as part of the Body of Christ, homosexual acts remain grave sins against chastity. Those with same-sex attraction are called to live chaste lives, a moral virtue that all people are called to live. An active prayer life and support from others within the faith community can help them to embrace the virtue of chastity through deepening friendships that are a sign of Christian love. ✳

UNIT 4

HMMMMM. . . What would be your list of reasons to not have sex before marriage?

Article 45

The Christian Vision of Marriage and Sexuality

Who has shaped your view of marriage? This is an important question to think about. For most people, it is their parents. If you come from a family where your parents have been loving, joyful, and faithful with each other, you most likely have a pretty positive view of married life. But for many of you studying this course, the opposite may be true. Your parents may be distant from each other, perhaps even divorced, and their relationship may be angry and bitter. It would be no surprise if your view of married life is a bit negative. Whichever might be true for you, it is important to understand God's beautiful and exciting purpose for marriage—and the role of sexuality in that purpose—and make that our goal if marriage is our vocation.

In the Sacrament of Matrimony, a husband and wife make sacred vows to love and cherish each other until the end of their lives. This sacrament calls a husband and wife to share God's love with each other, with their children, and with the wider community. The faithful love of couples who have been married for many years is a beautiful and inspiring witness to the love of God.

The Purpose of Marital Sex

Recall that in his teaching on the theology of the body, Pope Saint John Paul II says that our sexuality has both a nuptial and a generative meaning. These are sometimes also called the "unitive" and "procreative" ends of sexual intercourse. The nuptial meaning calls wives and husbands into intimate, loving communion; they are called to completely share themselves with each other, with total openness and honesty. Sexual intercourse is the most intense physical expression of that communion; it is literally two bodies joined together as one, bringing joy and pleasure to their union. But this physical union is also a visible sign of the emotional and spiritual union that is taking place.

The nakedness that a husband and wife share during sexual intercourse is a visible sign of the nakedness of mind and heart that they share. In strong marriages, there are no secrets; husbands and wives are spiritually one in body, mind, and heart. This unity helps them to grow in their love for each other, their love for God, their love for their children, and their love for their neighbors. Through the grace of the Sacrament of Matrimony, the Holy Spirit empowers them to be faithful and committed in their love so that they can be

Sex within marriage is a wonderful gift, creating greater intimacy and new life.

the very image of the love of Jesus Christ. The Letter to the Ephesians gives a biblical example of this call: "Husbands, love your wives, even as Christ loved the church" (5:25, see 5:21–33 for the complete teaching).

The committed love between a wife and husband is meant to be faithful and lifelong, just as Christ's love for the Church is faithful until the end of time. Adultery, polygamy, and divorce have no place in God's plan for married love. Adultery and polygamy harm the unity of marriage, and divorce separates what God has joined together. In the Sermon on the Mount, Christ emphasizes the permanence of marriage:

> It was also said, "Whoever divorces his wife must give her a bill of divorce."
> But I say to you, whoever divorces his wife (unless the marriage is unlawful)
> causes her to commit adultery, and whoever marries a divorced woman
> commits adultery. (Matthew 5:31-32, see also 19:3-9)

God intends marriage to be a faithful, lifelong, loving union, a union that is also open to the possibility of bringing new life into the world. Through the Sacrament of Matrimony, Christian spouses receive a special grace from Christ that enables them to perfect their love, strengthen their indissoluble unity, and welcome and educate children that may result from their union.

The Purpose of Marriage Annulments

You might be asking yourself, "If divorce is against God's plan for marriage, why does the Church allow **annulments**?" This is a good question, so keep this key principle in mind: Annulment and divorce are not the same thing. When a couple divorces, the marriage is dissolved in the eyes of the state but not the Church. Divorced people remain full members of the Church but are not permitted to remarry as long as their original spouse is alive. Remember Jesus' words: "But I say to you, whoever divorces his wife (unless the marriage is unlawful) causes her to commit adultery, and whoever marries a divorced woman commits adultery" (Matthew 5:32).

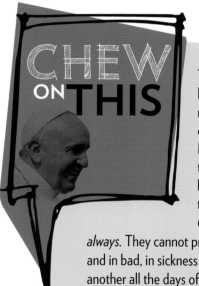

The call to married life . . . requires a heartfelt discernment of the quality of the relationship and a period of engagement to confirm it. To approach the Sacrament of Marriage, the engaged couple must establish the certainty that the hand of God is in their bond and that he precedes and accompanies them and will enable them to say: *With the Grace of Christ I promise to be faithful to you always.* They cannot promise each other fidelity "in good times and in bad, in sickness and in health," and to love and honor one another all the days of their lives, solely on the basis of good will or of the hope that it "will work out." They need to ground themselves on the solid terrain of God's faithful Love. And this is why, before receiving the Sacrament of Matrimony, there should be a careful preparation . . . because with love one's entire life is at stake, and one does not kid around with love. (Pope Francis, "General Audience," October 24, 2018)

annulment ➤ The declaration by the Church that a marriage is null and void, that is, it never existed as a sacramental union. Catholics who divorce must have the marriage declared null by the Church to be free to marry once again in the Church.

UNIT 4

There is an exception to this, however. In some cases, the married couple never truly achieves a sacramental or covenantal bond, recognized as a true union in the eyes of God. Church officials can declare such marriages null, and the two former spouses are free to marry again. This declaration is called an annulment. Receiving an annulment is not saying that a civil marriage (recognized by the state) never existed. An annulled marriage means that even though the couple was joined in a civil marriage, it was never a sacramental marriage.

Those who remarry without having an earlier marriage declared null are excluded from receiving Holy Communion but are not separated from the Church. "They should be encouraged to listen to the Word of God, to attend the Sacrifice of the Mass, to persevere in prayer, to contribute to works of charity and to community efforts for justice, to bring up their children in the Christian faith, to cultivate the spirit and practice of penance and thus implore, day by day, God's grace"[1] (*CCC*, number 1651).

The Openness to Life

The generative meaning of the gift of sexuality calls husbands and wives to be open to new life. Just as God's love brings all created things into existence, the love of a husband and wife can bring new human life into existence. A husband and wife are called to be open to sharing in God's power to bring life into the world whenever they have sexual intercourse. Bringing children into the world is an awesome gift and calling; it is a gift not to be taken lightly and without the complete commitment to raising a family. (This is another reason that pre-marital sex is wrong, as it risks bringing children into the world without the commitment to raising a family.)

For a married couple, eliminating the possibility of pregnancy while having sexual intercourse is a rejection of their call to share in God's power to bring life into the world. The refusal to be open to the transmission of life has no place in God's plan for marriage because it turns the couple away from a truly great gift of marriage: children. Although the Church recognizes that couples should act responsibly in having children, the spacing of children should be accomplished through a method such as natural family planning (NFP), which emphasizes the union of the couple and their openness to life. NFP teaches married couples how to recognize the wife's fertile periods and

© Jacob Lund / Shutterstock.com

One of the purposes of marriage is to support new life. How do married couples do this, even beyond the birth of children?

UNIT 4

practice chaste abstinence during those times to avoid pregnancy. All methods of **contraception**, including the use of chemicals, the use of barrier methods such as condoms and diaphragms, and surgical sterilization are morally wrong.

The gift of sexuality as expressed in marriage has a twofold end: to deepen the joyful, loving union of the spouses and to bring new life into the world if it is God's will. These two purposes are both necessary and should not be separated, especially during the act of sexual intercourse. To do so will have negative effects on the couple's relationship and their spiritual life. When the separation of these purposes (through practices such as artificial contraception) becomes widespread in society, it will have negative effects on the future of family life itself. ✳

 HMMMMMM. . .   Are you optimistic or pessimistic about the vocation of marriage? Who has shaped your views on this?

---

contraception ➤ The use of mechanical, chemical, or medical procedures to prevent conception from taking place as a result of sexual intercourse. Contraception is morally wrong because it violates the openness to procreation required of marriage and the inner truth of married love.

Article 46

Sins against the Dignity of Sexuality within Marriage

The Sixth Commandment clearly forbids adultery, but as we have seen in regard to other commandments, the New Law of Christ broadens our understanding of the moral law, helping us to see how the intent of the original commandment applies to other thoughts and actions. When applying the New Law to sexuality within marriage, anything that contradicts the twin purposes of sexual intercourse—sharing in God's faithful love and sharing in God's power to create new life—is a serious offense against the moral law.

Sins against Fidelity

Adultery, which occurs when a married person has sex with someone who is not his or her spouse, is a serious sin against the faithful, committed love that God intends to exist between a wife and husband. Adultery causes serious emotional and spiritual harm to everyone involved: the married couple, their family, the other person involved in the adulterous relationship, and even the wider community. A married relationship is based in trust and faithfulness, and when one of the spouses is sexually unfaithful, the trust in the relationship is extremely difficult to regain. This is why Jesus condemns even the desire for adultery (see Matthew 5:28). No intentions or circumstances can make adultery morally right. **Polygamy**, the practice of being married to more than one person, is in essence another form of adultery and is also condemned by the moral law.

Divorce is another serious offense against the dignity of marriage. The previous article discussed Jesus' condemnation of divorce. Here is another example from Matthew's Gospel of his strong teaching against this sin:

> Some Pharisees approached him, and tested him, saying, "Is it lawful for a man to divorce his wife for any cause whatever?" He said in reply, "Have you not read that from the beginning the Creator 'made them male and

UNIT 4

---

adultery ➤ Sexual activity between two persons, at least one of whom is married to another. Prohibited by the Sixth Commandment.

polygamy ➤ Having more than one spouse, an act contrary to the dignity of marriage and a sin against the Sixth Commandment.

female' and said, 'For this reason a man shall leave his father and mother and be joined to his wife, and the two shall become one flesh'? So they are no longer two, but one flesh. Therefore, what God has joined together, no human being must separate." They said to him, "Then why did Moses command that the man give the woman a bill of divorce and dismiss (her)?" He said to them, "Because of the hardness of your hearts Moses allowed you to divorce your wives, but from the beginning it was not so. I say to you, whoever divorces his wife (unless the marriage is unlawful) and marries another commits adultery." (19:3–9)

© fizkes / Shutterstock.com

The harmful effects of divorce go beyond the husband and wife and touch many lives. Who are some of the people affected when a married couple divorces?

As you can see from this passage, it was relatively easy for a husband to divorce his wife in Jesus' time. Jesus protects the dignity of marriage and also the equal dignity of women and men by insisting that in God's plan of creation, a husband and wife are permanently bonded in marriage. Jesus raises marriage to the dignity of a sacrament, offering married couples the grace with which to live out God's plan for marriage from the beginning of creation.

Cohabitation, or living together before marriage, is also a sin against the dignity of marriage because the couple lives together as if they were married,

---

cohabitation ➤ A man and woman living together before marriage. Prohibited by the Sixth Commandment.

There is a way for married couples to use natural means to better understand their fertility and plan their families. It is called natural family planning (NFP), and it helps married couples plan their pregnancies and can even increase their chances of conceiving a child. NFP is consistent with the Church's moral teaching, and when used correctly and consistently, it is just as effective at postponing pregnancy (97–99 percent) as most artificial means. Couples using it to become pregnant typically achieve pregnancy in two or three months instead of a year or more. Just as important, it empowers wives and husbands to better understand their bodies, to communicate more clearly and honestly, and to take shared responsibility for conceiving children. All this helps to deepen the love and intimacy of wife and husband.

UNIT 4

without the complete commitment of a sacramental marriage. Living together, even if the intention is a trial marriage, is not the same as a permanent commitment. Studies have shown that couples who lived together before marriage experience a higher rate of divorce than couples who do not live together.

When couples decide to experience the pleasure of sex without the lifelong vow, it is too easy to give up on each other and to walk away from the relationship. When a woman and man are called by God to marriage, when they work at nurturing their relationship before getting married (without having sex), and when they make a complete commitment to God and each other to be faithful for life, they will experience all the joys and be prepared to deal with all the challenges that marriage brings.

Sins against Natural Conception

Article 45 discusses how the use of artificial contraceptives is wrong because the husband and wife must remain open to the possibility of children in every act of sexual intercourse. In addition to this, the dignity of sexuality requires that children also be created naturally. This truth can be hard for married couples struggling to have children to accept. The emotional pain and suffering they experience is real and intense. Because of this, some people see prohibitions against artificially induced pregnancy as unnecessary or even cruel. However, this does not negate the moral truth that children must be the outcome of the loving union of a husband and wife in sexual intercourse and not conceived through some artificial means of conception.

These artificial means of conception include **in vitro fertilization**, which is creating a fertilized ovum in a laboratory and then implanting it in the wife's womb; **artificial insemination**, which is a fertility technique that artificially implants sperm in a woman's womb; and the use of **surrogate motherhood**, which is placing a fertilized ovum in another woman's womb, letting the baby grow inside her, and after birth giving the newborn infant to the baby's biological mother and father. These are all serious moral offenses. Likewise, human cloning is a grave moral offense.

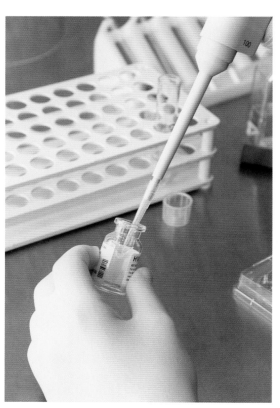

How would you explain to a friend why artificial means of conceiving a child—such as in vitro fertilization and artificial insemination—are against the will of God?

---

in vitro fertilization ➤ The fertilization of a woman's ovum (egg) with a man's sperm outside her body. The fertilized egg is transferred to the woman's uterus. The Church considers the process to be a moral violation of the dignity of procreation.

artificial insemination ➤ The process by which a man's sperm and a woman's egg are united in a manner other than natural sexual intercourse. In the narrowest sense, it means injecting sperm into a woman's cervical canal. The procedure is morally wrong because it separates intercourse from the act of procreation.

surrogate motherhood ➤ A medical process in which a woman becomes pregnant through artificial means, often carrying and delivering the child for someone else. The procedure is morally wrong because it separates intercourse from the act of procreation and pregnancy.

The Body of Christ, though, has great sympathy for husbands and wives who struggle with infertility. These couples share Christ's suffering, and Christ suffers with them. The Church actively encourages and supports research and medical treatments that increase their chances of naturally conceiving. But we must uphold the dignity of sexuality within marriage through the creation of children as God intended. As stated previously with other moral issues, good intentions cannot make an immoral act moral. ✳

HMMMMM. . . What are the most common offenses against marriage in our time?

UNIT 4

1. How is the gift of sexuality a reflection of the image of God?

2. Explain the two basic meanings of sexuality, according to the theology of the body.

3. Give a definition of a chaste person.

4. How can a person maintain purity of heart?

5. Define *fornication,* and explain why it is a sin.

6. Why is pornography a dangerous sexual sin?

7. Explain the twofold meaning and purpose of marital sexuality.

8. Why are artificial means of contraception wrong?

9. Who is harmed by adultery?

10. Name three artificial means of conception, and explain why they are wrong.

Hey! What u doing?

Nothing much. Just remembering the talk about sex in religion class.

I know, weird, right? But it is making me see things differently.

Me 2. I always thought the Church was just uptight and unreasonable about sex.

Right? But Mrs. J sure wasn't uptight and she made a lot of sense.

Exactly. I've never really thought about sex as a 🎁 to be cherished.

Cuz there are so many messages in our society that make it seem like no big deal.

And people are teased when they say they are saving it for marriage.

Yeah, but after Mrs. J's class, I'm getting how marriage is the best place for it. It just seems tough to wait that long.

🙂 True! That seems like a big ask.

What's Mrs. J always saying? The best things require sacrifice and patience?

I hate it when she says that!

Agreed! But I think she's right.

MAINTAINING CHASTITY
TEXT EXCHANGE

UNIT 4 HIGHLIGHTS

CHAPTER 10 The Fifth Commandment:
Respecting Life

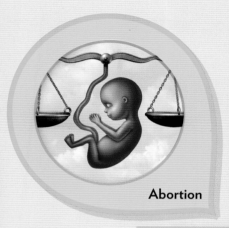

Abortion

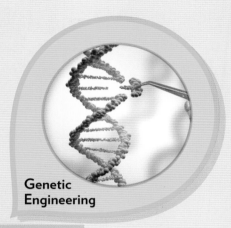

Genetic Engineering

Beginning-of-Life Issues

Prenatal Testing

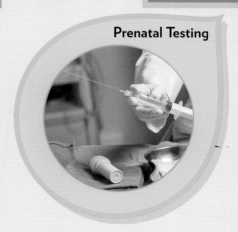

Stem Cell Research

Euthanasia

Suicide

End-of-Life Issues

Death
Penalty

Blessed Are the Peacemakers

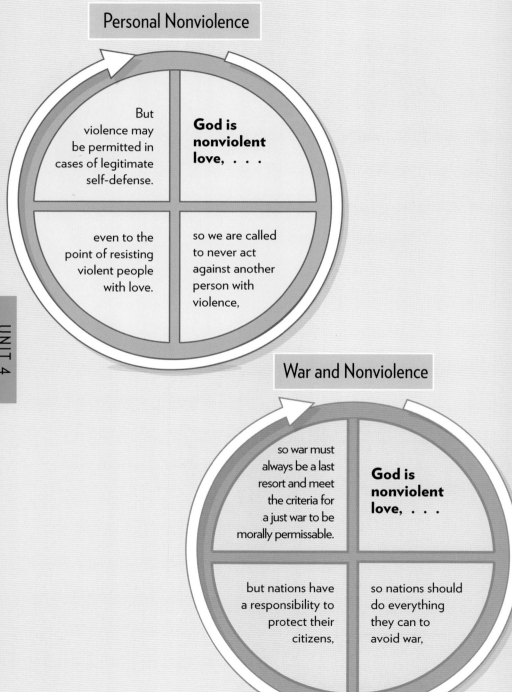

Personal Nonviolence

But violence may be permitted in cases of legitimate self-defense.

God is nonviolent love, . . .

even to the point of resisting violent people with love.

so we are called to never act against another person with violence,

War and Nonviolence

so war must always be a last resort and meet the criteria for a just war to be morally permissable.

God is nonviolent love, . . .

but nations have a responsibility to protect their citizens,

so nations should do everything they can to avoid war,

CHAPTER 11 The Sixth and Ninth Commandments: Respecting Sexuality

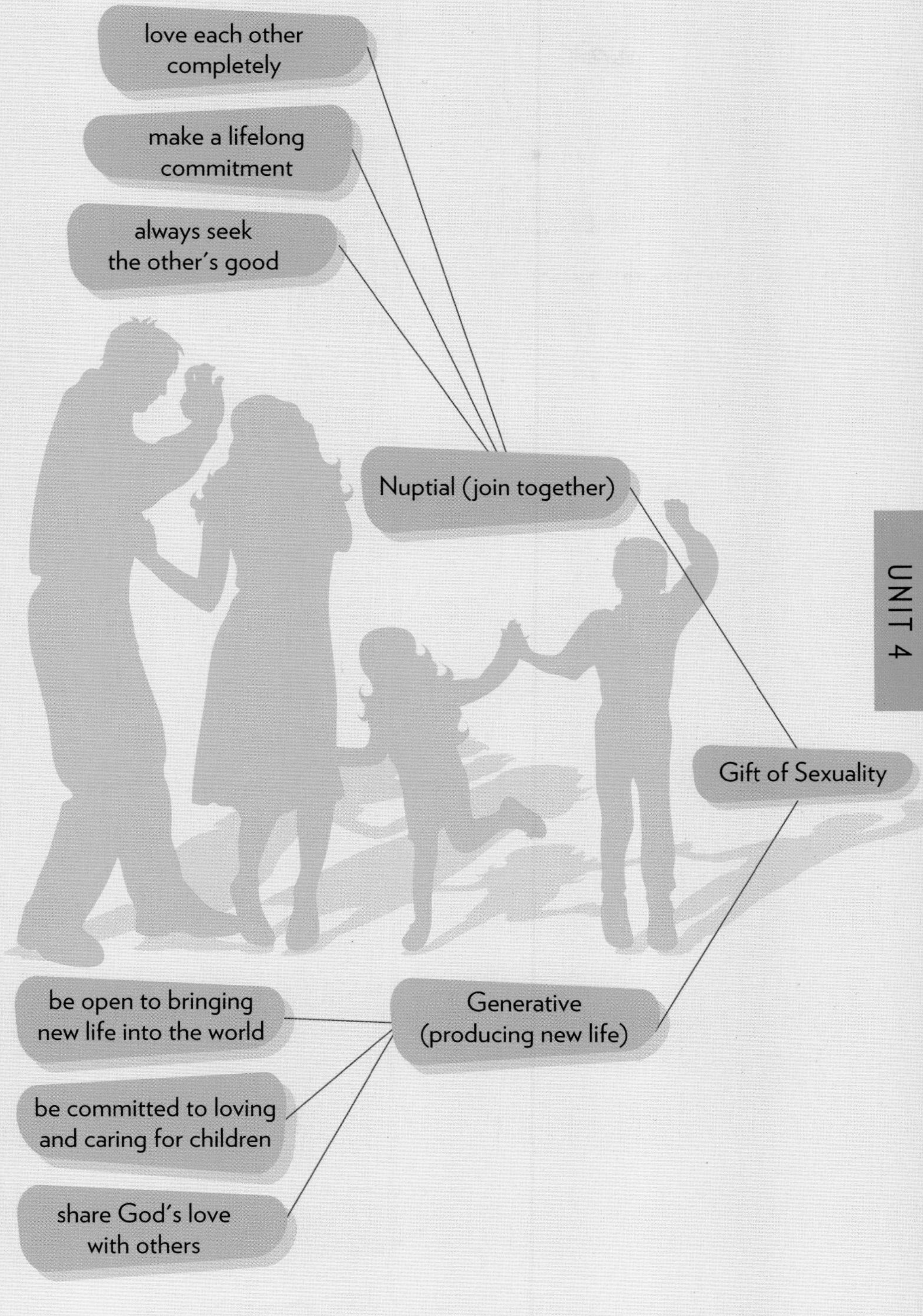

love each other completely

make a lifelong commitment

always seek the other's good

Nuptial (join together)

Gift of Sexuality

Images: Shutterstock.com

be open to bringing new life into the world

be committed to loving and caring for children

share God's love with others

Generative (producing new life)

Sexual Integrity
Purity of Heart
Healthy Relationships
Stronger Marriages
Respect for Others

WHAT IS CHASTITY?

Temperance
Modesty
Self-control
Reverence
Gratitude

No Pornography
No Premarital Sex
No Exploitation
Reject Media Lies
No Adultery

Sins against the Sixth and Ninth Commandments

Sins against Chastity

fornication Sexual intercourse between a man and a woman who are not married.

prostitution The act of providing sexual services in exchange for money, drugs, or other goods.

masturbation Self-manipulation of one's sexual organs for the purpose of erotic pleasure or to achieve orgasm.

pornography A written description or visual portrayal of a person or action that is created or viewed with the intention of stimulating sexual feelings.

Sins against Marriage

adultery Sexual activity between two persons, at least one of whom is married to another.

cohabitation A man and woman living together before marriage.

polygamy Having more than one spouse.

contraception The use of mechanical, chemical, or medical procedures to prevent conception from taking place as a result of sexual intercourse.

artificial insemination The process by which a man's sperm and a woman's egg are united in a manner other than natural sexual intercourse.

UNIT 4

UNIT 4
BRING IT HOME

HOW IS GOD CALLING ME TO RESPECT LIFE AND SEXUALITY?

UNIT 4

FOCUS QUESTIONS

CHAPTER 10   How can I show my respect for life?

CHAPTER 11   Why is sex okay in marriage only?

MATTIAS
Seton Catholic Preparatory School

UNIT 4

I can show respect for life by realizing the goodness that God has blessed us with here on Earth. In this unit, I learned that once you appreciate the great gifts of life and sexuality that God has given us, you will be inspired to show respect for these gifts all the time. We as humans are called to serve one another, listen to one another, help one another, or even just be there for one another. I will keep trying to maintain a healthy lifestyle. But I also need to remember that to truly care for others means that I must respect my life and the life of others, including the gift of sexuality.

REFLECT

Take some time to read and reflect on the unit and chapter focus questions listed on the facing page.

- What question or section did you identify most closely with?

- What did you find within the unit that was comforting or challenging?

UNIT 5
Making Good Moral Choices

HOW CAN I LIVE A GOOD LIFE, EVEN WHEN I SOMETIMES MISS THE MARK?

LOOKING AHEAD

Everyone makes mistakes. That is just life. Even though you sometimes miss the mark, you can still live a good life with the helping hand of God. God can help you learn the importance of life and how to enjoy it. Even though you can't physically talk to him, he's still there to lend a hand. There are many ways to live a good life. The struggle is just living in tune with God's will by finding what makes you happy. For example, going to Church or playing a sport could be something that makes you happy. One thing that helps me to be happy is helping those in need.

VICTORIA
Red Bank Catholic High School

UNIT 5

CHAPTER 12
Gifts and Guides

WHAT GUIDES SHOULD I LOOK TO WHEN MAKING A MORAL DECISION?

SNAPSHOT

Article 47

Called to Be Holy

There was a young woman who loved art. As a child, she drew picture after picture, which her parents proudly displayed in the family's kitchen and den. She worked hard in high school to get accepted into a college with a prestigious art program. She learned new and varied techniques for painting and sculpting. She spent long hours into the night painting the same image over and over to get the brush strokes just right. Finally, she graduated with honors, ready to begin her lifelong dream. She got a job as a commercial designer to pay her bills. But she also set up her own home studio where she could work on the art she really wanted to create.

TAKE IT TO GOD

Good and gracious God,
When I feel the lure of excess
and crave too much of a good thing,
help me to develop temperance,
the self-control that gives my life balance and wholeness.

When I feel driven to act on impulse,
give me prudence,
the wisdom to stop and think before I act.

When I find that I am preoccupied with myself,
my own wants and worries,
help me to see others with eyes of compassion
and to reach out to them with loving justice.

When I face obstacles to living morally
that tempt me to move away from you,
give me fortitude,
the courage to overcome the temptation.

Amen.

UNIT 5

However, she had a problem. Every time she started a project in her home studio, she rarely got further than her initial sketches. Or if she did start a painting, she would get halfway through, get disgusted with her work, and toss it out. After months of this, she made a lunch appointment with an art teacher she greatly respected. During lunch, she explained her difficulty. "What are you thinking about while you are painting?" the teacher asked. "I'm thinking about the technique I'm using and how I'm not getting it right," she replied.

"What gave you the desire to create art?" the teacher asked. "Try to remember what made you want to be an artist in the first place."

The woman replied, "I just loved making beautiful things."

"Then forget the techniques," said the teacher, "and just focus on making something beautiful. You've learned the techniques, and they are a part of you. Trust that they will work."

You can probably guess the end of the story. The artist focused on making something beautiful and trusted the techniques she had learned to create it. Her passion returned, and now she couldn't paint and sculpt fast enough.

Our moral life is like this. If you forget the goal of Christian morality, you can study moral theologians, papal documents, and the *Catechism of the Catholic Church*, and learn everything there is to know about Christian morality, and still struggle to live a good moral life. We must never forget that the goal of Christian morality is to live a holy life, a life that is purified from sin and

© Vladimir Vladimirov / iStockphoto.com

What is your goal for your life? What knowledge and skills must you master to live a happy, healthy, and holy life?

darkness and filled with love for God, others, and ourselves. This is what motivates the saints to put into daily practice the moral principles and teachings taught by the Church. When we pursue this goal as all the great saints have before us, in whatever vocation God calls us to, we will be passionate about living the moral life.

The good news is that through the Catholic faith God has given us an abundance of resources to strengthen and guide us. Being Catholic is like being at a free gourmet restaurant for moral living. In the Catholic faith, we find the best of all that we need: moral principles, the Theological Virtues, the Ten Commandments, the Beatitudes, Jesus' life and teachings, and two thousand years of wisdom and reflection on moral issues and principles. We have moral support from parents, priests, youth leaders, teachers, counselors, and peers who share our values. Grace, the Cardinal Virtues, and the sacraments are the gifts that help us to put all this wisdom into action. Conscience guides us in making reasoned, moral judgments about how to act. We truly have everything we need to live a holy, happy, and healthy life.

Disciples of Christ

The primary role and description of a Christian is that he or she is a disciple of Christ. And what is the primary characteristic of being a disciple? Jesus gives us the answer in the Gospel of John: "This is how all will know that you are my disciples, if you have love for one another" (13:35). Jesus teaches us, his disciples, that the Old Law was meant for one thing, to teach us how to love. The moral life, discipleship, and love are all connected; they are all different ways of expressing the same reality. And that reality is that God created us to be a holy people in full communion with the Father, Son, and Holy Spirit, and with one another.

Here is a great mystery of the Christian life: Human beings do not create love; we simply tap into and share God's love. We must live in Christ so that he can live in us. We cannot be holy on our own power. We need God's love working in us and through us. The First Letter of John contains a beautiful expression of this truth.

> In this is love: not that we have loved God, but that he loved us and sent his Son as expiation for our sins. Beloved, if God so loved us, we also must love one another. No one has ever seen God. Yet, if we love one another, God remains in us, and his love is brought to perfection in us.
>
> This is how we know that we remain in him and he in us, that he has given us of his Spirit. . . .

UNIT 5

. . . We know that we love the children of God when we love God and
obey his commandments. For the love of God is this, that we keep his
commandments. And his commandments are not burdensome. (4:10–13,
5:2–3)

Letting God's love fill us and flow through us is the only way that human
beings will overcome sin and grow in holiness. It is the reason for which we
were created and how we find our ultimate fulfillment and happiness.

Vocation and Holiness

Stephan raised his hand in religion class and asked the question he knew everyone was thinking. "All this talk of holiness sounds beautiful and everything,
but it doesn't feel like it really applies to us. I mean most of us aren't going to
be priests or nuns or even religion teachers. A lot of us aren't even Catholic. So
why are we talking about all this?"

His religion teacher thought for a long moment before replying. "Stephan,
we all have the same destination, no matter what our path in life is. That destination is knowing God's love and joy, both in this life and in the next. Really,
that's what holiness is, and we all get there the same way, by answering God's
call and sharing his love with others. And there are so many ways we can do
that. Of course, we won't all be priests or nuns; God loves diversity and creativity. You are—or can be—on the path to holiness right now by just striving
to be the best friend, the best student, the most loving son or daughter you
can be!"

There are many ways to live out our Christian calling. How do you see yourself
living out Christ's call to live a holy life?

In the most general sense, a vocation is the call from God to share his love with others and grow in holiness. All Christians share this common vocational call, grounded in the Sacraments of Baptism, the Eucharist, and Confirmation. Living that call happens in a variety of ways; these ways are responses to specific needs, to different states of life, and even to different temperaments. We must listen in prayer to how God is calling us to live our baptismal vocation and seek out opportunities to answer that call. The following are some examples of ways to live out our common vocational call:

- **A meaningful job** The most common calling is to share God's love with the world through employment that contributes to the good of society. Teachers, accountants, authors, medical workers, businesspeople, factory workers, media providers, support staff, managers, farmers, food service workers, and so many others share God's love by providing important goods and services with a joyful and caring attitude.

- **Volunteer work** Society is full of special needs that require the response of dedicated volunteers. Volunteering to visit people who are sick and homebound, to provide meals and hospitality for people who are homeless and hungry, to help raise money for important charities, to work for pro-life issues, and to help build homes for needy families are some ways that people share God's love through volunteer work and organizations. If you are attracted to one of these needs more than others, it is probably a sign that God is calling you to volunteer to help with that need.

- **Service to the Church** The Church needs people to help in a variety of ministries, whether as a volunteer or a full-time lay ecclesial minister. God might be calling you to help in outreach ministry, catechetical ministry, or liturgical ministry.

- **Missionary activity** God calls some people to travel to foreign lands to share his love with people who have little knowledge or experience of Christians and Christianity. This usually requires a commitment of several years or more.

- **Religious movements** Many different religious movements associated with the Church encourage and support our call to share God's love with others. For example, Catholic Charismatic Renewal focuses on the Gifts of the Holy Spirit. Communion and Liberation is a movement whose purpose is growth in Christian maturity and collaboration with the mission of Christ in all walks of life. Many other movements and programs like Teens Encounter Christ, Kairos, LifeTeen, and religious Third Orders can help you to grow in holiness.

UNIT 5

Vocation in the more specific sense is a lifelong commitment to live a holy life as an ordained minister, as a consecrated religious, in Christian marriage, or in the dedicated single life. Although the baptismal vocational opportunities mentioned previously can and probably will change over a person's lifetime, the vocations of marriage, the priesthood, the diaconate, religious life (brothers and sisters), and consecrated virgins are stable and lifelong. Living them faithfully purifies us of selfishness, dishonesty, envy, conceit, and lust. They offer us profound ways of receiving and sharing God's love with spouses, family, religious communities, and the People of God. They challenge us to put our complete trust in God's saving power.

Many people believe that Christian morality is simply a big list of fun things that you are forbidden to do. But this is not what Christian morality is at all. Yes, God's Law forbids us from doing things that appear to be fun, but if we are really honest, we recognize that those things are harmful to us and others. Christian morality is so much more than that; it is a challenging and joyful call to continual-

The vocation to the priesthood can be lived out in many ways: priests can be missionaries, they can teach in schools and universities, they can be chaplains in the military and in hospitals, and they can be parish pastors.

ly work toward holiness (see Matthew 5:48) as disciples of Christ, sharing in Christ's priestly, prophetic, and kingly ministries. It is the way we invite God's love to live in us and through us. It leads us to true and eternal happiness. We do this by focusing on all the things we can do to love one another and live our lives to the full potential God wants for us. We will be focused primarily on the positive, life-giving aspects of our faith rather than the things we "can't do." ✳

UNIT 5

Do you see living a moral life as a burden or a blessing? Why?

Article 48

Grace

Carmen was really struggling. She and Peter had broken up. Her parents had recently split, and they couldn't agree who she would be staying with most weekends. She couldn't focus so her grades were suffering, and she really let the volleyball team down in their last match. She looked at the drink in her hand and felt the growing buzz it was bringing her. "Why is God letting this happen to me?" she thought. "Why is he tempting me to give up, to give in, to make another stupid choice?"

When faced with powerful temptations, we can find ourselves asking, "Why is God doing this to me?" Scripture and Tradition call us to think differently. First, they teach that God is never the source of temptation. The Letter of James says: "No one experiencing temptation should say, 'I am being tempted by God'; for God is not subject to temptation to evil, and he himself tempts no one. Rather, each person is tempted when he is lured and enticed by his own desire [not by God!]" (1:13–14). The author of James tells us that we are tempted not by God but by our own passions and desires, the lingering effects of concupiscence.

© fizkes / Shutterstock.com

Grace is the gift of God's loving and active presence in the world. How do you experience God's grace in your life?

Second, Scripture and Tradition reveal that God provides the means to resist every temptation or difficulty we face. We read the following in the First Letter to the Corinthians: "No trial has come to you but what is human. God is faithful and will not let you be tried beyond your strength; but with the trial he will also provide a way out, so that you may be able to bear it" (10:13). What Saint Paul is saying is that God gives us the **grace** we need to resist moral temptations and live the commandments of the moral law. Let's go back to Carmen for a second. She is in a difficult time in her life, but she must trust that God is not tempting her to drown her sorrows. The temptation is there because she wants to escape the other painful parts of her life. By making a decision to trust that God wants the best for her, by trusting that God is with her in her struggles, and by leaning on the grace that God will supply, she can move past the pain without resorting to things that will only hurt her.

The word *grace* comes from the Greek word *charis*, which can also mean "favor," "talent," or "gift." Theologically defined, grace is the free and undeserved gift of God's loving and active presence in our lives, empowering us to respond to his call and to live as his adopted sons and daughters. Grace restores our loving communion with the Holy Trinity, lost through sin.

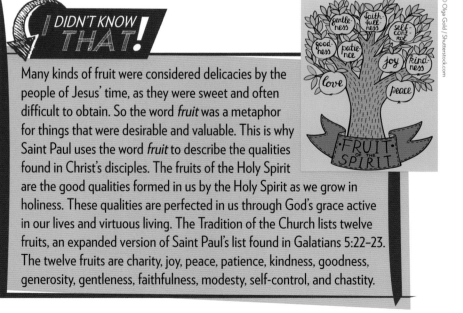

I DIDN'T KNOW THAT!

Many kinds of fruit were considered delicacies by the people of Jesus' time, as they were sweet and often difficult to obtain. So the word *fruit* was a metaphor for things that were desirable and valuable. This is why Saint Paul uses the word *fruit* to describe the qualities found in Christ's disciples. The fruits of the Holy Spirit are the good qualities formed in us by the Holy Spirit as we grow in holiness. These qualities are perfected in us through God's grace active in our lives and virtuous living. The Tradition of the Church lists twelve fruits, an expanded version of Saint Paul's list found in Galatians 5:22–23. The twelve fruits are charity, joy, peace, patience, kindness, goodness, generosity, gentleness, faithfulness, modesty, self-control, and chastity.

grace ➤ The free and undeserved gift of God's loving and active presence in our lives that God gives us to empower us to respond to his call and to live as his adopted sons and daughters. Grace restores our loving communion with the Holy Trinity, lost through sin.

Grace is God's initiative in preparing us for salvation. It is at work in our soul to help us realize that we need to respond in faith to God's invitation to be in relationship with him. Grace does not take away human freedom but helps us to use our freedom in responding to God's offer of friendship and salvation. In a real sense, God's grace is the source of our freedom; it enables our free response and perfects it.

Although all three Divine Persons of the Trinity confer grace, the work of grace is often associated with the Third Person of the Trinity, the Holy Spirit. *The Catechism of the Catholic Church (CCC)* talks about the Holy Spirit's infusing grace in our souls and that "grace includes the gifts that the Spirit grants us to associate us with his work, to enable us to collaborate in the salvation of others and in the growth of the Body of Christ, the Church" (number 2003).

Kinds of Grace

Article 4 discussed how God's grace frees us from sin and sanctifies us, that is, it makes us holy. We call this kind of grace **sanctifying grace**. Through our Baptism, the Holy Spirit gives us sanctifying grace to heal our wounded soul and make us whole again. He confers on us the righteousness of God by uniting us to the Passion and Resurrection of Jesus Christ. Sanctifying grace makes us sharers in God's own life and love. It is also called deifying grace (meaning it brings us closer to God) or habitual grace because it is always at work within us, disposing us to live and act in accord with God's will.

We human beings can do nothing to merit the initial movements of grace in our lives, which causes our awareness of the need for God and leads to conversion. But once we have responded with faith to the Holy Spirit's initial promptings, we can merit for ourselves and other people all the graces needed to sustain our earthly life and to attain eternal life. The *Catechism* identifies three kinds of these graces: **actual graces, sacramental graces,** and **special graces** (see numbers 2000–2004).

---

sanctifying grace ➤ The grace that heals our human nature wounded by sin and restores us to friendship with God by giving us a share in the divine life of the Trinity. It is a supernatural gift of God, infused into our souls by the Holy Spirit, that continues the work of making us holy.

actual graces ➤ God's interventions and support for us in the everyday moments of our lives. Actual graces are important for conversion and for continuing growth in holiness.

sacramental graces ➤ The gifts proper to each of the Seven Sacraments.

special graces ➤ Gifts intended for the common good of the Church, also called charisms.

Actual grace is the work of God in our lives, either preparing us for conversion or helping in our sanctification. An example of actual grace might be a friend who just happens to be there right when you need someone's support in making an important moral decision. Or it might be finding just the right Scripture passage that moves a person to talk to a priest about joining the Church. Actual grace is the strength the Holy Spirit gives us to make it through the grief of losing a loved one. It is important to ask God in prayer for what we need to follow his will because he will always provide the grace we need.

Sacramental graces are the special gifts we receive through the Seven Sacraments. The sacraments are effective signs, meaning they make the spiritual realities they symbolize present at the time and place they are celebrated. For example, in the Eucharist, we receive the grace of being spiritually nourished by Christ's Word and with his Body and Blood. In the Sacrament of Confirmation, we receive the grace of being strengthened so that we are better able to participate in the Church's mission. In the Sacrament of Anointing of the Sick, we receive the grace of being healed—spiritually, physically, or both.

Special graces, also called charisms, are given to us to build up the Church. Saint Paul teaches about these gifts in his letters, especially in his First Letter to the Corinthians:

The grace we receive in the sacraments makes the spiritual realities they symbolize present in our lives.

There are different kinds of spiritual gifts but the same Spirit; there are different forms of service but the same Lord; there are different workings but the same God who produces all of them in everyone. To each individual the manifestation of the Spirit is given for some benefit. To one is given through the Spirit the expression of wisdom; to another the expression of knowledge according to the same Spirit; to another faith by the same Spirit; to another gifts of healing by the one Spirit; to another mighty deeds; to another prophecy; to another discernment of spirits; to another varieties of tongues; to another interpretation of tongues. (12:4–10)

What special grace has God given to you for the good of the Body of Christ?

The Gifts of the Holy Spirit

The **Gifts of the Holy Spirit** are related to grace because they are also unmerited spiritual gifts bestowed on us by the Holy Spirit at Baptism and increased in us at Confirmation. Jesus possessed these gifts in their fullness. There are traditionally seven of these gifts, based on Isaiah 11:1–3.

Gifts of the Holy Spirit	
Wisdom	Through the gift of wisdom, the wonders of nature, every event in history, and all the ups and downs of our lives take on deeper meaning and purpose. The wise person sees where the Holy Spirit is at work and is able to share that insight with others.
Understanding	The gift of understanding is the ability to comprehend how a person must live their as a follower of Jesus. Through the gift of understanding, Christians realize that the Gospel tells them not just who Jesus is but also who we are.
Counsel	Also called right judgment, the gift of counsel is the ability to know the difference between right and wrong and then to choose what is good. It helps us to act on and live out what Jesus has taught.
Fortitude	Also called courage, the gift of fortitude enables us to take risks and to overcome fear as we try to live out the Gospel of Jesus.

Gifts of the Holy Spirit ➤ At Baptism, we receive seven Gifts of the Holy Spirit. These gifts are freely given to us to help us live as followers of Jesus and to build up the Body of Christ, the Church. The seven gifts are wisdom, understanding, right judgment or counsel, fortitude or courage, knowledge, piety or reverence, and fear of the Lord or wonder and awe.

Gifts of the Holy Spirit (continued)	
Knowledge	The gift of knowledge is the ability to comprehend the basic meaning and message of Jesus. Jesus revealed the will of God, his Father, and taught people what they need to know to achieve fullness of life and ultimately salvation.
Piety	Also called reverence, the gift of piety gives Christians a deep sense of respect for God. Through the gift of piety, we can come before God with the openness and trust of small children, totally dependent on the One who created us.
Fear of the Lord	The gift of the fear of the Lord, also called wonder and awe, might be better understood as being in awe in the presence of God. Though we can approach God with the trust of little children, we are also often aware of his total majesty, unlimited power, and desire for justice.

For Christian morality, tuning in to the Gifts of the Holy Spirit and grace is crucial. They are the help God gives us to respond to our vocation to be his adopted daughters and sons. Without any effort on our part, they connect us to the divine life of the Trinity. Through grace, God's infinite love is there before we realize it, preparing us and inviting us to respond to the invitation to love him back. Although we don't earn grace by being good, grace and the Gifts of the Holy Spirit help us to be good. When we are grace filled, we are at our best, living holy and happy lives. ✳

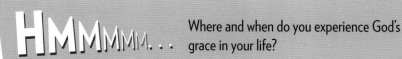

HMMMMM... Where and when do you experience God's grace in your life?

Article 49
The Cardinal Virtues

Virtues are habits that firmly direct us in making good moral decisions. Like mastering skills in any sport, virtues capitalize on the abilities God has already placed within us. For example, most people have the physical potential to shoot a basket, to dribble a soccer ball, or to master a swimming stroke. When athletes first learn to do these things, someone has to show them the technique. As they practice the technique, the skill becomes more natural, and they are able to play the game without having to be preoccupied with the basic skills required. In a similar way, virtues are moral skills that we need to develop by working at them. Virtues harness the power of grace within us.

Everyone has the moral potential to live a virtuous life. But most people benefit from having virtues explained and from being shown how to live them out in daily life. Then the more we intentionally practice these virtues, the more they will become part of us, and we will naturally apply them to moral decisions we face. This article looks at the human virtues called the **Cardinal Virtues**, and the next article considers the Theological Virtues.

Prudence, Temperance, Justice, and Fortitude

Human virtues are the virtues we develop by our own effort with the help of God's grace. They guide our intellect and our will in controlling our passions and in making good moral choices based on reason and faith. Four virtues play a pivotal role and accordingly are called Cardinal Virtues. They are prudence, justice, temperance, and fortitude. Every human virtue can be grouped around the Cardinal Virtues. As you develop the Cardinal Virtues in your life, you become a person of moral character. To have character means that you do the right thing, even under difficult circumstances.

Prudence is the opposite of being impulsive. Acting impulsively is okay for a two-year-old. It may even be appropriate for a grown person in certain settings that call for creativity or spontaneity. But making moral decisions impulsively can get you into trouble. Prudence directs you to approach moral

UNIT 5

Cardinal Virtues ➤ Based on the Latin word *cardo*, meaning "pivot," four virtues that are viewed as pivotal or essential for full Christian living: prudence, justice, fortitude, and temperance.

prudence ➤ The Cardinal Virtue by which a person is inclined toward choosing the moral good and avoiding evil; sometimes called the rudder virtue because it helps steer the person through complex moral situations.

CATHOLICS MAKING A DIFFERENCE

© MatteoFarina.com

In May 2020, Pope Francis moved ten people closer to sainthood. One of them was an Italian teenager, Venerable Matteo Farina, who lived from 1990 to 2009. He was by all counts a normal teenager, growing up in a strong Christian family. However, Matteo's life was built on justice, prudence, temperance, and fortitude, taking full advantage of all the gifts God offers us to live a holy life. Starting at eight years old, Matteo would regularly receive the Sacrament of Penance and Reconciliation. At nine years old, he read the entire Gospel of Saint Matthew as a Lenten practice. He also prayed the Rosary every day.

In September 2003, a month before his thirteenth birthday, Matteo began to have symptoms of a brain tumor. As he was undergoing medical tests, he began to keep a journal. He called the experience of the bad headaches and pain "one of those adventures that change your life and that of others. It helps you to be stronger and to grow, above all in faith." Over the next six years, Farina would undergo several brain operations and chemotherapy. In between hospitalizations, he continued to live the ordinary life of a teenager: he attended school, hung out with his friends, formed a band, and fell in love with a girl.

Matteo once wrote in his journal: "When you feel that you can't do it, when the world falls on you, when every choice is a critical decision, when every action is a failure . . . and you would like to throw everything away, when intense work reduces you to the limit of strength . . . take time to take care of your soul, love God with your whole being and reflect his love for others" ("Italian Teen Who Died in 2009 Declared 'Venerable' by Pope Francis," in *Catholic News Agency,* May 6, 2020). Matteo died surrounded by his friends and family on April 24, 2009.

problems thoughtfully and objectively. Also called wise judgment, prudence relies heavily on our reason. In fact, Saint Thomas Aquinas called it "right reason in action"[1] (*CCC*, number 1806). Prudence helps you to stop and think before you act.

Prudence

Justice is the virtue concerned with giving both God and neighbor what is their due. It is the habit of considering the needs of others as much as your own needs. It takes determination and dedication to be a just person. Remember that God takes justice a step further than simple fairness. Fairness is doing an equal share of work; justice is doing more because someone else can't. Justice is about loving and serving disadvantaged people and even loving your enemies.

Justice

Temperance is about balance in your life. You know that stress, greed, or sickness can come from too much of a good thing. The pleasures in life must be balanced with moderation. Too much play isn't good; neither is all work and no play. Exercise is good for our bodies, but too much can lead to problems. Food is another good we must learn to balance. Healthy food nourishes our bodies and gives us pleasure. Too much food can lead to obesity,

Temperance

Fortitude

and too little food can lead to eating disorders. The virtue of temperance is about self-control and balance in all areas of our lives.

Fortitude is the moral virtue that strengthens us to overcome obstacles to living morally. It is easy to be good when we have no strong temptation in

---

justice ➤ The Cardinal Virtue concerned with rights and duties within relationships; the commitment, as well as the actions and attitudes that flow from the commitment, that ensure we give to God and to our neighbor, particularly those who are poor and oppressed, what is properly due them.

temperance ➤ The Cardinal Virtue by which one moderates his or her appetites and passions to achieve balance in the use of created goods.

fortitude ➤ Also called strength or courage, the Cardinal Virtue that enables one to maintain sound moral judgment and behavior in the face of difficulties and challenges.

our lives. When you are not feeling the ecstasy of being in love, the Church's teaching on premarital sex makes perfect sense. If you are not angry, nonviolence is a worthy ideal. But when you are in the heat of any moment, whether it is sexual passion, anger, or some other strong feeling, fortitude gives you strength to overcome the temptation to give in to sinful desires. It is the habit of doing the right thing even though part of you wants to do the wrong thing. Fortitude is also called moral courage or moral strength.

Other Virtues

The word *cardinal* is derived from the Latin *cardo*, meaning "pivot," something on which many other things depend. So, the Cardinal Virtues of justice, prudence, temperance, and fortitude are the primary virtues on which many other virtues depend or pivot. If we develop these four good habits in our lives, many other virtuous habits are possible. For example, if we develop the virtue of temperance, it is easier to develop the virtues of patience and living a healthy lifestyle.

The following are some examples of other virtues: compassion, honesty, chastity, charity, caring for the Earth, caring for our bodies, expressing gratitude, and respecting life. The life of Christian virtue is an ongoing journey. Do you notice that when you practice a good habit, it becomes easier to do other good things and to avoid bad habits?

We must work hard to develop the Cardinal Virtues and the other virtues that might arise as a result so that they become habitual ways of thinking and acting. We do this through education in morality and by deliberately making prudent, just, temperate, and courageous moral decisions. We must persevere in this even when it is a struggle. The good news is that God is with us in our efforts to live virtuous lives. With God guiding our efforts through divine grace, the Cardinal Virtues will bring our moral lives to a higher level of integrity. ✳

HMMMMM. . . Which Cardinal Virtue do you most need in your life right now?

Article 50
The Theological Virtues

Carmen knew her grandmother had grown up in Europe during World War II and had lived through many difficult times. Despite this, her grandmother seemed so loving and peaceful. One day Carmen asked her grandmother, "Have you ever been really depressed or angry and just wanted to give up trying?"

"Oh, honey," answered her grandmother, "of course I have." "What's gotten you through it?" asked Carmen.

Without hesitation, her grandmother replied, "Faith, hope, and love. I learned about those three things as a little girl in religion class. They've always stuck with me. They were even part of the readings at my wedding. When I look back over my life, I see that faith, hope, and love have helped me through all the hard times. I ask God every day to keep them coming because I know I cannot make it without having them in my life."

"Faith, hope, and love" Carmen thought, "I could certainly use those three things in my life, too."

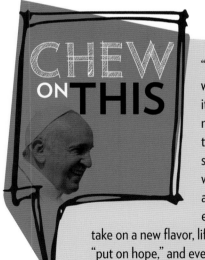

"Put on faith": what does this mean? When we prepare a plate of food and we see that it needs salt, well, we "put on" salt; when it needs oil, then you "put on" oil. "To put on," that is, to place on top of, to pour over. And so it is in our life, dear young friends: if we want it to have real meaning and fulfillment, as you want and as you deserve, I say to each one of you, "Put on faith," and life will take on a new flavor, life will have a compass to show you the way; "put on hope," and every one of your days will be enlightened and your horizon will no longer be dark, but luminous; "put on love," and your life will be like a house built on rock, your journey will be joyful, because you will find many friends to journey with you. Put on faith, put on hope, put on love! (Pope Francis, "Homily at the Opening Mass for World Youth Day," July 25, 2013)

Faith, hope, and love—the Theological Virtues—are the foundation from which all human virtues flow. *Theological* means "of the study of God." These virtues are theological because through them, we are drawn into deeper knowledge of and relationship with the Holy Trinity. They give life and meaning to all the other virtues.

Faith

Faith, Hope, and Love

Faith is belief in God. It is both a gift and a response. Faith is the gift of God inviting us to believe in him, never forcing our acceptance. Faith is also our response—we accept or reject the offer. Our belief in God affects every dimension of our lives; we can't just say we believe in God and leave it at that. As disciples of Christ, we must live our faith, confidently professing it and spreading it to others.

Hope

Hope in God is closely connected to our faith. It enables us to keep our eyes on the prize of Heaven and eternal life. It inspires us in this life, helping us to overcome discouragement. Even when a situation seems hopeless, maintaining our hope in God helps us to remember our ultimate destiny and gets us through difficulties. Hope, working together with faith and love, gives us confidence to live the higher purpose of our lives.

And then there is **love**, also called charity. This is the greatest of all the Theological Virtues. Love is the virtue that gives life to the commandment to love God above all things, and our neighbor as ourself. "Beloved, let us love one another, because love is of God; everyone who loves is begotten by God and knows God. Whoever is without love

Love

Images © Renata Sedmakova / Shutterstock.com

---

faith ➤ From the Latin *fides*, meaning "trust" or "belief," faith is the gift of God by which one freely accepts God's full Revelation in Jesus Christ. It is a matter of both the head (acceptance of God's revealed truth) and the heart (love of God and neighbor as a response to God's first loving us). Also, one of the three Theological Virtues.

hope ➤ The Theological Virtue by which we trust in the promise of God and expect from God both eternal life and the grace we need to attain it; the conviction that God's grace is at work in the world and that the Kingdom of God established by and through Jesus Christ is becoming realized through the workings of the Holy Spirit among us.

love ➤ Also called "charity," the Theological Virtue by which we love God above all things and, out of that love of God, love our neighbors as ourselves.

does not know God, for God is love" (1 John 4:7–8). Even though feelings of love are wonderful it's is more than a feeling is an attitude. At times, we must go beyond feelings and will ourselves to love others. Love like this is possible because of God, and it makes all things possible.

The Centrality of the Theological Virtues

Since the beginning of Christianity, the greatest teachers among the Church Fathers have affirmed the centrality of faith, hope, and love in the life of the Christian. Saint Paul, in his First Letter to the Corinthians, summarizes his teaching on the importance of love with the simple but profound sentence: "So faith, hope, love remain, these three; but the greatest of these is love" (13:13).

In his *Explanations of the Psalms* (AD 400), Saint Augustine teaches that unlike most every other thing, the Theological Virtues cannot be taken from us:

> What are you going to give (to God), that you did not receive from him?
> . . . He gave you faith, hope, and love: these you can offer to him, these you can sacrifice. But plainly, everything else can be taken from you against your will by an enemy; but these cannot be taken from you unless you are willing.

The Theological Virtues are the foundation of Christian morality; they give the Christian moral life its unique character. God has infused these virtues into our soul at Baptism. They are God's pledge that the Holy Spirit is active in our lives. ✳

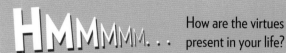

HMMMMM. . . How are the virtues of faith, hope, and love present in your life?

Article 51

The Sacraments

"The moral life is spiritual worship" (*CCC*, number 2031). What does the Church mean by this statement? It means that our worship of God is not limited to our liturgical celebrations. We also worship God by living a virtuous life. Saint Paul points to this in his Letter to the Romans, "I urge you therefore, brothers, by the mercies of God, to offer your bodies as a living sacrifice, holy and pleasing to God, your spiritual worship" (12:1). In other words, we offer God our praise, adoration, and sacrifice by living his Law of Love in our daily lives.

When it comes to our worship of God, the Seven Sacraments entrusted to the Church by Christ hold the highest place of honor. These "efficacious signs of grace" (*CCC*, number 1131) were instituted by Christ to lead us to his Father by the power of the Holy Spirit. The visible rites by which the sacraments are celebrated make present the grace which they signify in those people who receive them with faith and the proper disposition. The sacraments are necessary for our salvation; they are necessary for us to live a moral life; they are necessary for us to grow in holiness. Our Christian moral life is nourished and strengthened by the liturgy and the celebration of the sacraments. Let's look at how each of the Seven Sacraments offers us the grace and strength to live a moral life.

How is living a good, moral life a way of worshipping God?

The Seven Sacraments and Morality

The Seven Sacraments help us to remember that Christ, whom we encounter through the life of the Church, is the Sacrament of Salvation. Through the sacraments, we remember the life, ministry, and message of Jesus, and we celebrate his risen presence and saving power as it is made real in our lives. Here is a brief summary of each sacrament and its connection to the moral life.

The Seven Sacraments and the Moral Life	
Baptism	Through the sanctifying grace received at Baptism, we are welcomed into the Christian community, our sins—Original and personal—are forgiven, and we are spiritually reborn as a child of God. Our Baptism is the beginning of our Christian moral journey, and through it we receive the grace we need to turn our lives toward God and be faithful to his commandments.
Confirmation	Through Confirmation, the grace received at Baptism is perfected, strengthening our bond with the Church and enriching our lives with an outpouring of the Holy Spirit. We experience a growth in the Gifts of the Holy Spirit to help us to live virtuous lives in the name of Christ.
The Eucharist	The Eucharist is the source and summit of the moral life. Listening to the Word of God and receiving the Body and Blood of Christ nourishes and strengthens us to resist temptation and to make the sacrifices needed to share Christ's love and justice with the world. And we also bring our efforts at living virtuously to the Eucharist and offer them to God the Father in union with the sacrifice of Jesus, his Son.
Penance and Reconciliation	We will not be perfect in all our moral choices. Through the Sacrament of Penance and Reconciliation, we receive the grace of God's forgiveness, cleansing us from our sin and releasing us from shame and guilt. The sacrament reconciles us with God and with the Church.
Anointing of the Sick	Through the grace received in the Sacrament of Anointing of the Sick, our suffering is united with Christ's Passion. We regain mental and physical health if that is God's will, and we are prepared for our death if that be his will. The sacrament strengthens us to continue living virtuously even amid illness and physical suffering.
Matrimony	The grace received in the Sacrament of Matrimony helps a husband and wife to live the vocation of Christian marriage virtuously. It helps them to be faithful to each other in marriage and to be open to the gift of children. The sacrament helps them to guide and educate their children to follow God's commandments.
Holy Orders	The grace received in the Sacrament of Holy Orders helps bishops, priests, and deacons to live their clerical vocations virtuously. It enables them to live chastely and to love and serve God's people with all their heart and soul. The sacrament helps them to be an example of moral living for the People of God and to guide his people into holiness.

UNIT 5

Can you match each of the Seven Sacraments to their depictions in this stained-glass window? Can you describe the sacramental grace we receive in each sacrament?

If we truly wish to live virtuous lives, we must participate in the sacramental life of the Church. Christ gave the Seven Sacraments to the Church for our benefit, as an aid to living a holy life. If we desire and are open to the graces they provide, our moral journey will greatly benefit. ✳

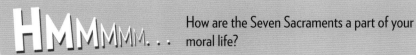

HMMMMMM. . . How are the Seven Sacraments a part of your moral life?

Article 52
The Role of Conscience

God has given us several guides to assist us in moral living. We have his Revelation, transmitted through Scripture and Tradition and authentically interpreted and taught by the Magisterium, to teach us moral truth. We have natural law, the God-given ability that enables us to understand what to do and what to avoid. We have the witness of the saints, who inspire us by their heroic moral virtues. We have parents, friends, and trustworthy leaders who point us to the right moral choices. We have been referring to these moral guides throughout this book, and they are all important. However, these guides will fail to direct and influence our lives if we choose to ignore them. In order to live as God calls us to, we must allow these guides—especially natural law and God's Revelation transmitted through Scripture and Tradition and taught by the Magisterium—to form our conscience, and we must learn how to listen to and follow our conscience.

Our conscience is at work through all stages of moral decision-making. It helps us recognize that a particular choice or action has moral consequences to consider. For example, our conscience will probably not be concerned about choosing what shirt or blouse to wear to school. But if that shirt or blouse conveys a verbal or nonverbal message of some kind, our conscience will prompt us to consider the impact of that message on others. Our conscience is also at work when we are making a moral decision. It helps us to apply reason in judging the most moral course of action in a particular situation. Finally, our conscience makes a judgment about the moral correctness of a specific act. If we have yet to perform the act, our conscience will give us moral certainty about

Some people think of conscience as a scale weighing right and wrong. But perhaps it is better to think of it as a compass pointing us in the best moral direction.

This chart outlines one moral decision-making process you might use to form and follow your conscience. It uses the acronym: FACTS.

Find the Facts	Identify the three elements of the moral decision: the object, the intention, and the circumstances. Are either the object or your intentions bad? What circumstances might put pressure on you to make a bad decision?
Assess the Alternatives	Consider all the possible actions that could be taken in responding to this situation. Do not leave any choice out because it seems too challenging.
Consider the Consequences	For each alternative action identified, evaluate how that action would affect your relationships with God, with other people, and with yourself. Which action leads to the truest sharing of God's love?
Think about God's Teachings	Be sure your conscience is properly formed before making this decision. Consider what the Old Law has to say about this issue. Which of the Ten Commandments has the most meaning in guiding your decision? Consider how Jesus' Law of Love can guide you. Which teachings or stories from the Gospels guide you and inspire you?
Seek Spiritual Support	As you consider your choice, ask the Holy Spirit for the gifts and virtues you need to make a good decision. Seek the wisdom of trusted spiritual mentors. Once your conscience is certain, draw strength from the Eucharist to carry out your decision.

UNIT 5

the right choice to make. If we have already performed the act, we experience the inner peace that comes from having done the right thing or the guilt that comes from having acted immorally. A guilty conscience prompts us to take responsibility for our sinful actions, seek forgiveness, and make reparation for any harm we have caused.

Conscience is not the moral opinion of the majority, because large groups of people can often be wrong. Conscience is not just a feeling, because feelings about moral decisions can change, but what is morally right stays the same. Your conscience is not a little voice in your head telling you what to do (although some people might describe it that way). "A voice in your head" sounds like something outside of you that is trying to intrude on your freedom. But conscience is not something foreign to us; it is part of us. The *Catechism* describes it as "a judgment of reason by which the human person recognizes the moral quality of a concrete act" (number 1796). Thus, the quality of our conscience depends largely on how well we use our reason to understand Divine Law and whether we follow the moral judgments made based on reason and Divine Law. Let's look more closely at both of these conditions.

Conscience Formation

To use reason well in making moral judgments, we must educate ourselves about Divine Law. This process is also called conscience formation. A well-formed conscience will lead us to make the right moral judgment, in keeping with God's commandments. It is principled, honest, and truthful. Because a well-formed conscience is so important to our moral life, we have a serious obligation to educate our conscience well. Here are some proven ways we can form our conscience:

- We can study the doctrine of the Church to learn the moral truth revealed by God. Reading this book is a good start. However, our education in faith is a lifelong process that we must continue, especially as we encounter complex moral issues that this book could only briefly describe.
- We can read and reflect on the Word of God in Scripture. God's Word is a "light for [our] path" (Psalm 119:105), and the more time we spend with it in study and prayer the more it influences our daily life and practice.
- We can examine the moral choices we have made at the end of every day or every week. The more we practice identifying our good and bad decisions, the more trained our conscience becomes at recognizing sinful choices before we make them.

- We can read the lives of the saints and other holy people, both ancient and modern. Their stories of moral courage and integrity will inspire us in forming and following our conscience.
- We can receive the Sacraments of the Eucharist and Penance and Reconciliation regularly. The graces we receive from these sacraments will strengthen our desire to seek moral truth and to follow it.

Reading and reflecting on the Word of God is an important way to form our conscience. What are some other ways you can properly form your conscience?

With a well-formed conscience, we are better prepared to respond to moral situations. When our conscience has been educated in the moral virtues, making good moral decisions comes more naturally. When our conscience has developed a habit of making good moral decisions in small matters, we are better prepared to make good decisions in more serious matters. When our conscience is regularly exercised, we are better prepared to make a good moral decision in situations that call for a quick decision.

Obeying Your Conscience

When it comes to following our conscience, there is one essential rule to follow: We must always obey the judgment of a certain conscience. When our conscience has been properly prepared and we are certain about the morally right course of action to take, we must take that action. To do otherwise would be a sin. This doesn't mean that following our conscience will always be easy.

There are times in most people's lives when they wish they did not have to follow their conscience. Following your conscience might mean sacrificing popularity, material wealth, or even your own safety (remember the martyrs). Christ himself faced these challenges but stayed true to his conscience despite them. So must we.

Keep in mind that a certain conscience is not always a correct conscience. When faced with a moral decision, our conscience can make either a right judgment in keeping with reason and Divine Law or it can make an erroneous judgment that is not in keeping with reason and Divine Law. Occasionally, our conscience can be erroneous through no fault of our own. Consider this example. A trusted tax authority tells someone that it is legal to take a certain tax credit, so the person takes it. However, it turns out that the tax credit does not apply to that person and taking it is illegal. But the person taking the credit did not commit a sin because his conscience was in error through no fault of his own. Should he find out later that the tax credit was not legal, he would be morally responsible for correcting the mistake.

Most of the time, we are at least partially responsible for any sin committed due to an erroneous judgment by our conscience. This is because in most cases we could have prevented the ignorance that caused our conscience to make the wrong judgment. This ignorance might happen because we never took the time to study the teachings of the Gospel, or because we rejected the Church's moral authority, or because we let ourselves be influenced by the bad example of other people. It could also happen because we let our conscience become dulled by sinful habits or vices. When our conscience leads us into erroneous moral judgments because of these things, we are still **culpable** for the sins we commit.

Our conscience is the greatest guide God has given us for living the moral life. It is the law that he has written on our hearts (see Jeremiah 31:33). Properly formed, it will faithfully direct us on our journey to holiness. Using it only requires that we take the time to be still, turn inward, reflect on our lives, and listen for the interior voice directing us on how best to love God, love our neighbor, and love ourselves. ✳

 What is the most important thing you can do to prepare your conscience for making good moral decisions?

culpable ➤ To be guilty of wrongdoing.

UNIT 5

1. What is the primary characteristic of being a disciple of Jesus Christ?

2. Describe four different opportunities that Christians have to live their baptismal vocation.

3. Define *grace*.

4. Name three kinds of grace, and give an example for each kind.

5. What are the four Cardinal Virtues, and why are they important for living a moral life?

6. How are the Theological Virtues different from the Cardinal Virtues?

7. What does it mean to say that "the moral life is spiritual worship" (*CCC*, number 2031)?

8. Choose three sacraments and explain how the graces of each sacrament are connected to living a moral life.

9. Why is a well-formed conscience important in Christian morality?

10. Describe three things you can do to form your conscience.

Moral Gifts and Guides

Sanctifying Grace

Sacramental Graces

Charisms

Conscience

GOOD

EVIL

Called to Be Holy

Gifts of the Holy Spirit

The Theological Virtues

The Cardinal Virtues

UNIT 5

Images: Shutterstock.com / © Masim Apnyatin / Shutterstock.com / © jorisvo / Shutterstock.com

CHAPTER 13
Forgiveness and Reconciliation

HOW CAN I FORGIVE SOMEONE WHO HAS DONE SOMETHING REALLY HURTFUL?

SNAPSHOT

Article 53

The Biblical Call to Forgiveness

Corrie ten Boom belonged to a Dutch family that was part of the Dutch resistance during World War II. In her book *The Hiding Place*, she tells how her family created a small secret closet that could hide up to six people, and they used it to hide Jewish people during Nazi searches. Her family was betrayed and sent to concentration camps, where her father and sister later died. Eventually Corrie was freed. Years later, after speaking about forgiveness at a church service, she met a German man whom she recognized as a guard at the concentration camp where her father had died. He thanked her for her message and held out his hand to shake hers. Corrie was so filled with anger that at first she could not bring herself to shake his hand.

At that moment, it seemed impossible to forgive the man. So Corrie said a prayer, asking Jesus to forgive him. She was then able to shake his hand, and as she did so, she had an extraordinary feeling and something like an electric current went down her arm and into him. Suddenly she was filled with love for the man, a love that did not come from her. She realized that along with the command to forgive your enemies, Jesus also gives the love itself.

© Hiraman / iStockphoto.com

UNIT 5

Corrie ten Boom was able to find the strength to forgive someone who was part of a terrible injustice her family suffered. How can someone find the strength to do this?

TAKE IT TO GOD

My God,
I am sorry for my sins with all my heart.
In choosing to do wrong and failing to do good,
I have sinned against you whom I should love above all things.
I firmly intend, with your help, to do penance,
to sin no more, and to avoid whatever leads me to sin.
Our Savior Jesus Christ suffered and died for us.
In his name, my God, have mercy.
(Prayer of the Penitent from the *Rite of Penance*, number 45)

The Word of God calls us to both seek and give forgiveness. We can seek forgiveness and reconciliation with God and the Church through the Sacrament of Penance and Reconciliation. We may also have to seek forgiveness from the people our sin has hurt and make reparation for the harm we have caused them. Granting forgiveness to others who have harmed us is just as important and possibly even more difficult. But until we have forgiven those who have hurt us, we cannot experience the fullness of God's forgiveness for ourselves.

The Example of Jesus

His only crime was calling for people to be faithful to their religious heritage and calling for justice for the poor. He was arrested by the leaders of his religion and brought before them, accused of crimes against their religion—in a secret hearing in the middle of the night! Those religious leaders brought him before their local governor and falsely accused him of planning a rebellion against the government. The governor, despite having no personal knowledge of the man and calling for no other witnesses, had him publicly humiliated and brutally whipped. When this punishment wasn't enough to placate the religious leaders, the governor ordered the man to be crucified—a torturous, prolonged death meant to discourage anyone else from committing the same crimes.

Despite all this—the unjust accusations, the secret trials, the brutal treatment, the torturous death—the man forgave his executioners while hanging on the cross. He prayed, "Father, forgive them, they know not what they do" (Luke 23:34). The man, of course, is Jesus Christ, the Son of God. Throughout his earthly ministry, he preached about the importance of forgiveness, and he lived what he preached right up until the end of his earthly life.

Contrast the value that Jesus placed on forgiveness with the value placed on revenge portrayed by many heroes in books and movies. The basic action book or film plot goes like this: The hero gets falsely accused, or someone close to the hero gets hurt or killed or abducted by villains. The hero vows to get revenge and tracks the evil people down. After overcoming many obstacles and dangers, the hero confronts the villains, brutalizes them, and very often kills them—the more violent and bloody the better—and the reader or the audience erupts into cheers. Let's be honest, sometimes revenge seems so satisfying and so right. So why doesn't Jesus endorse it? Why did he preach exactly the opposite? Why was he so emphatic that we must seek and grant forgiveness?

Old Testament Passages on Forgiveness

The Bible's teaching on forgiveness is huge, and exploring it would require another book. Even though there is a great deal of "just punishment" in the laws and stories of the Old Testament, the seeds for the importance of forgiveness are planted in its books. Consider these well-known examples.

- The Mosaic Law prescribed special sacrifices as guilt offerings for the forgiveness of certain sins (see Leviticus, chapters 4 and 5). One example:

  If someone does wrong and violates one of the Lord's prohibitions without realizing it, that person is guilty and shall bear the penalty. The individual shall bring to the priest an unblemished ram of the flock, at the established value, for a reparation offering. The priest shall then make atonement on the offerer's behalf for the error inadvertently and unknowingly committed so that the individual may be forgiven. (5:17–18)

UNIT 5

- Psalm 51 is a song attributed to King David, written after his affair with Bathsheba. In the Psalm, David asks for God's mercy and forgiveness:

  > Have mercy on me, God, in accord with your merciful love; / in your abundant compassion blot out my transgressions. / Thoroughly wash away my guilt; / and from my sin cleanse me. / For I know my transgressions; / my sin is always before me. / Against you, you alone have I sinned; / I have done what is evil in your eyes / So that you are just in your word, / and without reproach in your judgment. (Verses 3–6)

- Even after all of Israel's many sins, some of the prophets told of a day when the people would know God's mercy and forgiveness. We recognize in these prophecies the foreshadowing of the saving work of Christ. Here is an example from Jeremiah:

  > I will place my law within them, and write it upon their hearts; I will be their God, and they shall be my people. They will no longer teach their friends and relatives, "Know the Lord!" Everyone, from least to greatest, shall know me—oracle of the Lord—for I will forgive their iniquity and no longer remember their sin. (31:33–34)

From his agony on the cross, Jesus forgives those who crucified him. In what other ways did he teach us about the importance of forgiveness?

Jesus on God's Forgiveness

The seeds about God's forgiveness planted in the Old Testament come into full bloom in the Gospels. In Jesus' teaching, we come to understand that forgiveness is one of the most important attributes of God. Jesus' teachings on God's mercy and forgiveness were partially covered in chapter 3, but here are two more examples to consider.

The Parable of the Prodigal Son (see Luke 15:11–32) might be better called the Parable of the Forgiving Father. The parable's emphasis is really on the father more than the son. This father does the completely unexpected act of forgiving and welcoming his repentant son, rather than punishing and humiliating him (as his neighbors would have expected him to do). In fact, the father seems to be spending his days watching and hoping for his son's return. In this parable, Jesus is telling us that this is what God is like, just waiting anxiously to forgive us when we have done wrong.

When we compare a section of the Sermon on the Mount from Matthew (see 5:38–48) with the parallel section in Luke (see 6:27–36), we see something very interesting. In this section, Jesus tells us to do good to those who mistreat us and even love and do good to our enemies. In Matthew, Jesus ends this section by saying, "So be perfect, just as your heavenly Father is perfect" (5:48). But in Luke, Jesus ends by saying, "Be merciful, just as [also] your Father is merciful" (6:36). These parallel passages equate God's perfection and God's mercy and forgiveness. One cannot be perfect without also being merciful.

Seeking Forgiveness

Every human being—except Jesus and his mother, Mary—is guilty of sin and subject to death. However, what is even more unfortunate than being guilty of sin is denying our sinfulness. Denying our sin is easy to do; whether the cause is pride or shame, we find it hard to admit to God, ourselves, and other people that we have missed the mark. This denial is tragic because we cannot receive what we need—forgiveness—until we admit that we are sinners. And only by seeking God's forgiveness will we find the healing we need to repair the damage to heart and soul caused by our sin.

This is why Jesus has such high praise for those who acknowledge their sin and seek forgiveness. The Gospel of Luke tells about a time when Jesus is invited to the house of a Pharisee for dinner (see 7:36–50). While at dinner, a woman who is a known sinner comes into the house and bathes Jesus' feet with her tears, wipes them with her hair, and rubs them with ointment. Her wordless actions express her deep sorrow for her sins and her desire to be forgiven.

UNIT 5

The Pharisee is shocked that Jesus allows this sinful woman to even touch him. After telling a parable about debtors whose debts were forgiven, Jesus concludes by telling the Pharisee, "So I tell you, her many sins have been forgiven; hence, she has shown great love. But the one to whom little is forgiven, loves little" (verse 47). In praising the woman, Jesus makes a connection between forgiveness and love. Those who admit their sin and seek forgiveness experience an increase of love in their hearts—love for God, love for themselves, and love for others.

The Gospel of Christ calls us to seek forgiveness. We see this call expressed at the beginning of the Church. After receiving the Holy Spirit at Pentecost, Peter speaks to the crowds and shares the Good News of Jesus' life, death, and Resurrection (see Acts of the Apostles 2:14–39). Afterward, the crowds ask Peter and the other Apostles how they should respond. Peter says, "Repent and be baptized, every one of you, in the name of Jesus Christ for the forgiveness of your sins; and you will receive the gift of the holy Spirit" (verse 38). The same is true for us today. Those who are unbaptized must seek forgiveness through the Sacrament of Baptism, and those who are baptized who have committed serious sin must seek forgiveness through the Sacrament of Penance and Reconciliation. When we do this, God's love will heal our wounded souls and fill our empty hearts.

© WAYHOME studio / Shutterstock.com

Asking for and giving forgiveness require honesty, humility, and love. Which is more challenging for you: to ask for forgiveness or to forgive someone who has hurt you?

Giving Forgiveness

Forgiveness has another crucial side. Consider the Parable of the Unforgiving Servant in the Gospel of Matthew. In this parable, a king forgives a large debt owed to him by one of his servants. But then this servant goes out and has a fellow servant who owes him a much smaller amount thrown into prison. When the king finds out about this, he angrily summons the first servant before him. "You wicked servant!" says the king. "I forgave you your entire debt because you begged me to. Should you not have had pity on your fellow servant, as I had pity on you?" (18:32–33).

Jesus' point in telling the parable is this: We are like the first servant. Through the forgiveness of our sins, God has erased the huge spiritual debt caused by our sin. How then can we not be merciful and forgive those who have sinned against us? Clearly, we must not only seek forgiveness, but we must also be willing to forgive those who have sinned against us. These two sides of forgiveness are spiritually inseparable. Jesus makes this point in teaching his disciples the Lord's Prayer: "And forgive us our sins / for we ourselves forgive everyone in debt to us" (Luke 11:4). In still another place, he says: "Stop judging and you will not be judged. Stop condemning and you will not be condemned. Forgive and you will be forgiven" (6:37). All these teachings of Jesus lead to one inescapable conclusion: God's forgiveness of our sins depends on whether we forgive other people's sins against us. Put another way, it is a sin to withhold our forgiveness from someone who sincerely asks us for it. ✳

 How is your understanding of God connected to mercy and forgiveness?

UNIT 5

Article 54

Seeking Forgiveness and Reconciliation

The Mission (Warner Home Video, 1992) is a powerful movie about forgiveness and **reconciliation.** The movie is set during a time when Spanish Jesuit missionaries are establishing missions in the South American jungle to evangelize the native people living there. Part of the story is centered on a mercenary and slave trader named Mendoza, who kills his brother in a jealous rage. Overcome with guilt and remorse, Mendoza seeks forgiveness from God and from the native people he had previously enslaved. In a powerful scene, Mendoza does penance by climbing a treacherous waterfall, weighed down by the former tools of his trade, his weapons and armor.

When he finally reaches the top, the native warriors have to choose between killing this former enemy or forgiving him. They choose to forgive him, and in a symbolic act, cut off his armor and weapons and throw them over the waterfall. Having received the forgiveness of God and of the people he had sinned against, Mendoza is filled with God's love, and he joins the Jesuit order and becomes a missionary, serving the native people.

© United Archives GmbH / Alamy Stock Photo

Movies like *The Mission* emphasize the importance of forgiveness on our journey toward God. What other movies have you seen in which forgiveness is an important theme?

reconciliation ➤ The process of restoring broken relationships with God, with the Church, and with people who were directly offended by our sins.

Seeking forgiveness and reconciliation may indeed involve dramatic moments such as those portrayed in *The Mission*. But for faithful Christians, it often involves offenses much less serious than slave trading, sins such as telling white lies, gossiping, cheating, and harboring minor envies. But just because these sins may be less serious does not mean that they are harmless to our spiritual health. Venial sins that go unconfessed can easily become vices and lead to more serious sin. We must not wait until habits of unrepented sin lead us to commit a sin so serious that it causes a complete breakdown of our relationship with God and the people we love, as it did for Mendoza.

If we humans have the tendency to deny our sinfulness, what breaks through the denial and prompts us to seek forgiveness and reconciliation? It is the voice of conscience, that inner guide God has placed in every human heart. If our conscience is dull and poorly formed, it may take the impact of a serious sin for us to hear its call to repentance. That is why we must be attentive to our conscience and see that it is properly formed (see article 52). Two good ways to be attentive to our conscience is through a regular examination of conscience and by regular reception of the Sacraments of the Eucharist and of Penance and Reconciliation.

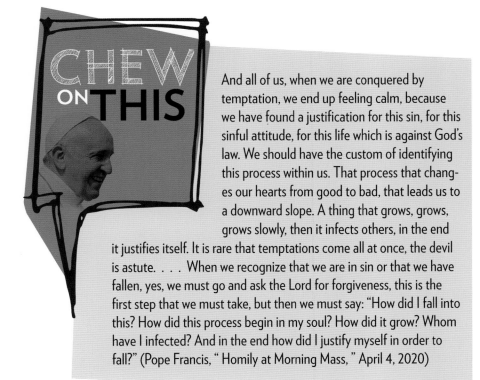

And all of us, when we are conquered by temptation, we end up feeling calm, because we have found a justification for this sin, for this sinful attitude, for this life which is against God's law. We should have the custom of identifying this process within us. That process that changes our hearts from good to bad, that leads us to a downward slope. A thing that grows, grows, grows slowly, then it infects others, in the end it justifies itself. It is rare that temptations come all at once, the devil is astute. . . . When we recognize that we are in sin or that we have fallen, yes, we must go and ask the Lord for forgiveness, this is the first step that we must take, but then we must say: "How did I fall into this? How did this process begin in my soul? How did it grow? Whom have I infected? And in the end how did I justify myself in order to fall?" (Pope Francis, "Homily at Morning Mass," April 4, 2020)

UNIT 5

Conducting an Examination of Conscience

A regular examination of conscience is a good way to see if our conscience is prompting us to seek forgiveness. This examination of conscience is based on the Ten Commandments and the two Great Commandments.

Love of God

- Is there anything that I am allowing to take God's place in my life?
- Do I pray regularly, and when I do pray, do I give my full attention to my prayer?
- Do I attend Mass and receive the Eucharist every week? Do I keep Sunday holy?
- Am I making a good effort to grow in my relationship with God by receiving the Sacrament of Penance and Reconciliation, spiritual reading, retreats, and other spiritual practices?
- Am I always reverent to God in my words and actions?

Love of Neighbor

- Have I treated anyone with disrespect, especially my parents, brothers and sisters, teachers, and other people in authority?
- Have I obeyed the rules and laws of my school, state, and country?
- Have I harmed another person intentionally or through my careless actions? Have I been unkind or cruel to others in thought, word, or deed?
- Have I harmed another person's dignity by engaging in gossip or spreading demeaning stories about the person?
- Have I protected my chastity at all times? Have I viewed pornography, engaged in lustful thoughts, or been sexually active in any way outside of marriage?
- Have I been truthful in all situations calling for the truth? Have I cheated or been dishonest in any way?
- Have I been envious of someone else in any way?
- Have I participated in or supported another person's sinful actions?
- Have I been of service to others who I was in a position to help? Have I reached out in some way to people in need?
- Have I encouraged others to avoid sin?

Seeking Forgiveness from God

Javier was really feeling down and depressed lately and decided to talk to his youth minister about it. It turned out that Javier had had a big fight with his girlfriend, accusing her of cheating on him. Later, he found out that his girlfriend has just been helping someone with a homework assignment. He had let his jealousy drive his anger, and he was completely in the wrong. "I apologized to my girlfriend, and she seemed to forgive me," Javier told his youth minister. "But I still don't feel right. Shouldn't that take care of things?"

"You might be missing something, Javier," his youth minister replied. "Have you confessed your jealousy and false accusation to God? Have you asked for God's forgiveness too? That's just as important as asking forgiveness of the person we offended. Knowing you have God's forgiveness will help your conscience and your soul be at peace."

Our relationship with God suffers when we are in a state of unrepented sin. If the sins are venial sins, our relationship with God has been weakened but not broken. When we realize we are guilty of a venial sin, we should

© Godong / Alamy Stock Photo

The Sacrament of Penance and Reconciliation is a powerful experience of God's forgiveness. There are many benefits in making it a regular part of your spiritual life.

confess it to God in prayer and ask for his forgiveness with a commitment not to sin again. Recognizing and turning away from our sin and committing not to sin again is called **contrition**, and having a contrite heart is essential when asking God for forgiveness. Venial sins do not require that we receive the Sacrament of Penance and Reconciliation, but it is strongly recommended that we also confess our minor faults in the sacrament. When we commit a mortal sin, our relationship with God is ruptured because we have intentionally turned away from God through a conscious and willful choice to disobey his commandments. Once we realize that we have committed a mortal sin and are contrite, we should ask for God's forgiveness in our private prayer and then confess our sins and receive absolution in the Sacrament of Penance and Reconciliation as soon as we can. When we are guilty of mortal sin, receiving the sacrament is the sure way of reconciliation with God and with the Church.

It is natural to wonder, "Why do I have to confess my sins to a priest?" This question has many possible answers, but let's consider two important reasons. First, the priest is the visible sign of the presence of Christ himself. Christ shares the power to forgive sins with the bishops of the Church (see John 20:23). Priests—and only priests—share the bishops' power to forgive sins. So when the priest absolves us from our sins in the Sacrament of Penance and Reconciliation, it is Christ himself who is forgiving us. Second, because human beings are creatures with bodies and souls, all the sacraments have both physical and spiritual realities. The visible, physical elements of the sacraments signify the spiritual realities made present through the visible rites and the power of Christ and the Holy Spirit.

In the Sacrament of Penance and Reconciliation, the physical elements include the confession of the person's sins to the priest and the priest's laying hands on the person while saying the words of **absolution**. Like Javier, we need to hear the following words spoken by the priest as God's agent: "I absolve you from your sins in the name of the Father, and of the Son, and of the Holy Spirit" (General Absolution from *The Rite of Penance*, number 46). These are powerful words to hear spoken aloud. Through the work of the Holy Spirit, these words and actions put us in touch with the spiritual reality of God's forgiveness of our sins.

---

contrition ➤ To have sorrow and hatred for our sin and a commitment not to sin again.

absolution ➤ An essential part of the Sacrament of Penance and Reconciliation in which the priest pardons the sins of the person confessing, in the name of God and the Church.

Seeking Forgiveness from Others

Receiving absolution takes away our sin but does not repair the harm caused to other people or even the harm we may have caused ourselves. So after confessing our sin, we must still seek to repair the harm caused by our sin and to grow in moral virtue, especially the virtue needed to avoid the same sin in the future. In the Sacrament of Penance and Reconciliation, the priest directs us to perform certain acts to satisfy this need. This satisfaction is called our **penance**. The penance assigned by the priest confessor could be prayer, a spiritual discipline, or acts intended to heal our relationships with the people who were harmed by our sins.

The penance we receive from the priest is not the only way we can seek forgiveness from others and make reparation for our sin. In fact, after we realize that we have directly sinned against another person and are truly sorry for the harm we have caused, we can express our sorrow to the person as soon as is reasonable. When making our apology, we must exercise the virtues of prudence and humility. For example, we should apologize in person rather than through a text message. This could be misunderstood to mean that our

© Prostock-studio / Shutterstock.com

When we seek forgiveness, our apology must be sincere. If we are not sincere, what is the likely result?

---

penance ➤ In general, an attitude of the heart in which one experiences regrets for past sin and commits to a change in behaviors or attitudes. In the Sacrament of Penance and Reconciliation, the priest assigns penitents a penance to help them make amends for their sins. Particular acts of penance may include spiritual disciplines such as prayers or fasting.

apology isn't sincere. Instead, we should apologize when we have privacy and time to talk. We will want to make the apology as positive as possible and not compound the hurt by having it appear insincere or poorly thought out. If necessary, we can seek advice from a trusted friend or counselor about how best to express our sorrow and ask for forgiveness.

Keep in mind that we may also need to make reparation in some concrete ways. If we steal something, we need to return it or make some other compensation of equal value. If we harm someone's reputation, we can set the record straight by telling people we were wrong in what we said about the person. If we are unsure about how to make reparation, we can also ask the person we have sinned against how we might compensate for our offense. We are not required, however, to make amends in any way that would harm ourself or another person.

Expressing our sorrow for our sins to the people we have hurt and making reparation for the damage caused by our sin is part of the healing process. We cannot control whether the other person chooses to forgive us. We can only do our best to express our sorrow and leave the rest to the work of the Spirit; some healing takes a great deal of time. We will get better at expressing our sorrow with practice; let us not compound our sin by being too proud to ask for forgiveness. ✳

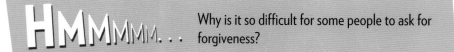

HMMMMM... Why is it so difficult for some people to ask for forgiveness?

Article 55

Granting Forgiveness

In September 2018, Botham Jean was sitting in his apartment, watching television and eating ice cream. An off-duty police officer entered his apartment, shot, and killed him. According to the officer's testimony, she somehow mistakenly thought the apartment was her own and entered it. Again, according to her testimony, she thought her apartment was being invaded by an intruder and thus shot and killed Botham Jean. The officer was brought to trial, convicted of first-degree murder, and sentenced to prison. But at her sentencing, something truly remarkable happened.

Botham Jean's younger brother, Grant, who was eighteen, forgave the police officer while giving his victim impact statement. "If you truly are sorry, I know I can speak for myself, I forgive you," said Grant. "And if you go to God and ask him, he will forgive you," he continued. Then he asked permission to leave the witness stand to give his brother's killer a hug. His amazing display of forgiveness was widely broadcast, prompting a national discussion on forgiveness.

Some people are inspired by powerful stories of forgiveness, while others are not. Why is granting forgiveness so hard to accept for some people?

UNIT 5

The Effects of Failing to Forgive

When we refuse to forgive others who have sinned against us, we hang on to resentments and the feelings of pain, sadness, and anger that accompany them. We may wish to harm the other person in retaliation. But the saints and spiritual leaders teach that it is important to forgive people who have hurt us, even if they have not asked for our forgiveness. "Remember," someone once said, "that reconciliation takes two, but forgiveness only requires one." We saw Jesus practicing this on the cross; he forgave the people who crucified him before they even asked for forgiveness. So why should we forgive someone who has hurt us, especially if the person has not asked us for forgiveness?

The answer of many authorities—both spiritual and medical—is because when we hold on to past hurts and refuse to forgive, we only continue to suffer ourselves. Saint Ambrose (ca. 340–397) once said, "No one heals himself by wounding another." Medical researchers have traced the lack of forgiveness to physical conditions such as higher blood pressure, depression, anxiety, chronic pain, and higher risk of alcohol and substance abuse. When someone sins against us, we often experience psychological and spiritual trauma. The more serious this trauma is, the more potentially damaging is the physical suffering we experience when that hurt goes unhealed.

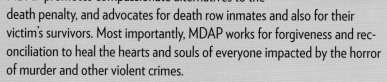

CATHOLICS **MAKING** A DIFFERENCE

DEATH ROW

The Ministry Against the Death Penalty (MADP) is an organization founded by Sr. Helen Prejean. Sister Helen has ministered to inmates on death row as well as to the families of their victims for nearly forty years. Her first book, *Dead Man Walking,* tells the story of how she first started ministering to death row inmates. MDAP promotes compassionate alternatives to the death penalty, and advocates for death row inmates and also for their victim's survivors. Most importantly, MDAP works for forgiveness and reconciliation to heal the hearts and souls of everyone impacted by the horror of murder and other violent crimes.

UNIT 5

This simple but profound reflection is associated with Saint Mother Teresa of Kolkata (Calcutta) and is based on a reflection written for students by Kent Keith. Let it inspire you to great acts of faith and forgiveness.

The Paradoxical Commandments

1. People are illogical, unreasonable, and self-centered. Forgive them anyway.

2. If you do good, people will accuse you of selfish, ulterior motives. Do good anyway.

3. If you are successful, you will win false friends and true enemies. Succeed anyway.

4. The good you do today will be forgotten tomorrow. Do good anyway.

5. Honesty and frankness make you vulnerable. Be honest and frank anyway.

6. The biggest men and women with the biggest ideas can be shot down by fearful people. Think big anyway.

7. People favor underdogs but follow only top dogs. Fight for a few underdogs anyway.

8. What you spend years building may be destroyed overnight. Build anyway.

9. People really need help but may attack you if you do help them. Help people anyway.

10. Give the world the best you have and you'll get kicked in the teeth. Give the world the best you have anyway.

(Adapted from Kent Keith, *The Silent Revolution: Dynamic Leadership in the Student Council*)

UNIT 5

Katherine's father deeply hurt her family through his sins of adultery and physical abuse. She was very angry and depressed because of her father's actions and told her friends that she was never going to forgive him. Many months passed, and Katherine realized that her anger and resentment was making her life miserable. She made the difficult step of forgiving her father in her heart and later forgiving him directly. Surprisingly, when she did this, her father asked for her forgiveness and promised he would change. Katherine's family decided to give him one more chance. "But even if he doesn't change," Katherine said, "I have to forgive him so that I can free myself of my anger and move on."

Perhaps the most important reason for forgiving others is because it is crucial to our spiritual well-being. Holding on to resentments and thoughts of revenge damages our relationship with God. When we live with anger and hate, we cannot be in full communion with God, who is all-loving. Article 53 discusses how Jesus made the connection between divine forgiveness and our forgiveness of others. God does not withhold forgiveness from us, but when we refuse to forgive others, we prevent ourselves from accepting his forgiving love. In a sense, when we withhold forgiveness from those who have hurt us, we are choosing our own spiritual suffering.

© 965 Creation / Shutterstock.com

UNIT 5

The process of forgiveness and reconciliation is often a difficult one. However, refusing to forgive keeps us trapped in our pain. We can move forward by asking for God's help.

It is important to remember that forgiveness and reconciliation are connected but not the same. As has been mentioned, you can forgive somebody who has not asked for forgiveness; however, you cannot be reconciled with that person until they are truly repentant and sorry for their sin against you. Forgiveness does not mean that you must allow an abusive person back into your life, nor does it mean that you must trust or be vulnerable with a person who continues to be untrustworthy.

From Hurt and Resentment to Forgiveness and Healing

In general, our culture is not a forgiving culture. This might be one reason that forgiving people who have hurt us seems like a foreign concept to many people. When true forgiveness is practiced, as it was with Grant Jean, some people find it difficult to believe it is even real. Although it is sometimes hard to understand and sometimes even harder to live, true forgiveness should be the norm for Christians, as Christ commands. When you find it hard to practice forgiveness—whether the hurt is great or small—here are some suggestions to move forward:

- Do not think of yourself as a victim. Do not let the person who has hurt you continue to control your life. You are a beloved child of God who has God's grace to strengthen you. Do the right thing—forgive and move on.
- Allow yourself to feel the pain of being hurt. Some people never get to forgiveness because they will not admit to being hurt. This is especially true for men.
- Make a decision to forgive. Forgiveness is not a feeling; it is a choice. You do not need to wait until you stop hurting to forgive.
- Do not wait for the person to change or to come to you and ask for forgiveness. Doing so only continues to put you in the role of the victim. In prayer, ask for the Holy Spirit's grace to strengthen you and guide you. Pray for the willingness to forgive when you find yourself not wanting to forgive someone. ✳

UNIT 5

 What role has forgiveness played in your life? Is there someone you need to forgive?

1. Why is it so important that we ask for God's forgiveness of our sins?

2. Give two examples from the Gospels in which Jesus teaches about the importance of forgiving those who have sinned against us.

3. How must we ask God's forgiveness for mortal sins?

4. What are some things to keep in mind when seeking forgiveness from other people?

5. What is the potential effect on ourselves when we fail to forgive others? What is the potential effect on ourselves when we extend forgiveness to others?

6. What are some things people can do to start the process of forgiveness?

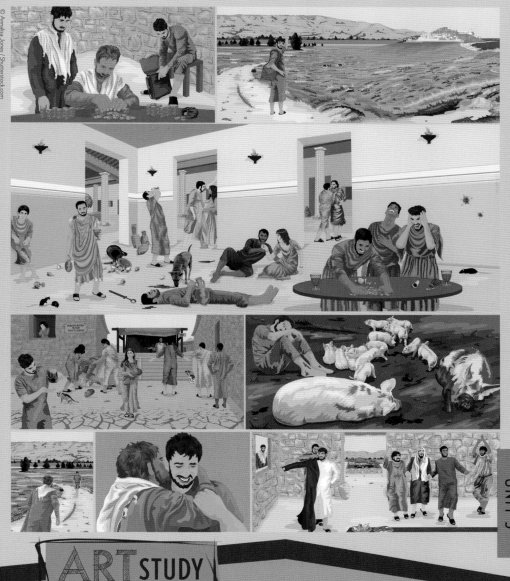

© Annalisa Jones / Shutterstock.com

ART STUDY

This image of the Parable of the Prodigal Son illustrates several scenes from this powerful story on forgiveness.

1. What parts of the parable do you recognize?

2. What parts of the image attract your attention?

3. Put yourself in the place of the older brother, who appears in the first and last panels. Why might he be struggling with forgiveness?

UNIT 5 HIGHLIGHTS

Gifts of the Holy Spirit

CHAPTER 12
Gifts and Guides

fortitude

prudence

temperance

justice

Cardinal Virtues

UNIT 5

Welcome to a life of holiness and love!
Theological Virtues
faith love hope
How can I live out my baptismal vocation?
Here are some ideas: missionary activity, religious movements, service to the Church, meaningful job, or volunteer work.

Sanctifying Grace

- Received at Baptism
- Heals our wounded soul

Actual Graces

- God's intervention and support
- Received in the daily moments of our lives

Grace

Special Graces

- Gifts intended for the good of the Church
- Also called charisms

Sacramental Graces

- Gifts proper to each Sacrament

Proven Ways to Form Your Conscience

Study Church teaching

Study God's Word

The Catholic Youth Bible

CATECHISM OF THE CATHOLIC CHURCH

Reflect on your choices

Be inspired by the saints

Receive the sacraments

A properly formed conscience is essential to guide us in making good moral decisions. We must always obey a well-formed, certain conscience.

CHAPTER 13   Forgiveness and Reconciliation

The Forgiveness of God

- "I will forgive their iniquity and no longer remember their sin."
- Parable of the Forgiving Father
- "Be merciful, just as your Father is merciful."

Jesus' Example of Forgiveness

- "I did not come to call the righteous but sinners."
- "Father, forgive them, they know not what they do."

Our Call to Forgive and Ask Forgiveness

- "Forgive and you will be forgiven."
- Jesus has high praise for those who ask for forgiveness.
- "Forgive us our trespasses as we forgive those who trespass against us."

UNIT 5

Celebrate Forgiveness!

Receive absolution!

Forgive others to heal yourself!

Do an examination of conscience!

Willingly accept penance!

Make
reparation!

Remember
forgiveness
is a choice!

Express
sorrow!

Be truly
contrite!

Do not
wait!

UNIT 5

Giving and receiving forgiveness is something to celebrate.
Make use of these practices to make forgiveness an essential
part of your spiritual life, especially in the Sacrament of
Penance and Reconciliation!

UNIT 5
BRING IT HOME

HOW CAN I LIVE A GOOD LIFE, EVEN WHEN I SOMETIMES MISS THE MARK?

UNIT 5

VICTORIA
Red Bank Catholic High School

Missing the mark is not the end of the world. You still have the potential to live a virtuous life with the helping hand of God. In this unit, I was reminded that to keep from making more mistakes, it is important to continuously listen to your conscience. My conscience is a wonderful gift from God that can aid in decision-making. Another thing to always remember is the power of forgiveness. When you make a mistake that impacts someone else, you should seek forgiveness. When someone makes a mistake that impacts you, you should give forgiveness. Forgiveness leads to healing and reconciliation between both parties. Let's find our ultimate happiness and fulfillment by being open to God's love and letting it fill our hearts!

UNIT 5

REFLECT

Take some time to read and reflect on the unit and chapter focus questions listed on the facing page.

• What question or section did you identify most closely with?

• What did you find within the unit that was comforting or challenging?

APPENDIX
Challenge Questions

The content of this course will raise some important questions for those who think seriously about their faith. This is especially true today when many people are asking hard questions about religious beliefs. We are not afraid of these hard questions because an honest search for answers will deepen our faith and understanding of what God has revealed. Here are some common questions about Christian morality with some key points for how to answer them. The references to paragraphs in the *Catechism of the Catholic Church (CCC)* are for further reading if you want to explore these questions more deeply.

QUESTION 1: If God created me free, doesn't that mean that I alone can decide what is right and wrong?

Western culture places a very high value on individual freedom, so is natural to ask this question in a discussion on morality. However, as this book has tried to show, this is a misunderstanding of human freedom. We are free to choose to do what is right or what is wrong and to resist the temptation to sin (see *CCC*, numbers 1730–1742). But we are not free to decide what is right and what is wrong, because we would have to be as wise as God to do so! Moral truth is objective truth; it is not subjective. This is why true freedom is following God's Law (see numbers 1954–1960).

Still someone might ask why we need to follow laws that were created thousands of years ago. If this is referring to the Ten Commandments and the New Law taught by Jesus, then these laws were not created thousands of years ago. They were created at the beginning of time. They are based in Eternal Law, which is true forever. Yes, it is true that the moral law needs to be applied to new historical situations and new scientific advances, but this is the work of the entire Church, not just one person.

One final thing to remember about this question: Following the moral law and doing what is good actually increases our freedom (see *CCC*, number 1733). Conversely, using our freedom to do whatever we want is a misuse of our freedom and results in our becoming less free, trapped by our sin. Think about the example of telling lies given in chapter 2. Over time, chronic liars are far less free than before they started lying. People who are chronically dishonest will tell you that staying on top of whom they told which lies to eventually consumes most of their attention. They become totally controlled by their fear of being discovered. They are trapped and are less free because of their sinful behavior.

QUESTION 2: Isn't it wrong to judge other people by telling them something they are doing is wrong?

Jesus Christ commands us to be forgiving people. But does that also mean that we should overlook the wrong things that other people do? You might ask: "What right do I have to tell friends who are shoplifting or drinking underage or involved in premarital sex that their actions are sinful? Didn't Jesus himself say, 'Stop judging, that you may not be judged' (Mathew 7:1)"?

The truth is that we cannot ignore the sinful acts of others. Caring for others means we want the best for them, which means a life free from sin. We would warn our friends if their reckless driving endangers their physical well-being. It is even more important to warn friends about the danger of sinful acts which endanger their spiritual well-being, their full communion with God in this life and the next (see *CCC*, number 1787). Sin is real, and its negative effects are real; encouraging others to avoid sin is truly an act of love (see numbers 1849–1869).

The challenge is in how we talk about this with our friends. There is an old saying, "love the sinner, hate the sin" (see how Jesus treats the woman caught in adultery, John 8:1–11; see also *CCC*, numbers 1465, 1846). This is what Jesus meant when he said, "Stop judging." He is telling us that we must never stop loving someone because of their sinful acts. When we take the difficult step of warning another person that something they are doing is objectively wrong, we must always do it out of loving concern for that person. We should pledge our support and friendship and never condemn the person or threaten to stop caring for them (see numbers 1793–1794).

We live in a culture that says we should be tolerant of other people no matter what they do. But tolerance is not a higher value than the Law of Christ. Being tolerant of sinful actions only leads to pain, chaos, and the spread of evil. Many people in our culture also wrongly embrace moral relativism— the belief that there is no objective morality and that what is right is whatever they decide is right. We must always remind one another that the eternal truth revealed by Christ applies to everyone at all places and at all times; this is not being intolerant or judgmental (see *CCC*, numbers 2477–2478).

QUESTION 3: Isn't it wrong for the Church to impose her views of morality on others?

Some people have a concern that the Catholic Church imposes her morality on people who are not members of the Church. Their concern is that in a free society, people should be free to make their own moral decisions. Should you ever face this argument from someone, here are some important points you can make in response.

- The moral law taught by the Church is not her invention but is God's universal law meant for all people (see *CCC*, number 1700). All people have the ability to understand the Church's basic moral teaching because God has written the natural law on the heart of every person (see *CCC*, numbers 1954–1960).

- For the good of individual souls and for society as a whole, the Church has a responsibility to teach God's moral law to all people and to do so as persuasively as possible.

- The Catholic Church does not try to impose her moral teaching on anyone, but part of the Church's mission is to share with all people the moral law revealed by God. Even though the Church does this as publicly as possible, she respects each person's right to accept or reject this truth (see *CCC*, numbers 1716–1724).

- The Catholic Church has a responsibility to influence public opinion to create laws and build social structures that support and defend the moral truths revealed by God. This is true in free societies, but it is even truer in dictatorships and other societies with limited freedoms. The Church's moral teaching is crucial for the common good. Imagine the chaos and suffering that would result if every person lived only by their own personal moral code. And remember the suffering and evil that happens in the world when states enact laws that are contrary to Divine Law.

The Church does not seek to take over the responsibilities of the state or to make Church law the law of the land. Catholics recognize the important distinction between the Church and the state and the dangers that come when one of these institutions tries to take over the responsibilities of the other.

QUESTION 4: Why can't we make up our own minds and be in control over everything?

All the explanation about what is required for a sin (see chapter 3) makes some people say: "I'll just make up my own mind about what is right and wrong. Why do I need help from anyone? God gave me a free will to control my own destiny." There is a lot of truth in this attitude but also some misconception. God has given us the freedom to make up our own mind about our actions and to determine our eternal destiny. The key is whether our moral decisions are based on an informed conscience, and we need help to have an informed conscience.

All human beings, no matter how experienced or how well educated, have a limited perspective. We cannot possibly know all there is to know about all the moral decisions we need to make. We need God's help—because God knows, sees, and understands more than we can—to make the best decisions about our actions. Through the Church, God has revealed the guidance we need when it comes to religious truths and moral law. The Church is not trying to make people's moral decisions for them. The Church only desires to share the truth human beings need to make the best possible moral choices, which is the truth revealed by God.

Should we require proof about the need people have for help in making good moral decisions, we just need to look at the world around us. The many abuses and tragic conflicts occurring in the world testify to our inability to make good moral choices using only our own knowledge and power (see *CCC*, number 2317). Our sinfulness cannot be overcome simply by our own efforts; it can only be overcome by the salvation we receive through Christ's life, death, and Resurrection (see numbers 619–623).

QUESTION 5: There's an old saying about charity beginning at home. Doesn't this mean I don't have to worry about helping anyone else until I have enough to take care of my family and me?

Some people object to paying taxes and to civic involvement based on the old saying "charity begins at home." They argue that if everyone just takes care of their own family, that should be enough. Or they ask why they should have to give time and money for other people's needs when their family does not yet have everything that they desire.

Although it is certainly important to take care of your family's needs, the New Law of Christ challenges us to have a broader vision. When Jesus told his disciples to "love your neighbor as yourself," he was teaching that we have a responsibility to care for people outside our own families. He made this perfectly clear by following up his teaching on the Great Commandments with the Parable of the Good Samaritan (see Luke 10:25–37), a parable that teaches that all people, including our enemies, are our neighbors.

In our modern society, an important way we love our neighbors is by being good citizens. And in the Parable of the Widow's Mite (see Luke 21:1–4), Jesus reminds us that our charity toward others is not measured by how much we give, but by how generous we are when we give. He calls us to be generous both within our families and to those outside our families. Our charity begins at home and continues by our reaching out to the entire human family.

GLOSSARY

abortion ➤ The deliberate termination of a pregnancy by killing the unborn child. It is a grave sin and a crime against human life.

absolution ➤ An essential part of the Sacrament of Penance and Reconciliation in which the priest pardons the sins of the person confessing, in the name of God and the Church.

actual graces ➤ God's interventions and support for us in the everyday moments of our lives. Actual graces are important for conversion and for continuing growth in holiness.

adulation ➤ Excessive flattery, praise, or admiration for another person.

adultery ➤ Sexual activity between two persons, at least one of whom is married to another. Prohibited by the Sixth Commandment.

agnostic; agnosticism ➤ One who believes we cannot know anything about God's existence or his nature; the belief that we cannot know anything about God's existence or his nature.

almsgiving ➤ Freely giving money or material goods to a person who is needy, often by giving to a group or organization that serves poor people. It may be an act of penance or of Christian charity.

anger (wrath) ➤ A desire for revenge that prevents reconciliation, one of the capital sins.

annulment ➤ The declaration by the Church that a marriage is null and void, that is, it never existed as a sacramental union. Catholics who divorce must have the marriage declared null by the Church to be free to marry once again in the Church.

apostasy ➤ The act of renouncing one's faith.

artificial insemination ➤ The process by which a man's sperm and a woman's egg are united in a manner other than natural sexual intercourse. In the narrowest sense, it means injecting sperm into a woman's cervical canal. The procedure is morally wrong because it separates intercourse from the act of procreation.

Asherah (also called Astarte or Ashtoreth) ➤ The Canaanite goddess of love and fertility, often represented by a serpent and worshipped in sacred groves. She was considered a false god by the Israelites but also worshipped by them when they fell away from the one true God.

atheist; atheism ➤ One who denies the existence of God; the denial of the existence of God.

Baal ➤ The Canaanite god of rain and vegetation, often represented by a bull and worshipped in the "high places." He was considered a false god by the Israelites but worshipped by them when they fell away from the one true God.

beatitude ➤ Our vocation as Christians, the goal of our existence. It is true blessedness or happiness that we experience partially here on earth and perfectly in Heaven.

blasphemy ➤ Speaking, acting, or thinking about God, Jesus Christ, the Virgin Mary, or the saints in a way that is irreverent, mocking, or offensive. It is a sin against the Second Commandment.

calumny ➤ Ruining the reputation of another person by lying or spreading rumors. It is also called slander and is a sin against the Eighth Commandment.

Canon Law ➤ The name given to the official body of laws that provide good order in the visible body of the Church.

capital sins ➤ Seven sins that lead to and reinforce other sins and vices. The seven are traditionally called pride, covetousness (greed), envy, anger (wrath), gluttony, lust, and sloth.

Cardinal Virtues ➤ Based on the Latin word *cardo*, meaning "pivot," four virtues that are viewed as pivotal or essential for full Christian living: prudence, justice, fortitude, and temperance.

catechism ➤ A popular summary, usually in book form, of Catholic doctrine about faith and morals and commonly intended for use within formal programs of catechesis.

catechist ➤ Catechesis is the process by which Christians of all ages are taught the essentials of Christian doctrine and are formed as disciples of Christ. Catechists are the ministers of catechesis.

chastity ➤ The moral virtue by which people are able to successfully and healthfully integrate their sexuality into their total person, leading to an inner union of body and spirit: recognized as one of the fruits of the Holy Spirit.

circumstances ➤ The specific conditions or facts affecting a moral decision. Circumstances can increase or decrease the goodness or evil of an action.

civil authorities ➤ Leaders of public groups that are not religious institutions, particularly government leaders.

civil disobedience ➤ Deliberate refusal to obey or an immoral civil law or an immoral demand from civil authority.

cohabitation ➤ A man and woman living together before marriage. Prohibited by the Sixth Commandment.

common good ➤ Social conditions that allow for all citizens of the Earth, individuals and families, to meet basic needs and achieve fulfillment.

commutative justice ➤ This type of justice calls for fairness in agreements and contracts between individuals. It is an equal exchange of goods, money, or services.

conciliar ➤ Something connected with an official council of the Church, normally an Ecumenical Council such as the Second Vatican Council.

concupiscence ➤ The tendency of all human beings toward sin, as a result of Original Sin.

conscience ➤ The "inner voice," guided by human reason and Divine Law, that enables us to judge the moral quality of a specific action that has been made, is being made, or will be made. This judgment enables us to distinguish good from evil, in order to accomplish good and avoid evil. To make good judgments, one needs to have a well-formed conscience.

consumerism ➤ The preoccupation with buying and having more material things.

contraception ➤ The use of mechanical, chemical, or medical procedures to prevent conception from taking place as a result of sexual intercourse. Contraception is morally wrong because it violates the openness to procreation required of marriage and the inner truth of married love.

contrition ➤ To have sorrow and hatred for our sin and a commitment not to sin again.

Corporal Works of Mercy ➤ Charitable actions that respond to people's physical needs and show respect for human dignity. The traditional list of seven works includes feeding the hungry, giving drink to the thirsty, clothing the naked, sheltering the homeless, visiting the sick, visiting prisoners, and burying the dead.

covenant ➤ A solemn agreement between human beings or between God and a human being in which mutual commitments are made.

culpable ➤ To be guilty of wrongdoing.

D

Decalogue ➤ The Ten Commandments.

detraction ➤ Unnecessarily revealing something about another person that is true but is harmful to his or her reputation. It is a sin against the Eighth Commandment.

divination ➤ The practice of seeking power or knowledge through supernatural means apart from the one true God; a sin against the First Commandment.

E

envy ➤ Resentment that we direct at others who have some success, thing, or privilege that we want for ourselves. It is one of the capital sins and contrary to the Tenth Commandment.

eschatology ➤ The area of Christian faith having to do with the last things: the Last Judgment, the particular judgment, the resurrection of the body, Heaven, Hell, and Purgatory.

Eternal Law ➤ The order in creation that reflects God's will and purpose; it is eternal because it is always true and never changes. All other types of law have their basis in Eternal Law and are only true if they reflect the truth of Eternal Law.

etiology ➤ A story that explains something's cause or origin.

euthanasia ➤ A direct action, or a deliberate lack of action, that causes the death of a person who is disabled, sick, or dying. Euthanasia is a violation of the Fifth Commandment against killing.

examination of conscience ➤ Prayerful reflection on, and assessment of, one's words, attitudes, and actions in light of the Gospel of Jesus; more specifically, the conscious moral evaluation of one's life in preparation for reception of the Sacrament of Penance and Reconciliation.

excommunication ➤ A severe penalty that results from grave sins identified in Church law. The penalty is either imposed by a Church official or happens automatically as a result of the offense. An excommunicated person is not permitted to receive Holy Communion or other sacraments until the excommunication has been lifted.

F

faith ➤ From the Latin *fides*, meaning "trust" or "belief," faith is the gift of God by which one freely accepts God's full Revelation in Jesus Christ. It is a matter of both the head (acceptance of God's revealed truth) and the heart (love of God and neighbor as a response to God's first loving us). Also, one of the three Theological Virtues.

fornication ➤ Sexual intercourse between a man and a woman who are not married. It is morally wrong to engage in intercourse before marriage, a sin against the Sixth Commandment.

fortitude ➤ Also called strength or courage, the Cardinal Virtue that enables one to maintain sound moral judgment and behavior in the face of difficulties and challenges.

free will ➤ The gift from God that allows human beings to choose from among various actions, for which we are held accountable. It is the basis for moral responsibility.

G

generative ➤ As a theological term, something related to the power of producing new life.

Gifts of the Holy Spirit ➤ At Baptism, we receive seven Gifts of the Holy Spirit. These gifts are freely given to us to help us live as followers of Jesus and to build up the Body of Christ, the Church. The seven gifts are wisdom, understanding, right judgment or counsel, fortitude or courage, knowledge, piety or reverence, and fear of the Lord or wonder and awe.

gluttony ➤ Excessive eating or drinking; a capital sin.

grace ➤ The free and undeserved gift of God's loving and active presence in our lives that God gives us to empower us to respond to his call and to live as his adopted sons and daughters. Grace restores our loving communion with the Holy Trinity, lost through sin.

Great Commandments ➤ Jesus' summary of the entire Divine Law as the love of God and the love of neighbor.

greed ➤ The desire to accumulate earthly goods beyond what we need. It is one of the capital sins and contrary to the Tenth Commandment.

H

heresy ➤ The conscious and deliberate rejection by a baptized person of a truth of faith that must be believed.

hope ➤ The Theological Virtue by which we trust in the promises of God and expect from God both eternal life and the grace we need to attain it; the conviction that God's grace is at work in the world and that the Kingdom of God established by and through Jesus Christ is becoming realized through the workings of the Holy Spirit among us.

I

idolatry ➤ The worship of other beings, creatures, or material goods in a way that is fitting for God alone. It is a violation of the First Commandment.

infallibility ➤ The gift given by the Holy Spirit to the Church whereby the Magisterium of the Church, the Pope and the bishops in union with him, can definitively proclaim a doctrine of faith and morals without error.

intellect ➤ The divine gift that gives us the ability to see and understand the order of things that God places within creation and to know and understand God through the created order.

intention ➤ The intended outcome or goal of the person choosing the object when making a moral decision.

in vitro fertilization ➤ The fertilization of a woman's ovum (egg) with man's sperm outside her body. The fertilized egg is transferred to the woman's uterus. The Church considers the process to be a moral violation of the dignity of procreation.

J

Johannine writings ➤ The Gospel of John and the three Letters of John.

justice ➤ The Cardinal Virtue concerned with rights and duties within relationships; the commitment, as well as the actions and attitudes that flow from the commitment, that ensure we give to God and to our neighbor, particularly those who are poor and oppressed, what is properly due them.

justification ➤ God's act of bringing a sinful human being into right relationship with him. It involves the removal of sin and the gift of God's sanctifying grace to renew holiness.

just war ➤ War involves many evils, no matter the circumstances. A war is only just and permissible when it meets strict criteria in protecting citizens from an unjust aggressor.

L

legitimate defense ➤ The teaching that you can use the amount of force necessary to defend yourself or your nation from an aggressor if attacked.

love ➤ Also called "charity," the Theological Virtue by which we love God above all things and, out of that love of God, love our neighbors as ourselves.

lust ➤ Undisciplined, unchecked desire for self-enjoyment, especially of a sexual nature. It is one of the seven capital sins.

M

magic ➤ The belief in supernatural power that comes from a source other than God; a sin against the First Commandment.

Magisterium ➤ The Church's living teaching office, which consists of all bishops, in communion with the Pope, the Bishop of Rome. Their task is to interpret and preserve the truths revealed in both Sacred Scripture and Sacred Tradition.

mammon ➤ An Aramaic word meaning wealth or property.

masturbation ➤ Self-manipulation of one's sexual organs for the purpose of erotic pleasure or to achieve orgasm. It is a sin because the act cannot result in the creation of new life and because God created sexuality not for self-gratification but to unify a husband and wife in marriage.

merit ➤ God's reward to those who love him and by his grace perform good works. To have merit is to be justified in the sight of God, free from sin and sanctified by his grace. We do not "merit" justification or eternal life; the source of any merit we have is due to the grace of Christ in us.

monotheism ➤ The belief in and worship of only one God.

morality ➤ Refers to the goodness or evil of human acts. The morality of an act is determined by the nature of the action, the intention, and the circumstances. God's grace empowers us to choose good acts and live virtuous lives in obedience to Eternal Law.

moral law ➤ The moral law is established by God and is a rational expression of eternal law. Moral law reflects God's wisdom; it is the teaching that leads us to the blessed life he wants for us.

mortal sin ➤ An action so contrary to the will of God that it results in a complete separation from God and his grace. As a consequence of that separation, the person is condemned to eternal death. For a sin to be a mortal sin, three conditions must be met: the act must involve a grave matter, the person must have full knowledge of the evil of the act, and the person must give full consent in committing the act.

N

natural law ➤ The moral law that can be understood through the use of human reason. It is our God-given ability to understand what it means to be in right relationship with God, other people, the world, and ourselves. However, our ability to know natural law has been clouded by Original Sin.

New Law ➤ Divine Law revealed in the New Testament through the life and teaching of Jesus Christ and through the witness and teaching of the Apostles. The New Law perfects the Old Law and brings it to fulfillment. Also called the Law of Love.

nuptial ➤ Something related to marriage or a marriage ceremony.

object ➤ In moral decision-making, the object is the specific thing—an act, word, or thought—that is being chosen.

Old Law ➤ Divine Law revealed in the Old Testament, summarized in the Ten Commandments. Also called the Law of Moses.

original holiness ➤ The grace given to Adam and Eve in their original state by which they lived in close friendship with God.

original justice ➤ The original state of Adam and Eve before the Fall. Due to their friendship with God, they were at harmony within themselves, with each other, and with all creation.

Original Sin ➤ From the Latin *origo*, meaning "beginning" or "birth." The term has two meanings: (1) the sin of the first human beings, who disobeyed God's command by choosing to follow their own will and so lost their original holiness and became subject to death, (2) the fallen state of human nature that affects every person born into the world, except Jesus and Mary.

pantheon ➤ All of the gods of a people or religion collectively.

parable ➤ Generally a short story that uses everyday images to communicate religious messages. Jesus used parables frequently in his teaching as a way of presenting the Good News of salvation.

Paschal Mystery ➤ The work of salvation accomplished by Jesus Christ mainly through his life, Passion, death, Resurrection, and Ascension.

penance ➤ In general, an attitude of the heart in which one experiences regrets for past sin and commits to a change in behaviors or attitudes. In the Sacrament of Penance and Reconciliation, the priest assigns penitents a penance to help them make amends for their sins. Particular acts of penance may include spiritual disciplines such as prayers or fasting.

Pentateuch ➤ A Greek word meaning "five books," referring to the first five books of the Old Testament

perjury ➤ The sin of lying while under an oath to tell the truth. It is a sin against the Second and Eighth Commandments.

perpetual adoration ➤ The practice of people committing to pray before the Blessed Sacrament in a designated location so that someone is always in the presence of Christ, twenty-four hours a day, 365 days a year.

plagiarism ➤ Copying someone else's words or ideas without permission or giving proper credit to the person.

polygamy ➤ Having more than one spouse, an act contrary to the dignity of marriage and a sin against the Sixth Commandment.

pornography ➤ A written description or visual portrayal of a person or action that is created or viewed with the intention of stimulating sexual feelings. Creating or using pornography is a sin against the Sixth and Ninth Commandments.

poverty of heart ➤ The recognition of our deep need for God and the commitment to put God above everything else in life, particularly above the accumulation of material wealth.

Precepts of the Church ➤ Sometimes called the Commandments of the Church, these are basic obligations for all Catholics, dictated by the laws of the Church and intended to guarantee for the faithful the indispensable minimum in prayer and moral effort.

pride ➤ Believing one is better than others, often resulting in despising or disrespecting other people; one of the capital sins.

profanity ➤ Speaking disrespectfully about something that is sacred or treating it with disrespect.

prostitution ➤ The act of providing sexual services in exchange for money, drugs, or other goods. It is a serious social evil and is a sin against the Sixth Commandment.

providence ➤ God's divine care and protection.

prudence ➤ The Cardinal Virtue by which a person is inclined toward choosing the moral good and avoiding evil; sometimes called the rudder virtue because it helps steer the person through complex moral situations.

R

reconciliation ➤ The process of restoring broken relationships with God, with the Church, and with people who were directly offended by our sins.

reparation ➤ The act of making amends for something one did wrong that caused physical, emotional, or material harm to another person.

S

Sabbath ➤ In the Old Testament, the "seventh day" on which God rested after the work of Creation was completed. In the Old Law, the weekly day of rest to remember God's work through private prayer and communal worship. Christians fulfill the Sabbath observance on the Lord's Day, celebrated on Sunday, the day on which Jesus was raised, which Catholics also observe with participation in the Eucharist.

sacramental graces ➤ The gifts proper to each of the Seven Sacraments.

sacred ➤ The quality of being holy, worthy of respect and reverence; set apart for God.

sacred art ➤ Art that evokes faith by turning our minds to the mystery of God, primarily through the artistic depiction of Scripture, Tradition, and the lives of Jesus, Mary, and the saints.

sacrilege ➤ An offense against God. It is the abuse of a person, place, or thing dedicated to God and the worship of him.

salvation history ➤ The pattern of specific events in human history in which God clearly reveals his presence and saving actions. Salvation was accomplished once and for all through Jesus Christ, a truth foreshadowed and revealed throughout the Old Testament.

sanctify, sanctification ➤ To make holy; sanctification is the process of becoming closer to God.

sanctifying grace ➤ The grace that heals our human nature wounded by sin and restores us to friendship with God by giving us a share in the divine life of the Trinity. It is a supernatural gift of God, infused into our souls by the Holy Spirit, that continues the work of making us holy.

scandal ➤ An action or attitude—or the failure to act—that leads another person into sin.

simony ➤ Buying or selling something spiritual, such as a grace, a sacrament, or a relic.

sin of commission ➤ A sin that is the direct result of a freely chosen thought, word, or deed.

sin of omission ➤ A sin that is the result of a failure to do something required by God's moral Law.

sloth ➤ Habitual laziness; failing to put forth effort and take action; one of the capital sins.

social doctrine ➤ The teaching of the Church on the truth of Revelation about human dignity, human solidarity, and the principles of justice and peace; and on the moral judgments about economic and social matters required by such truths.

social justice ➤ The defense of human dignity by ensuring that essential human needs are met and that essential human rights are protected for all people.

social sin ➤ The impact that every personal sin has on other people; sin that directly attacks others' life, freedom, dignity, or rights; and the collective effect of many people's sins over time, which corrupts society and its institutions by creating "structures of sin."

solidarity ➤ Union of one's heart and mind with those who are poor or powerless or who face an injustice. It is an act of Christian charity.

soul ➤ Our spiritual principle, it is immortal, and it is what makes us most like God. Our soul is created by God at the moment of our conception. It is the seat of human consciousness and freedom.

special graces ➤ Gifts intended for the common good of the Church, also called charisms.

state ➤ Any organized political authority in a specific area, such as a kingdom, a nation, a country, or a state within a country.

suicide ➤ Deliberately taking one's own life. It is a serious violation of the Fifth Commandment, for it is God's will that we preserve our own lives.

superstition ➤ Attributing to someone or something else a power that belongs to God alone and relying on such powers rather than trusting in God; a sin against the First Commandment.

surrogate motherhood ➤ A medical process in which a woman becomes pregnant through artificial means, often carrying and delivering the child for someone else. The procedure is morally wrong because it separates intercourse from the act of procreation and pregnancy.

T

temperance ➤ The Cardinal Virtue by which one moderates his or her appetites and passions to achieve balance in the use of created goods.

Theological Virtues ➤ The name given for the God-given virtues of faith, hope, and love. These virtues enable us to know God as God and lead us to union with him in mind and heart.

tithe ➤ A commitment to donate a tenth or some other percentage of our income to the Church and other charitable causes.

V

venerate ➤ To show respect and devotion to someone or something.

venial sin ➤ A less serious offense against the will of God that diminishes one's personal character and weakens but does not rupture one's relationship with God.

vice ➤ A practice or habit that leads a person to sin.

virtue ➤ A habitual and firm disposition to do good.

vocation ➤ A call from God to all members of the Church to embrace a life of holiness. Specifically, it refers to a call to live the holy life as an ordained minister, as a vowed religious (sister or brother), or in a Christian marriage. Single life that involves a personal consecration or commitment to a permanent, celibate gift of self to God and one's neighbor is also a vocational state.

INDEX

Note: Charts are indicated with "C".

ACKNOWLEDGMENTS

The scriptural quotations contained herein marked *NRSV* are from the *New Revised Standard Version* of the Bible, Catholic Edition. Copyright © 1989, 1993 by National Council of the Churches of Christ in the United States of America. All rights reserved worldwide.

All other scriptural quotations and excerpts used in this work are taken from the *New American Bible, revised edition* © 2010, 1991, 1986, 1970 Confraternity of Christian Doctrine, Inc., Washington, DC. All Rights Reserved. No part of this work may be reproduced or transmitted in any form or by any means, electronic or mechanical, including photocopying, recording, or by any information storage and retrieval system, without permission in writing from the copyright owner.

The excerpts marked *CCC* are from the English translation of the *Catechism of the Catholic Church* for use in the United States of America, second edition copyright © 1994 by the United States Catholic Conference, Inc.—Libreria Editrice Vaticana (LEV). English translation of the *Catechism of the Catholic Church: Modifications from the Editio Typica* copyright © 1997 by the United States Catholic Conference, Inc.—LEV.

The excerpt by Pope Francis on page 15 is from Vatican News, "Message for World Communications Day," January 24, 2018, at *www.vaticannews.va/en/pope /news/2018-01/pope-world-communications-day-message-2018-truth-journalism-fake.html*. Copyright Copyright © Libreria Editrice Vaticana (LEV.)

The excerpt by Pope Francis on page 40 is from "Address of His Holiness Pope Francis to Participants at the World Conference on Xenophobia, Racism, and Populist Nationalism in the Context of Global Migration," September 20, 2018, at *www.vatican .va/content/francesco/en/speeches/2018/september/documents /papa-francesco_20180920_conferenza-razzismo.html*. Copyright © LEV.

The excerpt on page 41 is from Saint Augustine, "On The Trinity," Book XIV, chapters 15 and 21, at *www.newadvent.org/fathers/130114.htm*.

The excerpt by Pope Francis on page 69 is from "General Audience," March 30, 2016, at *www.vatican .va/content/francesco/en/audiences/2016/documents /papa-francesco_20160330_udienza-generale.html*. Copyright © LEV.

The quotations on pages 82 and 83 are from *The Pastoral Constitution on the Church in the Modern World* (*Gaudium et Spes*, 1965), number 26, at *www.vatican .va/archive/hist_councils/ii_vatican_council/documents /vat-ii_cons_19651207_gaudium-et-spes_en.html*. Copyright © LEV.

The quotations in the sidebar on page 83 are from "Pope, Latin American bishops urge action to save burning Amazon rainforest," August 23, 2019, in *Catholic News Service*. For more of the article go to, *www.ncronline. org/news/earthbeat/pope-latin-american-bishops-urge-action-save-burning-amazon-rainforest*.

The excerpts on pages 99 and 135 are from the English translation of *The Roman Missal* © 2010, 1923 International Commission on English in the Liturgy Corporation (ICEL) (Washington, DC: United States Conference of Catholic Bishops, 2011), pages 326 and 208. Copyright © 2011, 1973 USCCB, Washington, DC. All rights reserved. Used with permission of the ICEL. Texts contained in this work derived whole or in part from liturgical texts copyrighted by the International Commission on English in the Liturgy (ICEL) have been published here with the confirmation of the Committee on Divine Worship, United States Conference of Catholic Bishops. No other texts in this work have been formally reviewed or approved by the United States Conference of Catholic Bishops.

The excerpt by Pope Francis on page 109 is from "General Audience," August 1, 2018, at *www.vatican .va/content/francesco/en/audiences/2018/documents/papa-francesco_20180801_udienza-generale.pdf*. Copyright © LEV.

The excerpt by Pope Francis on page 120 is from "General Audience," August 22, 2018, at *www.vatican .va/content/francesco/en/audiences/2018/documents/papa-francesco_20180822_udienza-generale.html*. Copyright © LEV.

The excerpt by Pope Francis on page 147 is from "General Audience," September 5, 2018, at *www.vatican .va/content/francesco/en/audiences/2018/documents/papa-francesco_20180905_udienza-generale.pdf*. Copyright © LEV.

The excerpt on page 149 is from "Homily of John Paul II: Mass in the Church of the Holy Sepulchre," number 4, at *www.vatican.va/holy_father/john_paul_ii/travels /documents/hf_jp-ii_hom_20000326_holy-sepulchre_en.html*. Copyright © (LEV).

The excerpt by Pope Francis on page 170 is from "General Audience," September 19, 2018, at *www.vatican .va/content/francesco/en/audiences/2018/documents/papa-francesco_20180919_udienza-generale.pdf*. Copyright © LEV.

The excerpt by Pope Francis on page 192 is from "General Audience," November 14, 2018, at *www.vatican .va/content/francesco/en/audiences/2018/documents/papa-francesco_20181114_udienza-generale.pdf*. Copyright © LEV.

The excerpt by Pope Francis on page 218 is from "General Audience," November 7, 2018, at *www.vatican .va/content/francesco/en/audiences/2018/documents/papa-francesco_20181107_udienza-generale.pdf*. Copyright © LEV.

The excerpt by Pope Francis on page 231 is from "On Care for Our Common Home" (*"Laudato Sí"*), number 2, at *www.vatican.va/content/francesco/en/encyclicals/documents /papa-francesco_20150524_enciclica-laudato-si.pdf*. Copyright © LEV.

The excerpt by Pope Francis on page 234 is from "General Audience," November 21, 2018, at *www.vatican.va/content/francesco/en/audiences/2018/documents/papa-francesco_20181121_udienza-generale.pdf*. Copyright © LEV.

The excerpt by Pope Francis on page 261 is from "Invocation for Peace," June 8, 2014, at *http://w2.vatican.va/content/francesco/en/prayers/documents/papa-francesco_preghiere_20140608_invocazione-pace.pdf*. Copyright © LEV.

The excerpt by Pope Francis on page 280 is from "General Audience," October 17, 2018, at *www.vatican.va/content/francesco/en/audiences/2018/documents/papa-francesco_20181017_udienza-generale.pdf*. Copyright © LEV.

The quotation by Pope John Paul II on page 290 is from "General Audience," February 20, 1980, at *www.vatican.va/content/john-paul-ii/en/audiences/1980/documents/hf_jp-ii_aud_19800220.pdf*. Copyright © LEV.

The excerpt by Pope Francis on page 306 is from "General Audience," October 24, 2018, at *www.vatican.va/content/francesco/en/audiences/2018/documents/papa-francesco_20181024_udienza-generale.pdf*. Copyright © LEV.

The quotation on page 340 is from "Italian Teen Who Died in 2009 Declared 'Venerable' by Pope Francis," in *Catholic News Agency*, May 6, 2020.

The quotation by Pope Francis on page 343 is from "Homily at the Opening Mass for World Youth Day," July 25, 2013, at *www.vatican.va/content/francesco/en/speeches/2013/july/documents/papa-francesco_20130725_gmg-giovani-rio.pdf*. Copyright © LEV.

The excerpt on page 358 is from the English translation of *Rite of Penance* © 1975, ICEL, number 45, in *The Rites of the Catholic Church*, volume one, prepared by the ICEL, a Joint Commission of Catholic Bishops' Conferences (Collegeville, MN: The Liturgical Press, 1990). Copyright © 1990 by the Order of St. Benedict, Collegeville, MN. Used with permission of the ICEL. Texts contained in this work derived whole or in part from liturgical texts copyrighted by the International Commission on English in the Liturgy (ICEL) have been published here with the confirmation of the Committee on Divine Worship, United States Conference of Catholic Bishops. No other texts in this work have been formally reviewed or approved by the United States Conference of Catholic Bishops. Used with permission.

The excerpt by Pope Francis on page 365 is from "Homily at Morning Mass," April 4, 2020, at *www.vatican.va/content/francesco/en/cotidie/2020/documents/papa-francesco-cotidie_20200404_ilprocesso-dellatentazione.pdf*. Copyright © LEV.

The excerpt on page 368 is from the English translation of *The Rite of Penance* © 2002, International Commission on English in the Liturgy Corporation (ICEL), number 46. All rights reserved. Used with permission of the ICEL. Texts contained in this work derived whole or in part from liturgical texts copyrighted by ICEL have been published here with the confirmation of the Committee on Divine Worship, United States Conference of Catholic Bishops. No other texts in this work have been formally reviewed or approved by the United States Conference of Catholic Bishops. Used with permission.

The quotation on page 371 is from "Brother of Man Shot Dead by Ex-Dallas Police Officer Forgives and Hugs Her in Court," in *The Telegraph*, October 3, 2019. To read more, go to *www.telegraph.co.uk/news/2019/10/03/brother-murdered-man-forgives-hugs-former-dallas-police-officer*.

The Paradoxical Commandments on page 373 are adapted from *The Silent Revolution: Dynamic Leadership in the Student Council*, by Kent Keith (Cambridge, MA: Harvard Student Agencies, 1968). Copyright © 1968 by Kent Keith.

To view copyright terms and conditions for internet materials cited here, log on to the home pages for the referenced websites.

During this book's preparation, all citations, facts, figures, names, addresses, telephone numbers, internet URLs, and other pieces of information cited within were verified for accuracy. The authors and Saint Mary's Press staff have made every attempt to reference current and valid sources, but we cannot guarantee the content of any source, and we are not responsible for any changes that may have occurred since our verification. If you find an error in, or have a question or concern about, any of the information or sources listed within, please contact Saint Mary's Press.

Endnotes Cited in Quotations from the *Catechism of the Catholic Church*, Second Edition

Chapter 2
1. St. Thomas Aquinas, *Dec. præc.* I.

Chapter 4
1. *Gaudium et spes* 19 §3.

Chapter 6
1. Saint John Chrysostom, *De incomprehensibili* 3, 6: J. P. Migne, ed., Patrologia Graeca (Paris, 1857–1866) 48, 725.

Chapter 9
1. Cf. *Gaudiem et spes* 69 § 1.

Chapter 10
1. Congregation for the Doctrine of the Faith, *Donum vitae* I, 2.
2. John Paul II, *Evangelium vitae*, 56.
3. Francis, *Address to Participants in the Meeting Organized by the Pontifical Council for the Promotion of the New Evangelization*, 11 October 2017: L'Osservatore Romano, 13 October 2017, 5.

Chapter 11
1. *Familiaris consortio* 84.

Chapter 12
1. St. Thomas Aquinas, *Summa Theologiae*, II–II, 47, 2.